Culture and Society

HOW TO GET YOUR OWN WAY

HOW TO GET YOUR OWN WAY

Who's Manipulating You...?

Craig Shrives & Paul Easter

153

Kyle Books

For Penny and Liisa

First published in Great Britain in 2013 by
Kyle Books, an imprint of Kyle Cathie Ltd
67–69 Whitfield Street, London, W1T 4HF
general.enquiries@kylebooks.com
www.kylebooks.com

ISBN: 978-0-85783-158-3

Text © 2013 Craig Shrives and Paul Easter
Design © 2013 Kyle Books

Editor: Catharine Robertson
Editorial Assistant: Laura Foster
Designer: Jane Humphrey
Proofreader: John Westbrooke
Index: Lisa Footitt
Production: Lisa Pinnell

A Cataloguing In Publication record for this title is available from the
British Library.
Printed and bound by CPI Group (UK) Ltd, Croydon, CR0 4YY.

FOREWORD

If influence were visible like torchlight, we'd all be lit up like the actors on a West End stage. As we go about our lives, we are constantly bombarded with other people's words and images which they have designed to manipulate our actions.

More often than not, the aim of their messaging is to turn your money into their money. The people attacking you (some by instinct and some with training) know what makes you tick. They have learned to get inside your head and steer you around like a remote-controlled automaton. Too often, your decisions are in fact their decisions.

The noise of modern life is riddled with influencers. Adverts are the most overt type, but they only represent a small proportion of the attack you're enduring from far more people than you might realise. Everyone from politicians to market-stall holders is deliberately employing well-tested mind games to persuade you to act in their favour.

The levers in your brain that they're pulling are deeply rooted, and it takes training and practice to feel these levers being pulled and to counter the effects.

But it's not all bad news. With a bit of training, you can get your hands on other people's levers and start influencing them to turn their money into yours or to get them to do things for you.

Unfortunately, becoming a black belt in influence is not a quick process. I'm sure that today's Bruce Lees would have been pretty deflated by their very first Kung Fu lesson. Bowing in and out of class, saluting the teacher and learning how to tie your belt properly are a long way from kicking drug lords through glass windows, but they're a necessary foundation for all that later heroism.

The aim of *How To Get Your Own Way* is to teach you how to read your surroundings, to show you the main techniques used to influence, and then to release you into the wild to protect what's yours and take what's theirs. Don't forget, though – we've got some bowing in and out of class to learn first.

Chapter 1:
Write to get the job done

About nine seconds. That's how long it takes for someone to determine how quickly they're going to skim over your written work or whether they're going to read it at all. It's about how much time you've got to stamp your ideas into their heads or to encourage them to invest more time in your efforts.

Of course, polite people will feign interest in your work, but really no one cares what you've got to say unless it affects them or entertains them, and that's the first lesson in this book. Don't worry, though – there are techniques for tattooing your thoughts on people's retinas and stealing their time, and that's what Chapter 1 is about.

Chapter 1 talks a lot about how to write for effect. It's about business writing. It's about improving your ability to influence others using the right words and the right formats. If you're new to business writing, you might find Chapter 1 quite hard work, and you might wonder what it's got to do with influence and mind games. But hang in there. Writing is the tool with which you'll wield most influence. It will become your nunchucks (a martial-arts weapon comprising two wooden batons connected at one end with a short chain).

Chapter 2:
Guard against your biases and exploit theirs

Whether you like it not, your head is full of "gremlins" that influence how you behave. They interfere with how you reach decisions, and they are at play every time you walk into a shop or a meeting. They influence everything you do, and they never rest. But you can tame them. They're called your biases. In Chapter 2 of this book, we're going to cover about two dozen of the most common biases and learn to dissect people's arguments.

Understanding biases will give you the tools to help you get your own way, and it will help you to defend yourself against others' mind games.

If you can recognise these little cognitive "viruses" in you and others, you will be able to:

- Influence people by exploiting their biases.
- Defend yourself against attacks on your biases.
- Improve your decision-making.
- Argue far more effectively.

The first thing we should say about these biases is that you're probably aware of at least half of them, even if you don't know what they're called. We all encounter these biases on a daily basis, and we have learnt to deal with them instinctively. But with a bit of know-how, it is possible to do better than "instinctively". One of the purposes of this book is to firm up in your mind how each of these gremlins works, give it its proper name and help you to formulate deliberate strategies to ensure you get your way.

The other good thing about understanding biases and how arguments are made up is that it will allow you to use more convincing language to explain why others' opinions are flawed. If you can say stuff like "your assertion is based on a false premise resulting from your Confirmation Bias" as opposed to just "you're wrong", your ability to influence will rocket. Being able to discuss people's arguments at the argument-component level is a useful skill for pulling their ideas to shreds, and it will really strengthen your arguments. For that reason, your boss at work will love it when you wield words like those on your company's behalf. But, and it's a big but, your other half and your family will hate it, so the terminology and tricks we're going to teach you in this book are not to be used on loved ones. Do you promise? Okay, let's crack on.

There will be plenty of experts in Critical Thinking out there who won't like the sections in this book covering biases. For them, our wording won't be academically pure enough. Well, we're quite comfortable with that. We learnt this stuff on the job as military intelligence analysts, so we're coming at the subject from a vocational perspective, not an academic one. Over the years, we've learnt it's far more effective to impart ideas using possibly imperfect, understandable definitions than perfect ones that only professors of Critical Thinking can appreciate.

Over the years, we've also learnt that most people need to hear the ideas behind the biases more than once before the ideas click. For that reason, we explain each bias at least five times using different words and contexts. That repetition is deliberate. For each bias, we:

1. Warm you up to the idea (usually in the form of some plain advice).
2. Explain it again with a more formal definition.
3. Show you at least one example.
4. Show you how to apply it in a real-life situation.
5. Summarise the idea by telling you how to spot it in others.

When we wrote the definitions, our drivers were readability and applicability. Occasionally, these trumped academic purity. So, if you're a Critical Thinking geek, and you don't like our definitions, I'm afraid you're going to have to tut yourself to sleep each night until you get over it.

Chapter 3:
Reading body language

"I discovered I scream the same way whether I'm about to be devoured by a great white shark or if a piece of seaweed touches my foot."

The reason for including this quote is to highlight that you often can't trust what comes out of people's mouths. Some people lie. Some people are not as confident as their words would suggest. Some people won't like you, and some people will like you a little too much. All of these things are often detectable by reading body language, and that's what Chapter 3 covers. Here's a word of warning before you get to this chapter. Don't expect to spot a lie (or anything else) because the speaker carried out a specific action, like scratching his nose as he spoke. It really doesn't work like that. That would be like trying to guess the meaning of a sentence by looking at just one word. You have to take in the whole picture and the context and then make an informed decision on what all that arm-waving, eye movement, leg-positioning and gesticulation are likely to mean.

Chapter 4:
See through statistics

Whenever you make a point, you should expect your audience to say something like "prove it". Well, there's probably no better way of doing that than offering them some statistics. People like statistics. They're the bridge between opinion and fact. At least, sound statistics are the bridge between opinion and fact. The big, well-documented problem is that statistics can be spun to look like that bridge. But, all too often, they're no more than opinion masquerading as evidence. In Chapter 4, we'll look at how politicians, reporters and marketeers deliberately spin their figures to influence you and at the dangers of presenting defective statistics.

Clearly, we can't all be experts at everything. So, we have no choice but to rely on specialists in certain fields to tell us what's going on. Unfortunately, lots of those specialists are supporting people who are trying to sell you stuff, and an uncomfortably high number of their experiments produce results that improve the saleability of their companies' wares, when they shouldn't. The aim of Chapter 4 is to help you develop a more critical eye for the statistics assaulting your daily life and to help you create your own scrutiny-safe ones.

Chapter 5:
Shop smarter

A frighteningly high proportion of the bargains you see in shops aren't bargains. They're just tricks to make you think they are. You probably knew that. What you might not know though is that, at the point of buying, your brain will dismiss that knowledge and convince you the bargain is real.

If you think you're doing your own thing when it comes to shopping (e.g. choosing which shop to use, buying only the things you want and choosing your own route and pace through a store), then you need to think again and learn how to put your defences up.

Chapter 5 is not all about defending yourself from retailers, though. There are some tricks being used on you that you can turn against the shops, and there are techniques you can employ if you're in the selling game. Also, at certain times, retailers (like car salesmen and travel agents) have pressures on them to sell their wares quickly, and, with a bit of planning, you can exploit those pressures to win a bargain. Chapter 5 is about staying savvy during your lifetime shopping experience.

The sections in the book

Throughout the book, we've sought to use real-life examples and layman's language to walk you through the following ideas:

- Busy people don't care what you've got to say unless it directly affects them or entertains them.

- People are hardwired to make decisions, and they see the world through "them"-tinted glasses.

- When people talk to you, their mouths say one thing, but their eyes and limbs often say something else.

- A scary proportion of the statistics you encounter will have been manipulated to influence you.

- You are being bombarded with messages that influence your buying decisions.

Now, that seems like quite an eclectic mix of ideas, but they all contribute to those influence spotlights which would be illuminating you if influence were visible. In writing *How To Get Your Own Way*, our aim was to show the relationships between these ideas by referencing backwards and forwards between the sections in the book. And that's why the book has been presented in short, bite-sized sections. We don't really see this as a dip-in reference book, like a dictionary. It was written to be a cover-to-cover read, like a novel. However, we do recognise that Chapters 1 and 2 are quite geeky, and there's only a slim chance you'll "lose yourself" in them as you might with a real novel. As there's a fair chance not all of the academic gumpf will gel after just one reading, the sections and the index will help you to locate a concept in the future should you require a quick refresh.

It doesn't make you a bad person. Influencing others through mind games doesn't make you a bad person. It just gives you an edge that will help you slice through the noise of modern life to get more done and to defend yourself from those trying to manipulate you.

You apply it to you. I would wager the examples we've given you won't apply directly to your situation. Our thinking is that we provide the idea and then you apply it to you. We recently taught some of this stuff to a large Norwegian oil-exploration firm. We gave them an example about how to make a killing by selling TVs. Within 90 seconds, they'd applied the idea to themselves to ensure the big oil companies bought their most lucrative services. So, we'll present the idea, and you apply to it you. That's the plan. There's a plan?

CONTENTS

Numbers indicate sections

Chapter 1 – Write to Get the Job Done

Chapter 2 – Guard against your biases and exploit theirs

Chapter 3 – Reading Body Language

Chapter 4 – See Through Statistics

Chapter 5 – Shop Smarter

Write to Get the Job Done

INTRODUCTION

(1)   Writing is the weapon of choice

Writing is the most common way of asking someone to do something. This chapter is about crafting your writing to increase your chances of getting them to do it.

Later in this book, we will discuss how people think and how you can influence them, but before we cover that, we need to ensure your interaction with those you want to influence is tuned for maximum effect. As writing (e.g. emails, letters, reports) will be your main communication tool, we're going to start this book with how to create business writing that gets the job done.

How To Get Your Own Way is the work of two ex-military intelligence officers. The British Intelligence Corps' motto is *Manui Dat Cognitio Vires* (Knowledge gives strength to the arm). The chapters after this one will improve your knowledge of how to influence. The aim of this chapter is to boost the biceps of the arm that will deliver that knowledge: your writing.

(2)   What is business writing?

Before we look at how to tune your business correspondence for optimal effect, we should have a quick look at what business correspondence is. I reckon this covers it:

> Business writing is writing to get something else done.

Stories and poems are <u>not</u> examples of business writing. They are self-contained. You read a story to understand the story. You read a poem to enjoy the poem. You don't do that with business writing. You read a business report to help you smash the competition off the face of the planet.

3   No one cares what you've got to say

It's Monday. I'm late for work, and I haven't ironed my shirt yet. I'm now praying for some miracle with the traffic, because there's an email I need to send before 9 o'clock. I also need to find 20 minutes to go over the presentation that I'm giving at half past nine. Oh joy, the gas bill has just landed on the doormat. The electricity bill too. Great. Roll on 10 o'clock when I will be able to settle into the day's routine.

There are also some longer-term things bothering me. My annual personal appraisal report is not looking as good as I'd hoped this year, and my promotion is starting to look pretty unlikely. What if I don't get promoted? How will we afford the Maldives holiday? Whack it on the credit card? Err, no. Remortgage? Err, definitely no.

Does that sound like your life? Probably not. But I bet you could write something similar based on your own family, money and work issues. That's the point I am trying to make. People have lots of things going on in their lives. No one has time for irrelevant stuff.

To ensure your writing is effective, you need to understand the environment you're sending it to. You should think of that environment as a busy one – too busy for your detailed ramblings. Here's the idea I want you to keep in your head from now on:

> No one cares what you've got to say unless it affects them or entertains them. No, really, they don't.

So, when putting your business correspondence together, you have two choices:

- Make it short, or
- Make it entertaining.

Or both.

Twenty years ago, the average human attention span was 20 seconds. Today, it is a mere... yeah, whatever.

(4)   Subordinates' and dunces' emails are deleted first

We also need to talk about another dynamic at play with business writing: the writer-reader relationship.

I bet you read emails from your boss more carefully than those from your peers or subordinates. Provided we're talking generally, I reckon that's a safe bet. But if we examine more closely how much time you allocate to emails, we would find that the "boss factor" is only one reason for being a little more patient.

There are other factors determining how much time you dedicate to things like emails. High on the list is the credibility of the person writing to you. Your patience will diminish if you think the writer is a bit thick. Unfortunately, this is not just something you do. It's something everybody does. So, to improve the chances of your business writing being read or actioned, you must ensure you come across as an intellectual peer... or at least in the same league.

(5)   Protect your credibility to avoid being ignored

Whether it's right or wrong, readers make assumptions about a writer's capabilities and education when they read the writer's correspondence. I don't think there's anything wrong with that. Someone's writing is usually a good indicator of their abilities. I'm not alone in that opinion either.

In 2011, internet entrepreneur Charles Duncombe conducted an experiment on one of his retail sites which showed that a single spelling mistake cut his online sales in half. This is a common story cited by many online retailers. I can remember hearing a story of one internet store that had a promotion on a specific mountain bike. Frustrated because he'd sold almost none, the sales manager logged on to look at his promotion. To his horror, he spotted a basic grammar error in the advert, which he hurriedly had corrected. Sales starting rolling in immediately, and, within a week, the bike had sold out.

It's a simple equation: bad writing = not credible. And retaining credibility is a crucial aspect of business correspondence.

Imagine this. Your boss's inbox has 80 unread emails in it. He just clicked on your email. Because you are subordinate to him, his mouse cursor is already hovering over the next email. As he skim-reads yours, he is looking for the key points. While scanning for the key points (because they're not immediately obvious), he encounters a couple of basic grammar mistakes. At this point, you're toast. Your credibility is shot. He clicks his mouse, and now he has 79 unread emails in his inbox. Well done, you. A great day's work. You've had no effect, and your credibility has taken a punch in the kidneys.

YOUR GRAMMAR

6   Bad grammar will kill your credibility

English grammar is a set of rules that govern how our language is structured. Don't worry. I'm not going to talk about that now. Besides, I don't have to. If you're a native English speaker, your grammar is probably close to perfect. The problem, however, is that little gap between close to perfect and perfect. That little gap can cause a lot of damage. Do you remember the Space Shuttle Columbia Disaster in 2003? Columbia's thermal protection system was almost entirely intact. It was close to perfect. Heartbreakingly, "almost entirely intact" wasn't good enough, and on 1st February 2003, Columbia disintegrated over Texas shortly after launch, killing everyone on board. It was a tragic example of how a small flaw can cause a disaster. Similarly, even a tiny gap in your grammar know-how can "kill" you.

I can pretty much guarantee your writing is intelligible, but intelligible does not mean credible. A dodgy apostrophe or an erroneous capital letter can sink you. If you write *"We have identified two solution's",* that incorrect apostrophe in *solution's* will tell your readers that you're not as bright as they are. Your solutions might be amazing, but they won't save your credibility. That will already have been wrecked by the apostrophe. If you are presenting ideas that challenge existing preconceptions, your job will be made much harder if your writing contains grammatical errors. Those you are challenging could write off your ideas without confronting their preconceptions because of your poor grammar. They'll think something like this: *"Someone who doesn't even know the difference between it's and its isn't telling me what to think."*

I am not saying you have to form beautiful, grammatically sound sentences every time. Far from it. That last "sentence" of mine wasn't even a sentence. There is a whole section coming up dedicated to using non-sentences and, in particular, one-word "sentences". Techniques like this are useful for impact and to keep your writing natural. But these are deliberate deviations from formal grammar, and I fully expect readers to get that. Real grammar mistakes, on the other hand, are a different story. Stick a few of those in a letter, and you're instantly earmarked as bottom of the class.

> Grammar: the difference between a company that knows its shit and one that knows it's shit.

7   Grammar errors listed by their ability to make you look stupid

There are different levels of grammar wrongdoing. For me, there are three categories of grammar error residing in that space between close-to-perfect grammar and perfect grammar:

- Mistakes that make you look stupid.
- Mistakes that damage your credibility.
- Mistakes that take the shine off your work.

Here are the worst culprits in each category:

Mistakes that make you look stupid:
- Inserting apostrophes in the wrong place.
- Confusing *its* and *it's*.
- Writing *should of*.
- Confusing *your* and *you're*
- Confusing *they're, there* and *their*.
- Using capital letters for important words.

Mistakes that damage your credibility:
- Using commas instead of full stops.
- Using semicolons incorrectly.
- Confusing *affect* and *effect*.
- Confusing *compliment* and *complement*.
- Confusing *fewer* and *less*.

Mistakes that take the shine off your work:
- Using dangling modifiers.
- Using *you* and *I* incorrectly.
- Using *myself* incorrectly.
- Confusing *i.e.* and *e.g.*

We're not going to get into grammar in this book, but if I've just frightened you with these lists, you might want to start Googling some of these topics. (You could even buy *Grammar Rules: Writing with Military Precision* by Craig Shrives. Please forgive the plug.)

(8) **Bad grammar and being "clever" are poor bedfellows**

For now, it suffices to say that you will not be forgiven for grammar errors. This is especially true if you're trying to be clever. Here are some examples I've come across of people trying to be clever but failing:

"The days of this society is numbered."
(Should be: *"The days of this society are numbered."*)

I saw this quote on some **lanky stud**ent's home-made T shirt. I'm sure he has some profound **reasoning for** believing society is ending, but whatever it is, I don't care. **His gram**mar error suggests he's not likely to have the sharpest of minds, and, therefore, whatever he has to say is not likely to be convincing.

"If your going through hell, keep going."
(Should be: *"If you're going through hell, keep going."*)
I saw this on the internet. These words were tattooed on a skinhead's head in bold letters. Confusing your and you're is a basic mistake. I mean, come on, if you're going to get something tattooed on your skull, at least check the grammar and spelling. It might be a wrong conclusion, but that particular tattoo smacks of a low intellect. His encouragement to keep going in times of adversity is commendable, but who wants to take advice from someone with a primary-school-level error tattooed on his swede?

"Recruitment at it's best."
(Should be: *"Recruitment at its best."*)
This was a neon sign I saw outside a recruitment agency in Northern Ireland. If you don't know the difference between its and it's, then you're hardly likely to be the best at anything. That's probably unfair, but this was my first, and last, impression of that agency.

"Nothing under $5.If you don't like the prices, to bad."
(Should be: *"If you don't like the prices, too bad."*)
This was a sign in a shop in the US. The sign tells us the proprietor is aggressive and does not suffer fools. Unfortunately for him, it also tells us he is one.

So, to conclude, you cannot afford to put grammar errors in your work. Those who think that's hogwash, need to think again. Remember, first impressions play a key role when people form opinions.

9 Don't let poor grammar undermine your effectiveness

The four factors that ensure your work is read are your seniority, credibility, choice of words and structure.

It's like this. You only have four levers to pull to ensure your work is read: your seniority, your credibility, your choice of words and your structure. You can't change your seniority quickly, but you can pull on the other levers every time.

In broad terms, there are three levels of grammarian:

Level 1 (bad at grammar). People who don't think about grammar. They make dozens of basic mistakes and don't care. Usually, their chosen professions do not demand good writing skills. These people are not the ones who need help.

Level 2 (think they're good at grammar). People who are quick to point a finger at those in Level 1 and think they're in Level 3.

Level 3 (good at grammar). People who discuss things like how the need to eliminate ambiguity overrides local writing conventions and a striving for consistency.

It would be great if we were all at Level 3, but we're not, and getting there would be a time-consuming and painful process. The best thing to do (and this applies to everyone) is to get someone else to check your writing. The chances of the gaps in your grammar know-how being exactly the same as someone else's are pretty slim. For example, you might struggle with affect and effect, and they might struggle with capital letters, but overlaid, your grammar know-hows will provide an intact grammar shield. (There's a little more on proofreading later.)

10   Unfortunately, ignorance is <u>not</u> bliss

Many of those operating at Level 2 (and that's most of us) are suffering from the Dunning-Kruger Effect (see Section 51). This effect occurs when a person's incompetence prevents him from seeing his incompetence. It is well captured with the adage "Ignorance is bliss."

Picture this. Toby, our Level 2 grammarian, is happily typing away. Every few paragraphs, he types a nasty little grammar error, but he doesn't know they're mistakes. He knows that "two solution's" would be wrong, but he doesn't know that the "compliment" he just typed should be "complement" and that the "Client" should be "client". In ignorant bliss, Toby carries on. When he presses "Send", his message and his "grammar incompetency badge" go whizzing off to the addressees. The Dunning-Kruger Effect stopped Toby seeing his incompetence, but all the addressees can now see it. Another effect now kicks in: the Halo Effect (see Section 56). This ensures that a good or bad trait (and in this case, it's a bad trait) permeates throughout everything, even things that aren't related to the trait. So, Toby's bad grammar is now undermining everything he typed in his message. A quick check with a grammar programme <u>and</u> by another person, and his grammar errors would probably have been spotted, making his whole message far more credible.

11   Grammar checkers don't always work

Grammar-checking software can be a great help, but you need to understand what it is doing for you. If you think a grammar-checking program is going to solve all your grammar issues, then you need to adjust your expectations. Native English speakers should expect a grammar checker to spot around half of their grammar mistakes. They should also be aware that it will routinely highlight correct things as incorrect. For example, when I typed the "three levels of grammarian" paragraph above, my grammar checker told me to consider "People who doesn't think about grammar." (Obviously, I meant to type "don't" not "doesn't", so that suggestion got the old "Ignore Once" treatment.)

Grammar checkers perform a "mathematical check" on the grammar. They do not understand the words, and this is the main reason why they're not 100% effective. Here are some examples:

They often can't spot erroneous apostrophes

Example: *I have one dog. My dogs' kennel is green.*

Even in this simple example, the grammar checker is unable to determine that the kennel belongs to one dog (i.e. it should read: "My **dog's** kennel is green.") This is because it does not link the two sentences or even understand them. Mathematically, "dogs' kennel" is feasible as a standalone piece of English.

They often can't help with capital letters

Example: *The church is near the tube station.*

In this example, the church refers to a pub called "The Church". Therefore, "church" should start with a capital letter. With no context, however, there is nothing grammatically wrong with the sentence, and a grammar checker would ignore it.

They often can't help with that and which

Example: *He has selected the model which Tony developed on Monday.*

The latest grammar checkers would recommend the use of "that" instead of "which" in this example. (Both are correct.) However, grammar checkers would also wrongly suggest ", which" (with a comma) as an option. This is not a subject for this book, but it suffices to say:

"which" = "that"
", which" does not equal "that"

They Often Confuse the Meanings of Simple Words

Example: *Sandra was seen by the bridge.*

In this example, a grammar checker is likely to suggest the version "The bridge saw Sandra". This is because it does not realise that the word "by" is being used to mean "near".

They Can't Work Out If Some Words Are Plural or Singular

Example: *People who don't think about grammar.*

In this example, a grammar checker is likely to suggest the version "People who doesn't think about grammar". This is because it does not realise that the word "who" relates to the plural word "people". It knows that "who" can be singular or plural, so it offers the one you didn't choose to make you check. Grammar checkers do this a lot. For example, many will suggest "allude" if you type "elude" (and vice versa) to encourage you to check you've used the right one.

Don't get me wrong. I think the people who writes these grammar programmes is geniuses. (That was a deliberate, below-the-belt dig at them, by the way.) Nevertheless, these simple examples illustrate some of the flaws in grammar checkers.

Right, that's enough on grammar, but if you still need to be convinced that a single apostrophe can sink you, check this out:

"Were the best butchers in St. Helens!"
(Should be: *"We're the best butchers in St. Helens!"*)
No explanation needed, I feel.

Okay, you're about one third of the way through the business-writing chapter now. Remember, the aim of *How To Get Your Own Way* is to present a holistic system to improve your ability to influence and to protect yourself from those trying to influence you. Don't forget that writing is the tool you'll most often use to wield that influence, and a key part of that writing is your choice of words.

YOUR CHOICE OF WORDS

(12) ## Don't use words no one understands

One very smart guy I work with loves the word "concatenate", which means "to link things together in a chain or series" (Yes, I've just Googled it again.) Actually, I quite like the word "concatenate" too. It just sounds like a great word. It's wonderfully rhythmic. I feel I want to write a poem just so I can use it. But that's where my praise for "concatenate" ends. When his paper with "concatenate" was passed around the office, everyone (to a man) made some comment about it, and no one knew what it meant.

"Any word you have to hunt for in a thesaurus is the wrong word. There are no exceptions to this rule."
(Author Stephen King)

There is a simple message here: don't use words no one understands. But that's not the end of the story, unfortunately. That's just the extreme edge of what not to do. Your choice of words is important to make your writing easy to read, and easy to read does not just mean understandable. It covers all of the following:

Understandable. Using words people understand and presenting ideas clearly.

Flowing. Keeping your writing natural-sounding without the speed bumps of bureaucratic language.

Succinct. Making key points leap off the page, removing irrelevant detail and saying things just once.

Unambiguous. Using clear language that can only mean one thing and having a clear opinion.

Interesting. Making the content relevant and, if appropriate, throwing in a few linguistic tricks like metaphors.

Writing to sound professional is the biggest mistake people make. Trying to sound professional causes two problems:

- It makes writers select unnatural words.
- It makes writers use too many nouns.

13   Take Churchill's advice: Use "German" words

Consider the words *axiomatic* and *obvious*. Which one sounds the more professional? What about *ameliorate* and *improve*? What about *acquire* and *get*? Well, the answer to the question depends on what professional means. If professional means sounding like a 19th century lawyer, then the first word is the winner. But professional does not mean that. To most people, it just means being good at your job. Note I said being good at your job and not looking good at your job. They are different things. If you communicate your message clearly, you are being good at your job. If you make it hard for your message to be understood because you've chosen unnatural words, you are not. So, to be professional, natural-sounding words trump posh words.

So, what are natural-sounding words and what are posh words? You will know by instinct which words you can get away with. If you think a word sounds a bit too contrived, then it probably is. But here's a bit of history to assist you in your choice of words:

The Anglo-Saxon settlement of Britain in the fifth century caused an influx of Germanic words into Britain which were adopted by the general public. These words became the words of the everyday man and are still very natural sounding to the British ear. However, our language was also affected by another invasion, which started in 1066 with the Battle of Hastings. It was a war between Duke William I (Norman-French) and King Harold II (English). William won, as we know, and it wasn't long before we had a new French-speaking aristocracy. As a result, French-derived words (which often came from Latin) were the words of the upper classes. So, Germanic words sound natural, and French words sound posh. That idea still holds true today.

Look at these examples:
- Better from Besser (Germanic)
- Ameliorate from Amelior (French)
- Riding from Reiten (Germanic)
- Equestrian from Equitation (French)

As a general rule, the Germanic words will be short and easily understood. Often Germanic verbs (doing words) will be made up of more than one word (e.g. to look after, to put off, to get together). French words tend to be a little longer and a bit highbrow. Sometimes the meaning is clear (e.g. acquire, obtain), but sometimes they push the bounds of most people's understanding (e.g. militate, mitigate). Verbs will often be single words (e.g. nurture, postpone, congregate).

People like to read Germanic words, because that's how they speak.

"Broadly speaking, the short words are the best, and the old words best of all."
(Sir Winston Churchill)

However, writers like to use "French" words (they're actually called Latinate words), because it makes them look more classy and more educated. So, there is a balance to be struck. The first ruling is easy: don't use words nobody understands, like "concatenate". After that, it's up to you to decide what proportion of Germanic and Latinate words you go for. Here's a good rule of thumb: write how you speak. We'll examine that idea a bit more in a second, but, before we do, we need to talk about contractions.

Contractions are words like *don't, isn't, won't* and *can't*. (In other words, they are words that have had letters replaced by apostrophes to reflect how we speak.) Should you use contractions in formal writing? Well, that depends who you are. I was in the military. I can tell you that in 25 years of bashing out formal documents, I have never used a contraction – not one. It was forbidden. Contractions don't fit with the image the military seeks to portray in its formal correspondence. Hey, don't get me wrong. I've used thousands of contractions in day-to-day emails and memos. But, in those circumstances, I'm representing me, not my unit or the military. However, if I were to work for someone like Virgin or Red Bull, both of whom like to engage with their customers using very natural-sounding language, then I'm sure I'd be using contractions all over the place.

(14)　Write how you speak

There is a well-used saying that will guide us through the next section:

> "If your writing reads like writing, then re-write it."

Speaking is great. It's clear, full of personality and structured naturally. In my opinion, that last point (structured naturally) is its most fantastic trait. Writing, on the other hand, can be boring, corporate, predictable and structured abnormally. What do I mean by "structured abnormally"? Well, mostly, I mean an overuse of nouns (i.e. naming words). Look at these examples (nouns in bold):

Unnatural: I was under the mistaken **assumption** you performed the **dance**.
Natural: I mistakenly assumed you danced.

Unnatural: We promise an **undertaking** to show **support** for your **actions**.
Natural: We promise to support you.

Unnatural: They are in **agreement** with us.
Natural: They agree with us.

Unnatural: She will be in **attendance** at the **meeting**.

Natural: She will attend the **meeting**.

Unnatural: He was in **violation** of several **regulations**.
Natural: He violated several **regulations**.

Unnatural: Will it have an **effect** on our **procedures**?
Natural: Will it affect our **procedures**?

It's true that people overuse nouns when they're trying to sound official, but there is another way to look at the problem. Quite often the right verb (i.e. a doing word) will remove the pomp from your sentence. In the examples below, a good solid verb (shown in bold) gets the job done far more naturally:

Unnatural: This rule is applicable to both teams.
Natural: This rule **applies** to both teams.

Unnatural: The treaty is binding for all parties.
Natural: The treaty **binds** all parties.

Unnatural: The solution is derived from three universities' work.
Natural: The solution **derives** from three universities' work.

Unnatural: The Jamaican sunrise is influential in his work.
Natural: The Jamaican sunrise **influences** his work.

There are entire books dedicated to writing succinctly and naturally, but to get a 90% fix, you don't have to read them or even understand what's going on with the grammar. All you have to do is say what you want to say aloud and then write it down. Provided you don't trick yourself into talking like someone you're not, you'll end up with a natural-sounding text (with good solid verbs and just enough nouns to get the job done).

Hang on. Let's be a bit more realistic about this. You're not really going to say every sentence out loud before writing it down, but you could do that for the odd one if you're struggling with the structure of a sentence. Quite often, writers tie themselves up in knots with a sentence because they're trying to express too many ideas in an unnatural way (i.e. using too many Latinate words and nouns). The best thing to do if a sentence is starting to run away with you is:

(1) Stop.
(2) Say what you want to say (out loud if it helps).
(3) Write it down.
(4) Carry on.

That's a technique to free a brain block if you get yourself bogged down. More generally, here's what to do:

(1) Write as naturally and as simply as you can.
(2) Read your writing out loud when you've finished.
(3) If you can read it naturally, your sentence structure and word choice will be good.
(4) If you have to warble like a demented politician to get through the sentences (i.e. stressing words in a way that only you as the author could), you need to rethink your sentence structure and word choice.

Think of writing as speaking+

"Think like a wise man but communicate in the language of the people." (Irish poet and playwright William Butler Yeats, 1865–1939)

You could think of writing as "speaking plus". Write as you would speak, but:

(1) Make tweaks to improve the choice of words.
(2) Remove any repetition.
(3) Remove any ambiguity.
(4) Improve succinctness.

15   **Be yourself, and the right words will appear**

Don't be afraid to be yourself. Let your personality show through.
It's a great way to give your writing a natural flow and to make it
more interesting. A few years ago, I came across a terrific example of
someone tripping up by trying to be someone else:

For some reason, I was watching *America's Next Top Model*. Don't ask
me why. One of the contestants was being asked questions to give the
judges some insight into her personality. She was asked, "What's your
favourite film?" Trying to be sophisticated, she announced "I really
love *Dinner at Tiffany's*." The ensuing silence alerted her to her error.
She then said with waning confidence, "*Lunch at Tiffany's*?" Another
silence. Somewhat unimpressed, one of the judges said, "*Breakfast.
Breakfast at Tiffany's*". "Yes, that's it", she blurted, "*Breakfast at
Tiffany's*. That's my favourite film." I didn't watch any more of the
show, but I'm guessing she didn't get much further in the competition.

   Now, that's a pretty extreme example of what can happen if you
try to be someone you're not. The point here is just be yourself. That
honesty will improve your writing, particularly the structure of your
sentences. It will also engender trust between you and your readers,
and it will win the day in the end, I promise.

   Here's an idea. Don't take this too literally. It's only included to
encourage you to use shorter words. I believe there might be three
standards of writing:

Level 1 (the worst writers) – People who use *get* and *don't*
Level 2 (competent writers) – People who use *acquire* and *refrain*
Level 3 (the best writers) – People who use *get* and *don't*

If you think you're at Level 3 and you know your audience knows
you are, then crack on *getting, gotting, don'ting* and *won'ting*. But, if
you're unsure, play safe and write at Level 2. That's where I am when
it comes to formal writing, because I'm not confident my audience
would recognise the difference between Level 1 and Level 3.

I'm not sure Level 3 even exists in some fields. I don't think a brochure about over-the-horizon radar ought to be written in a speaking style. Many topics deserve a level of seriousness and respect that gets and don'ts would undermine.

Here's the bottom line: Write clearly using words fitting for your audience. Don't show off. If you do, you're setting yourself up to fail.

(16) Don't be lazy. Write parallel lists

People like reading bullet points. That's because there's one introduction and then a list of important information that's presented in easy-to-find, bite-sized chunks. Bullet points are great. Whenever you're writing a list, don't string it out in a long line of text as part of a sentence. Get it chopped up into bullet points. (Besides, punctuating lists in sentences can be a nightmare.)

I've been told I suffer from obsessive-compulsive disorder (OCD) when it comes to lists. That's rubbish. If I suffer from anything, it's CDO. I couldn't possibly suffer from something that doesn't have its letters in alphabetical order.

Seriously though, it is an excellent idea when writing lists to ensure that each list item is written in the same style. When list items are written in the same style, the list is said to be parallel. Bullet points are great, but parallel bullet points are great with a cherry on top.

You will have to invest some brainpower to make a list parallel, but a parallel list is much easier to read and far clearer. It will also portray you as a clear thinker. Once you've learned how to make lists parallel, there will be no going back. So, if you don't want to suffer from list "CDO", you need to skip this section. I wouldn't advise it though. I am confident you will grow to love parallel lists.

Here's a non-parallel list:

Risk-mitigation levers:
- *The updating of the memorandum of understanding.*
- *Engage with stakeholders on a monthly basis.*
- *Completed tender by January.*

Here's a parallel version:

Ways to reduce risk:
- *Update the memorandum of understanding.*
- *Engage with stakeholders on a monthly basis.*
- *Complete the tender by January.*

(Note: The two introductions above are not related to parallel lists. I just wanted to make the point that "Ways to reduce risk" is clearer than "Risk-mitigation levers". Have the confidence to write simply.)

The non-parallel list is fairly clear, but I hate it. The first bullet starts with a noun (notwithstanding the "The"), the second with a verb and the third with an adjective (well, a participle). The grammar's not important. What's important is that they all start with a different type of word. Even if you can't rattle off what nouns, verbs etc. are (and most people can't), it doesn't matter one jot. You will instinctively know how to make your list parallel if you're minded to do so.

Here's another example:

I would advise visitors to avoid:
- *Bathing in the river.*
- *Driving in the town.*
- *The local tapas bar.*

That's not bad, but it's not quite parallel. This would be parallel:

I would advise visitors to avoid:
- *Bathing in the river.*
- *Driving in the town.*
- *Eating in the local tapas bar.*

Parallel lists will make your writing far clearer. If you look back at the first set of lists (Risk-mitigation levers), it's not clear from the non-parallel version that there is an action required for each bullet. However, that is very clear on the parallel version. When dealing with risk to your business, you really don't need any ambiguity surrounding how you're going to reduce your risks. This reminds me of some advice I once heard on an Army junior leadership course back in the late 1980s. We were taught to nominate a person when barking out a quick instruction. "Jacko, call an ambulance" is far clearer than "Will someone call an ambulance?" The first version is far more likely to get the job done than the second. Well, that's how I feel about parallel lists over non-parallel lists.

Just to be clear, not every list item has to be an action, but each one does have to start with the same kind of word.

A quick word on formatting. The most common way to format bullet points is to start each one with a capital letter and end each one with a full stop. (In PowerPoint, people tend to drop the full stop.) Unless you have a company policy on this, there are no strict rules governing what you should do – except one. Pick whatever formatting you want and then be consistent.

Here's a quick example of why you should write bullet points.

"Please don't light fires, damage trees and take your litter home."
(National Trust sign at Wembury near Plymouth)

I think it's pretty clear from this sign what you're not allowed to do, but the English is broken. (For me, the National Trust's credibility dropped a bit when I saw this sign.) If they'd used parallel bullet points, they'd have written a much more credible sign, and they wouldn't have tied themselves in knots with the sentence structure.

They should have written this:

Please do not:
- *Light fires.*
- *Damage trees.*
- *Leave litter.*

(17) If your reader thinks it's jargon, it's jargon

What is jargon? Here's a good definition:

> "Special words used by a particular group that are difficult for others to understand."

Should you use jargon? Well, yes and no. Using jargon is an efficient way of communicating if you're talking to someone in your group, but it's a disastrous way of communicating with people outside your group. So, don't use jargon on outsiders. Sorted.

The problem, unfortunately, is a little more complicated than that. This is because it's not always easy to determine who's in your group and who's not. For example, an oil company that wants to hire a percussion rotary air-blast drilling rig (whatever one of those is) from your company can probably handle lots of jargon relating to the equipment and the environment it's needed for. However, the insurance company covering your workers in that environment would need a jargon-free version of the drilling activities. It's all about knowing your audience. You mustn't think your readers are like you. If you do, you're Mirror Imaging (see Section 60), and that's a certain path to filling your correspondence with incomprehensible jargon. The way to overcome Mirror Imaging is red teaming (see Section 60). This is a technique that involves you pretending to be the people you're examining (or in this case, writing to). Remember, this section is about creating business writing that gets the job done. Writing stuff the reader can't understand does not align well with that aim at all.

To a reader, jargon often looks like superfluous detail or clouding, and it can make the reader suspicious. George Orwell was all over this idea:

"The great enemy of clear language is insincerity. When there is a gap between one's real and one's declared aims, one turns as it were instinctively to long words… like a cuttlefish spurting out ink."
(English novelist George Orwell, 1903–1950)

Blurting superfluous detail is also a technique people use to mask a lie, and humans have learned to become pretty wary of people who do that.

Jargon, by definition, tells your readers they're not in your group. It can make them feel excluded, and that can't be good if you want them to do something for you.

(18) The other kind of jargon: business speak

Business speak does not fit well with the standard definition for jargon, because its use doesn't lead to a lack of understanding. It does, however, lead to groans from your readers or, more usually, your listeners.

Here are some examples of business speak:

- Out of the loop
- On the same page
- Synergy
- Drill down
- Think outside the box
- Win-win
- Low-hanging fruit
- Work smarter

- Hit the ground running
- Reinvent the wheel
- Blue-sky thinking
- Push the envelope
- Pre-prepare
- Touch base off-line
- Increased granularity
- Not enough bandwidth

I once heard this in a meeting:

"a synergistic systems-of-systems approach to leverage a long-term solution"

It wasn't a mickey-take either.

Personally, I don't think using these terms is anywhere near as bad a crime as using unintelligible jargon, but so many people tell me they're turned off by it, I felt I had to talk about it. You will of course have heard about Business Bingo, a game in which meeting attendees armed with lists of these expressions tick them off as they're spoken by the presenters. That game has done little to improve the acceptance of these terms, but, I think some of them are quite efficient. Take "low-hanging fruit" and "push the envelope". They express ideas that would otherwise take far more words to explain. Later, we will talk about avoiding old metaphors and creating new ones to keep your writing vibrant. I don't think these business-speak terms ought to be categorised as tired metaphors, but be aware that some people do. Where does that leave you? Should you use them or not? Here's my advice: Use them at will in meetings, informal briefings and peer-to-peer emails, but avoid them in formal writing.

You could also invent some of your own. Here are some computer-related ones:

Mouse potato: Like a couch potato, but relating to a computer, not a TV.
Percussive maintenance: Fixing by whacking.
Plug-and-play employee: Someone who doesn't need training.
Plug-and-pray employee: Someone who still needs training.
Treeware: Paper.
Uninstalled: Fired (also, decruitment).

19   **Avoiding tautology and redundancy**

Every time you use a word that adds nothing to your message, a small child somewhere stops believing in the Easter Bunny. It's a bad thing. Remember, no one really cares what you've got to say, and they're not going to spend much time reading your stuff (especially if it's long), so you must strive to get your message across in as few words as possible.

"The length of your letter is directly proportional to the speed of your readers' skim-reading."
(BBC Monitoring editor Ashley Brewer)

All that said, avoiding tautology and redundancy is not really about saving your readers' time, it's more about showcasing your proficiency with words. If you can write sentences with no redundant words, your writing prowess becomes very apparent – even to those who don't know what redundant words are. So, it's more about your credibility.

Some words in a sentence add nothing to the meaning, and these are the ones you should look to eliminate. You could do this as you're going along, but that might stifle your creativity and flow. In my experience, redundant words are best removed as part of the proofreading process. Look at these two sentences:

Starting version:
"Given a choice between two theories, take the one which is funnier."
Proofread version:
"Given a choice between two theories, take the funnier one."

Yes, well chuffed. I've managed to delete "which is" without any loss of meaning. I'm really pleased. The sentence now fits on one line, which is an added bonus!

Hang on. Did I just say "added bonus!" Do I really need the word "added"?

"Bonus" usually means "a payment or gift added to what is usual or expected." So, actually, there's no need for me to use "added". The notion of "added" is already included in the word "bonus". Therefore, "added" can be deleted without any loss of meaning. Bonus!

Here are a few common terms with deletable words:

~~Armed~~ gunman	~~New~~ innovation
Ask ~~the question~~	~~Past~~ experience
Attach ~~together~~	~~Temper~~ tantrum
Commute ~~back and forth~~	~~Three-way~~ love triangle
Depreciate ~~in value~~	~~Unintentional~~ mistake
Evolve ~~over time~~	~~Unexpected~~ surprise
~~Frozen~~ ice	Warn ~~in advance~~

All the crossed-out words are redundant.

Sometimes, redundant words are words that are just not needed.

Fetch the book ~~which is~~ by the fire.

But, sometimes, words are redundant because they say the same thing as something you've already said. When this happens, the redundant words are said to be tautological. The term with the idea expressed twice is called a tautology. For example:

He left at 3 a.m. in the morning.
(This is a tautology – a.m. means in the morning)

In our assessment, we think he is alive.
(In our assessment means we think)

Be careful though. Something that looks like tautology might not be:

Present a short summary.
(Argument: Summaries are always short. Delete short. Counter-argument: Are they? You could have a 5-page summary. Is that short?)

She died from a fatal dose of heroin.
(Argument: Of course it was a fatal dose. That's why she died. Counter-argument: She could have died from a non-fatal dose of heroin, i.e. it wouldn't have killed most people.)

Enter your PIN number in the ATM machine.
(Argument: PIN means Personal Identification Number. You don't need to repeat the word number. ATM means Automated Teller Machine. You don't need to repeat the word machine. Counter-argument: True, but don't you think PIN and ATM have become words in their own right? In the interest of clarity, it's best to leave the redundancy in.)

So, sometimes, you might have a debate on your hands about whether words are redundant or not. In all cases, your striving for clarity must trump your efforts to avoid redundancy. (And, that's why I left "or not" in "redundant or not" in the first sentence of this paragraph.)

This next point is important. Redundant words aren't just the odd word here and there (as in the common terms on the previous page). Often, redundant words are whole sentences or paragraphs which repeat something you've already said. Get 'em deleted. Keep the Easter Bunny in gainful employment.

20 Removing ambiguity

> "Never hit a man with glasses. Hit him with a baseball bat."

If using redundant words is shoplifting a bag of crisps, then inserting ambiguity is holding up the till with sawn-off shotgun. It's a far worse crime. Look at this sentence:

The extremists will develop their plans to attack in the next two days.

Now, imagine you're in charge of defending a facility against the extremists. You'd be on the phone pretty quickly to the person who wrote that sentence asking what it meant. Does it mean the planning will take place over the next two days, or does it mean the attack will take place over the next two days? That's a pretty important distinction if you're the one responsible for doubling the guard force. Ambiguous writing will show your readers that you're not a clear thinker, and it will confuse and annoy them. Here are some more ambiguous sentences:

The policeman shot a terrorist with a Kalashnikov assault rifle.
Cycling uphill quickly strengthens your legs.
We need a French and German teacher.
I await your comments on Facebook.
Her sister gave her cat food.

Because the author knew what he meant to say, he is usually the worst person to spot any ambiguous words he's written. For example, when the author wrote "The policeman shot a terrorist with a Kalashnikov", he imagined a terrorist holding a Kalashnikov. He didn't for one second think the policeman could be the one with a Kalashnikov. However, to the reader, it's ambiguous. Without context, the reader would have no idea who was holding the Kalashnikov. The author's "mind video" of the incident ensures he fails to see the ambiguity. I like to call this "author blindness".

Author blindness also affects the author's ability to see typos. Knowing what the text is supposed to say, the author's brain fails to register what it actually says. I always omit the word "be" for some reason. I only tend to spot this error the next day if I'm re-reading what I've written or if a proofreader points it out. The bottom line is this: there's a fair chance you won't spot anything ambiguous you've written, and you're likely to miss an uncomfortably high percentage of your own typos.

You might be surprised at your brain's ability to cope with jumbled or missing letters and words. It's trying to do you a favour, but – when it comes to proofreading – it's not. If you've been anywhere near the internet in the last decade, you'll probably have seen something like this before, but it's still useful to highlight how good your brain is at "helping" you:

Dno't tsrut yuorslef to sopt mesktais in yuor wrinitg. Yuor barin has the ablitiy to see waht was maent to be wtriten

If it's an important piece of business writing, get it proofread. Proofreaders rarely do you a disservice.

But don't worry. There is at least one great grammar checker out there. It's called the "Send" button. As soon as you send something, your typos will leap off the screen at you. Unfortunately, by the time it's worked its "magic", you'll be wishing you'd had your work proofread. So, do worry. Use a proofreader.

Here's a tip. Ask your proofreaders to annotate their markings with:

- "**1**" to express a minor concern (but the writing is still good to go).
- "**2**" to suggest a rewrite before sending (but the writing is still adequate).
- "**3**" to highlight something that definitely needs changing; i.e. typos, grammar errors, formatting errors, factual errors, ambiguity, redundancy or just very poor wording.

Armed with these options, your proofreaders will find the process much easier, because you've given them a way to express opinion without having to decide whether each observation is a reportable error. They'll do a more thorough job for you, I promise.

If you routinely check writing others do for you to sign there's an added benefit to this method of proofreading. It will help the writers "get in your head" (as we used to call it in the military) more quickly, and they'll be writing in your preferred style sooner, making the whole letter-drafting process more efficient. Communicating your amendments downwards (i.e. to your team) is a great investment. For example, you can either spend half your life deleting the word "that" from your drafters' letters or you can show them once that you deleted the word "that" nearly every time they used it.

21   How to ask people to do things for you

So, how do you get people to do stuff for you? Well, there are a few aspects to this. The first thing we need to talk about is your choice of asking words.

When talking to your seniors (or clients), use these words:

I propose that…
It is proposed that…

When talking to people at your level, use these words:

You are requested to…
I request that you…
It is requested that…

When talking to your subordinates, you can either use the words above, or, if you need to be a bit more authoritative, these words:

You are to…
Bill is to…

Now, these suggestions have been stripped back to their bare bones, and in this form they look a bit formal. Of course, your surrounding sentences can be used to remove some of that formality. Also, trust yourself. You will know instinctively whether words like "you are requested" and "you are to" are appropriate for using on the people you work with. If they're not appropriate, just use the words that come naturally, like "Please…" or "Please could you…". The suggestions above are for when some formality is required.

There are dozens of ways of asking people to do stuff, but the list above will hopefully take the thinking out of it for you. If the whole list doesn't seem right for you (e.g. it's too proscriptive or unnatural sounding), then just remember this: If you are talking to someone senior or a client whom you can't afford to rankle, then *propose* something. It's clear. It's polite. It's businesslike. It's a great word. But expect them to take your proposal, make it their own, call it their own and then do it. From your perspective, job done.

22 Thank them, praise them or agree with them, and then influence them

Crowbarring your request or your opinion into other people's busy lives is difficult because you have to overcome their natural resistance to run with your idea (as opposed to theirs) or to do something new. We've got a whole chapter on biases coming up later. It will cover why people like their own ideas and why they are resistant to new ideas, so we won't dive into that just yet. What we are going to look at though is how to make them think they're running with their idea and not yours.

Look at this quotation:

"Everyone is in love with his own ideas."
(Swiss psychiatrist Carl Jung, 1875–1961)

In my experience, that's accurate. It's why people work more enthusiastically on their own ideas than others' ideas. So, how can you divert their enthusiasm on to your idea? Easy. Do one of the following:

- Make them think their idea is contributing to your idea.

You: *We need to move that horse manure from the boss's car-parking space. Has anyone got any ideas?*
Johnny: *We could use that bucket in the coffee room.*
You: *Great idea. Off you pop.*

- Make them think your idea is contributing towards their idea.

You: *Would you like to use that horse manure in the boss's car-parking space for that rose garden you were talking about?*
Johnny: *Yes.*
You: *Great. Help yourself to all of it.*

- Make them think your idea was their idea.

You: *We'd probably get a fiver from the garden centre for all that horse manure in the boss's car-parking space.*
Johnny: *We could use it on the rose bed.*
You: *Great idea. Off you pop.*

How do think Johnny would feel if you said: "Johnny, can you use that bucket in the coffee room to move that horse shit from the boss's car-parking space to your rose garden?"

It's my bet that, if he did it at all, it would be with less enthusiasm than in any of the scenarios above. Obviously, this is a made-up simple scenario, but I believe the lesson is a good one. I don't really see this "influence dance" happening over a three-sentence conversation like the ones above. In some jobs, they can last months and involve dozens of correspondence exchanges. Unless your idea is an obvious solution which no one else has thought of (often called a "silver bullet") or a Eureka-moment gem, you could spend hours debating the merits of your idea to achieve buy-in, and you probably will. Remember, everyone loves his own idea. Therefore, they won't love yours. So, you're not starting from a good position when trying to sell an idea. Of course, you can pay people or order people to carry out your ideas without bothering to shoehorn in their ideas, but I bet they take every second of every coffee break that's due to them and more if you do.

"Don't worry about people stealing your ideas. If your ideas are any good, you'll have to ram them down people's throats."
(Computing pioneer Howard Aiken)

"The only people in the world who can change things are those who can sell ideas."
(American author Lois Wyse)

So, converting or aligning their ideas to yours is a great way to sell your idea. But how does this idea manifest itself in business writing? Well, early in the document, weave in lines of this nature:

Thank you for your idea/work...
Your idea/work was really useful...
We agree with your idea/work...
We liked your idea/work...

Later in the document, weave in lines of this nature:

We can develop this to [do what I want to do].
We can use this to inform [the stuff I want to do].
This aligns well with [what I want to do].
One observation is that [it's not what I want to do] so we might need to tweak that bit.
I have been thinking about your idea, and it could support [the stuff I want to do].
Your idea would also help the company [do what I want to do].

The secret to winning enthusiasm for your idea is to make it look as though your idea is a piece of their jigsaw or to encourage them to make their idea fit your jigsaw.

"A mediocre idea that generates enthusiasm will go further than a great idea that inspires no one."
(American businesswoman Mary Kay Ash)

Stealing their enthusiasm for their idea is a sure way to generate the necessary enthusiasm for yours. None of the words offered above may be a perfect fit for your specific scenario, but the bottom line is this: recognise their efforts and then start moulding them towards your aim.

(23) ## Make people think you're great by using moderation, modesty and evidence

Telling people you're great will have the opposite effect. People like moderation and evidence. If you apply those traits to what you write, you will win people over. And that's what we'll cover in this section.

"Modesty is the only sure bait when you angle for praise."
(Philip Dormer Stanhope 4th Earl of Chesterfield, 1694–1773)

People use way too many very's, extremely's and excellent's in their writing. Removing them is a good start. Your message is usually far more powerful without them. Unless they're backed up by evidence, words of this nature look like exaggeration or desperation. They don't even look like confidence. They do nothing for you. Your readers have become immune to them. To me, they just look like lazy writing. Let's examine this idea a bit more.

How have you described your communication skills on your CV? "Excellent communication skills"? If the answer is yes, go and stand with the other 95% of job applicants who wrote the same.

Will the employer reading your CV believe you've got excellent communication skills because that's what you wrote? No chance. The word "excellent" will have no impact at all. The employer will look at how you've written and laid out your CV to determine whether you've got "excellent" communication skills. But he will also be aware that your CV might not be your own work. Here's how it works:

Obviously, a badly written CV tells him your communications skills are poor. However, a well-written CV does not provide him with conclusive evidence that your communication skills are good or excellent. He still needs to make a judgement on that. For me, this brings to mind a great saying we had in the Intelligence Corps: Absence of evidence is not evidence of absence. In other words, when faced with a well-written CV, the employer has no evidence that your communication skills are bad, but he will instinctively know that it doesn't mean they're not bad. So, to score the most points you can for "communications skills", you need to do two things. You need to present a well-written CV (obviously) and offer some *evidence* that they're excellent. You could try a line like this:

"Sound communication skills developed over two years as a [insert previous job where communications skills were key] and honed with [insert something else you did more recently where communication skills were essential]"

First, you've used the word "sound". That shows modesty, and it's believable. Second, you've provided some evidence, so now it's very believable. You've written "sound communications skills", but the employer will be thinking "excellent communication skills".

The practice of using moderation and presenting evidence doesn't just work on CVs. It works on everything (emails, letters, adverts, etc.) Look at these two examples from my local paper:

"I am an extremely experienced plumber who'll do an excellent job."

"After a job well done, you can post a review on my website."

The second one is a cracker. He's so confident in his plumbing abilities, he's letting the customer hold him by the throat (not literally) to ensure he does a good job. That's about as much customer confidence ("evidence") as you can cram into one sentence. Also, the words "a job well done" show moderation. They're believable.

Unfortunately, Mr "a job well done" was booked up for two months, so I went with Mr "excellent job". He was a very good plumber, to be fair. He just wasn't good at selling himself, and that's why he was available.

To make people think you're great, chip away at them with words that show moderation and words that provide evidence.

(24) **Use moderation when reprimanding**

On occasion, you might be required to disagree with someone or reprimand them. In my experience, this is far more powerful when moderation is applied. It's the equivalent of the headmaster telling you he's not angry but disappointed or that you've let yourself down.

Sometimes it's not appropriate to deliver a straight-talking telling-off. Either because of your standing or theirs, it can be inappropriate to use words full of emotion. Calmer words are the order of the day.

Now, I'm not suggesting you should use backhanded compliments and become passive aggressive. Even passive aggressive is too aggressive. Here are some witty examples to explain what I mean by backhanded compliments:

- *"Remember, Russ, it's just as important to stay behind and guard the women and children."*
- *"It's nice that you can wear tight jeans without that unsightly bulge that most men have."*
- *"What I like about your toupee is it says, 'Hey, I have better things to spend my money on!'"*
- *"You have four cats? It only smells like one."*
- *"Lee, it's great that you're so self-confident, you can wear anything."*
- *"He is a modest man, and he has much to be modest about."*
(Attributed to Sir Winston Churchill)

To reprimand calmly, you need to come down one notch from passive aggressive to what I like to call "possibly aggressive". Here are some examples of "possibly aggressive":

- *"Mark is full of untapped potential."*
- *"The meeting was perfectly adequate."*
- *"Thank you for your comprehensive letter."* (This is a secret code. It always means your letter was too long and detailed.)
- *"The meal was nutritious."* (You think this is a compliment? Try it on your spouse.)
- *"I was a little surprised to see you had recommended Simon over Alan."* ("I was a little surprised" is a calm way of saying "What the hell were you thinking?")
- *"With a little more tempering, this man will be an excellent officer."*

This is not really about delivering a powerful reprimand. It's about expressing some displeasure without damaging your relationship or losing that hard-earned air of control. You can't expose your "iron fist". That's bullying. And where are you going to go from there? You just need to let people know you're the one wielding the power even if you don't express it through shouting.

"Iron fist in a velvet glove"
(Attributed to French military leader and emperor Napoleon Bonaparte, 1769–1821)

25   # Guard against the empty words of consultancy

> "Nothing gets ignored like a 30-page document, except legal small print"

Before we start this section, I need to say that I'm an advocate of getting stuff done by asking for it with clarity. However, on occasion, it might serve your purpose to throw in wads of jargon and detail to cloud an issue. Companies that are required by law to tell you something but don't really want you to know it employ this technique all the time. The next time a payment comes out of your bank account for a free service you tried three months ago, you'll know you've been subjected to this technique. Sometimes, however, this clouding effect (called obfuscation – see Section 73) is far more subtle, to the extent that it might not even be deliberate.

I'm going to switch tack now. I'm going to write the rest of this section from a how-to-defend-yourself perspective and not a how-to-attack-others one. And I'm going to do it through the "medium" of slagging off consultants.

There's an old saying:

"Consultants will steal your watch and tell you the time."

I also like this one:

"Tell us your phobias, and we will tell you what you are afraid of."
(American humorist Robert Benchley, 1889–1945)

That's close to how many consultants operate, but it doesn't quite describe the situation accurately enough.

Consultants are usually brought in by a company to fix a specific problem. If you look at just their daily rate, they normally get paid a fortune. A thousand pounds plus per day per man is not uncommon.

Now, knowing how much they're getting paid, the consultants feel they need to do a good job. That's fair enough. However, many consultants think the number of pages they produce in their reports is directly proportional to the value they're providing. I don't think word count and value for money are related, but I do know something that's related to word count: the will-it-ever-be-read factor.

What happens next with the consultants' weighty tome is terrific for the consultants. Their report tells the company that the problem is complicated. In fact, it's complicated to the tune of a hundred or so pages of detail. A situation then develops which sees the senior management ignoring the consultants because they're talking in lengthy, over-detailed, for-experts-only jargon. However, the management become resistant to removing the consultants because they think, given the volumes they're writing and how much they're costing, their findings must be important. Still in work, the consultants keep typing and typing and typing. Before long, the management trains itself to stop listening, and, before it knows it, the company ends up with a fattening leech hanging off its corporate torso.

This next tip probably only applies to the public sector or massive corporations where consultants can feed off their hosts without killing them. If you employ consultants, tell them you want a one-page report of their achievements. Not two pages. One. (This will improve your ability to kick them out if they're not delivering.) If they try to give you a 30-page document, they're probably not presenting 30 pages' worth of benefits but 30 pages of obfuscation in the interest of maintaining the status quo. Remember, if you want to dive into the detail, they can always show you it in their weighty tome. (Your request for a one-pager doesn't get them off that hook!)

Okay, I'll now give consultants a tiny bit of credit. In my experience, consultants tell a company what it already knows, but the value is that the company hear it from someone else – someone they're predisposed to believe because they're paying them. Hearing an idea from someone else always makes the idea more convincing.

Put your guard up against people employing these mantras:

> "If you can't convince them, confuse them."
> "Bullshit baffles brains."

This is related to the Obfuscation Fallacy (see Section 73). The extract below from the 80s satirical sitcom "Yes Minister" is one of my favourite examples of bullshit baffles brains:

Permanent Secretary: *"The Special Branch has reason to believe that the threat to your life [from the IRA] has been diminished."*
Prime Minister: *"How do they know?"*
Permanent Secretary: *"Surveillance. They overheard a conversation."*
Prime Minister: *"What did it say?"*
Permanent Secretary: *"Oh, I don't think it is of any..."*
Prime Minister: *"Come on, Humphrey, I have a right to know!"*
Permanent Secretary: *"Well it was a conversation to the effect that, in view of the somewhat nebulous and inexplicit nature of your remit, and the arguably marginal and peripheral nature of your influence on the central deliberations and decisions within the political process, there could be a case for restructuring their action priorities in such a way as to eliminate your liquidation from their immediate agenda."*
Prime Minister: *"They said that?"*
Permanent Secretary: *"That was the gist of it."*

Of course, the real message is "The IRA thinks you're not important enough to assassinate." But, like the communications of some consultants, this is a competent-looking message that has failed to communicate. In this case, deliberately.

The bottom line is this: if someone presents you with a document that is too hard or too long for you to read, then treat it as his fault. Get him to reshow his work in a more digestible format. If you let his work slip down your in-tray into the it's-never-going-to-be-read zone, you'll probably find yourself making an 11th-hour decision on something you know nothing about (possibly under the advice of the self-serving, obfuscating author of that nasty document you ignored).

26   Brainstorming – working out what to say

I'm going to end these sections under the heading "Your Choice of
Words" with a few words about brainstorming. Brainstorming is a
fantastic technique which will ensure you're never left staring at a
blank document wondering what on Earth you're going to write.

> "When you don't know what to do, do brainstorming."

Often at the end of an intelligence briefing, a general will pose a
seemingly unanswerable question to his intelligence staff. Sometimes,
he's just thinking out loud, but that doesn't matter. In any army, when
a general asks a question, it gets answered – no matter how hideous
the question and no matter how much the general really wants it
answered. And, that's how quite a few intelligence assessment papers
are conceived.

When I was in Kabul, I can remember my general wondering
out loud what would happen if the Taliban seniors based in
Pakistan stopped, for whatever reason, providing leadership to the
Afghanistan-based Taliban. Within 10 minutes of his departure, the
phone rang, and we were asked the question formally. It was now
our job to write an assessment paper on that subject. My head was
saying "How on Earth [or words to that effect] are we supposed to
know?" but my mouth was saying "No problem, we'll provide a brief
for you on that by tomorrow". That's because I had confidence in
brainstorming, a technique which allows you to magic great ideas
from thin air.

These three quotations capture how brainstorming works:

*"If you have an apple and I have an apple and we exchange these
apples, then you and I will still each have one apple. But if you have
an idea and I have an idea and we exchange these ideas, then each of
us will have two ideas."*
(Irish playwright George Bernard Shaw, 1856–1950)

"Ideas are like rabbits. You get a couple and learn how to handle them, and pretty soon you have a dozen."
(American author John Steinbeck, 1902–1968)

"The way to get good ideas is to get lots of ideas and throw the bad ones away."
(American chemist Linus Pauling, 1901–1994)

Done properly, brainstorming is far more productive than just sitting around a table and having a chat about your issue. Lots of people do that, and they call it brainstorming. But that's not really brainstorming. I would call that sitting around a table and having a chat about your issue. Here's a quick overview of how we were taught to brainstorm in the British Army. It really works.

There are three roles in a brainstorming session: the facilitator, the writer and the participants.

The Facilitator. The facilitator's tasks are:

Let 'em know who's boss. The facilitator prepares the room and meets the participants (e.g. shows them where the coffee and biscuits are or shows them where to sit). This is useful to make it clear who's running the show and to give an air of formality to the meeting. Brainstorming can easily break into chaos (e.g. lots of debates going on at once), so establishing authority early is more necessary than you might think.

Define the problem. The facilitator defines the problem to be tackled before the session starts. The first thing he does after his welcome is to seek agreement for his words that define the issue. Once done, the writer (we'll come on to him in a sec) writes the problem down in a place clearly visible for everyone. This is important to keep the session on track.

"A problem clearly stated is a problem half solved."
(New York-based editor Dorothea Brande, 1893–1948)

Outline the rules. Once he's defined the problem, the facilitator outlines the rules of brainstorming. These are the key to brainstorming's effectiveness.

Participants must:
• Understand that all ideas are potentially useful and not pass judgement.
• Strive for quantity over quality.
• Build on ideas.

Encourage participation. Throughout the session, it's the facilitator's job to encourage participation. He does this with responses to the participants' ideas like "Yes, and…", "Like it. What else?" and "How can we develop that idea?" He must avoid words like "Yes, but…" and "That would never happen". And, laughing at someone's contribution is a real no-no.

The Writer. The writer has the hardest job. The first thing he does, as we've just said, is to write the problem to be tackled in a place that's clearly visible. After that, his job is to capture all the ideas offered by the participants on a whiteboard (or whatever) that everyone can see. He should try to group the ideas in themes and write sufficient words to ensure everyone can remember what the idea was. The writer must be someone with the authority to tell the participants to slow down and to challenge the participants to present their ideas more succinctly or more clearly. "Hang on. One at a time. Jack, can you say your idea again?" (That sort of thing.)

The Participants. The participants' job is to generate ideas and state them to the rest of the group. Because the writer's job is so hard, each participant should also record his own ideas on a sheet on paper and hand it in at the end of the session. I've noticed over the years, that even the most formal brainstorming sessions don't do this. It's a mistake. Get your participants to log their own ideas and hand them in at the end. These notes will help you decipher the writer's scribblings. The facilitator and writer are both active participants too.

At the end of the session, gather all the ideas, remove any duplicates, the impractical and the ridiculous, and use what's left to solve your problem or write your paper or whatever. Brainstorming is dynamic and productive. It's fantastic for freeing up mental blocks, for team building and for knowledge transfer between participants.

On several occasions in my military career, I felt my future as an intelligence officer was dependent on being able to answer some pretty nasty-looking questions. Brainstorming saved me on each of those occasions. I'm a fan. A big fan. I doubt any of the individuals sitting in our sessions could have created the final product by themselves. It's almost magical how ideas materialise as the participants are triggered by the other participants' contributions. Armed with brainstorming, you can tackle anything.

"No problem can withstand the assault of sustained thinking."
(French philosopher François-Marie Arouet or "Voltaire", 1694–1778)

In the next few sections, we're going to talk about how to structure a document. However, I can't switch to another topic without first offering this classic quote as a reminder of the key points so far:

"I have made this [letter] longer, because I have not had the time to make it shorter."
(French mathematician Blaise Pascal, 1623–1662)

And this:

"Words as with sunbeams – the more they are condensed, the deeper they burn."
(English poet Robert Southey, 1774–1843)

YOUR DOCUMENT STRUCTURE

27   Write like a hammer, not a Christmas tree

I would wager that hardly anyone reads a newspaper from cover to cover, and that's because there's no need. You might not have noticed it, but stories in newspapers start with the important facts and then the information gets less important as you read down. A bit like this:

> **Bristol Man Wins Lottery Again.** Simon Jones from Bristol has won a major prize on the lottery for the second time in two years. After winning a £2 million jackpot in 2010, Simon has now bagged a further £500,000. He said he used the same numbers on both occasions. Simon did not move houses after his first win, and his neighbours say his fortune hasn't changed him. Simon worked as school caretaker before his first win, but bought himself a small sheet-metalwork business with his jackpot. Simon's wife said he still gets up at 6 o'clock every morning to walk the dogs before going to work.

With newspaper articles, there is no conclusion, no big twist and no ending. You could stop reading the story at any point and leave happy. Journalists are trained to write like this. It allows the editor to flex the story to fit the page.

"A newspaper consists of just the same number of words, whether there be any news in it or not."
(English novelist and dramatist Henry Fielding, 1707–1754)

If you were to represent this journalistic style graphically, it would look like an upside-down pyramid.

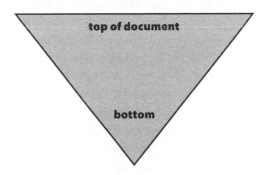

To be effective, business writing needs to adopt a fairly similar structure. All the key points need to be summarised at the very top. Quite often, these are presented as bullet points, but a summary paragraph is also common. The rest of the document adds the relevant detail. Often, the document will have an ending like a conclusion, which will be a close copy of the key points at the top. There ought to be no surprises in the ending. It is only there to reinforce the key points and to provide a fitting ending to the main body. If you were to represent this structure graphically, it would look a bit like a hammer.

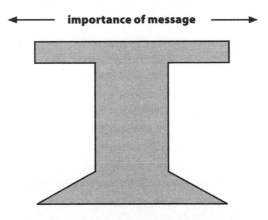

Whatever you do, don't hide the key points at random places in your document. You might have spent three days writing a beautiful report, but your readers don't care about that. You need to spoonfeed them the key points while they've got an appetite, and that means sticking the key points at the top. If they have to read through your whole document and find the key points for themselves, your writing is doomed. It will quickly make its way to the read-later pile. At this point, your document is highly vulnerable to a demotion from the read-later pile to the read-never pile. If you were to represent a bad writing structure graphically, it would look like a Christmas tree.

One of the most important aspects of asking people to do stuff is to make it very clear what you want them to do. The best way to make your request clear is to stick it right at the top of your letter or email. For example, start your email like this:

Dear all,

The purpose of this email is to request that you:

- *Submit your weekly returns by 1200 hrs on Thursday as opposed to Friday.*
- *Meet in the foyer at 0800 hrs on Friday morning.*

If needed, the justifications for these requests and the background can come next. However, if you start with the justification and the background and hide these requests amongst the text, you increase the likelihood of people failing to respond.

Remember, write like a hammer not a Christmas tree.

28   You're sending your emails into a hostile environment

Just before I left the Army, I can remember a fellow officer coming into my office and saying, "I think we're in email gridlock". He looked tired. And no wonder. There were so many emails landing in his inbox, his working day was hardly long enough to read them all, let alone respond to them. "Email gridlock" was exactly where we were. Prioritisation of emails was a key skill. But there were so many emails, the process of prioritising them – by necessity – created two never-seen-by-me-before categories: the-delete-without-reading category and the ignore-what-they've-asked category. These might be well-known categories to any very senior people reading this book, but it seems to me that junior and middle managers of all types are increasingly being forced to treat emails in the same way. So, how do we fix it?

Some companies have adopted a ruling which states: if you can phone it or go to their desk and say it, don't email it. Provided you're not talking about moving documents or data about, that's a great rule. It would cut down the number of emails hugely. More people should adopt it. But, for now at least, I think we'd be fighting the tide on that one. (Crikey, I often email my wife who's in the next room to ask what time we're taking the dogs out. I even email myself as a way of putting a knot in the handkerchief.) We've become really dependent on emails.

But, what about this:

I can remember sending a fairly senior officer an email. He was on leave. His automated out-of-office reply said, "I am on leave. Your email has been deleted."

Deleted! I nearly fell off my chair. That's not really the Army way. In the Army, out-of-office messages are more likely to offer half a dozen points of contact to assist, a promise your email will be actioned immediately upon return or, if it's important, a mobile phone number to ring the guy on his honeymoon or wherever. I thought it was quite unprofessional at first, as did others. For a few days, it was the talk of the officers' mess. But, actually, it was very smart. This officer was years ahead of us all. He completely got the fact that loads of his emails were trivial, and, if they were important, the sender would find another solution or await his return and resend it. He had created the perfect junk filter and email-prioritisation system, which was working at 100% efficiency while he took a well-earned break. I also heard a story of one very senior officer who deleted all his emails as a matter of routine, knowing the important stuff would find another route through the system. So, are emails a help or a hindrance? Actually, the answer to that question is irrelevant because we're stuck with them. So, why am I talking about them?

I am trying to get you to distrust the environment you're sending your emails to. Unless you're the one paying everyone's wages, you can't expect your emails to be read with the same love with which they were compiled. The window of interest afforded to your emails might be tiny. You might only have a few seconds to get your point across or to get the reader into the meat of your message.

And, don't think you're protected by the "audit trail" an email gives you. We're past that stage with emails. If your email is not actioned, it will become your fault for not chasing it. The answer "I sent him an email" got you off the hook 10 years ago, but not nowadays. It's lame. Your boss will start questioning your ability to get things done if you use that more than once.

Whenever I mentioned this "instructions up front" idea (i.e. write like a hammer) to my mates in the Army, there was lots of head-nodding, but not much change in the way people positioned their calls to action in their emails. In other words, they just kept doing it the old way and continued complaining about how everybody was too busy to respond to their emails. Those who did try it though have never gone back.

Here's my advice. Give "instructions up front" a bash. It's a simple idea, and it works. Even if getting things done isn't a problem in your organisation, you will save wads of time and become more efficient if you adopt the "hammer" format with your business correspondence.

"To get things done at work, put your killer bullet at the top of your document. The alternative might be putting it in the roof of your mouth."
(Adjutant of Defence School of Intelligence, Ginger Reilly)

29 Write the title, work out what you need to say

Great, you're now churning out writing structured like a hammer and not a Christmas tree. This is guaranteeing your key points are being seen by your readers. The next task is to entice them down into the main body of your document to give them a better understanding of your issues. To do this, you need to set some traps. You need to bait up your paragraphs.

Here are the main ideas:

• Make sure your paragraphs are important enough (from your readers' perspective) to be in the document.
• Title each paragraph with a succinct summary of its contents.
• Make sure your document flows, i.e. there is a logical reason for ordering the paragraphs.

Let's look at each idea in a little more detail.

Business correspondence should not be treated as your big chance to show the rest of world how busy you've been or to tell them all about your project. It is not the medium to showcase your knowledge. If you treat it as such, you are increasing the risk of everyone ignoring your message. You must only write about what the reader needs to know. Whenever I mention this concept, someone always talks about the danger of missing out important detail. It's a fair point. But, in my experience, less is more, and readers are amazingly receptive to that idea. Besides, if they want more detail, they can get back to you.

When I was learning to drive back in the 80s, I can remember my driving instructor asking, "When do you turn your lights on?" I wanted to blurt out "When it gets dark", but I refrained. I suspected he wanted an answer in lux or lumens (or whatever you measure light in), but I was wrong. The answer was "As soon you think about whether you need your headlights, you do." I quite liked that idea as a means of testing, and I think we can apply it here. How about this? As soon as you question whether some point of detail is required in your document, it isn't. I wouldn't take that idea too literally if I were you, but hopefully it will raise your threshold of what makes it into your document and what doesn't. Remember, you are writing for your readers, not for you.

The other reason people ramble on is they're thinking while they're writing. This is a pretty simple problem to fix. Do your thinking up front. It's simple, and it's effective. Do this:

(1) Start by writing a title.
(2) Next, write a list of paragraph headings and order them logically.
(3) Write the first draft of the summary.
(4) Check the title is still good.
(5) Write all the paragraphs and re-title them if necessary.
(6) Write the final conclusion and re-write the summary.
(7) Check the whole lot over.
(8) Get it proofread. Get it proofread. Get it proofread.
(9) Press Send.

"Nine things! I'm never going to remember that", I hear you say. Nah, me neither. So, just write the paragraph headings first, have a quick pop at the summary and then just do what comes naturally. In essence, you're just putting the skeleton in place for your hammer-shaped document.

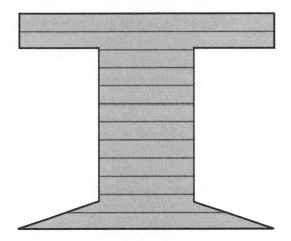

(30) ## Title each paragraph with a succinct summary of its contents

Your paragraph titles are your bait. These are the words that will drag your reader from the summary at the head of your document into its belly. Don't use single words like "Costs", "Support", "Insurance", "Challenges", "Proposals" for your paragraph titles. Nah, use whole sentences that summarise the paragraph. Your readers should be able to skim-read the paragraph headings (which is probably what they'll do) and be left with a 50% version of the whole lot. Remember, you don't have to eat all the soup to know whether it's nice or not, but you do have to try some. And, if your paragraph heading is something that interests them, they'll read the whole thing.

YOUR CHANCE TO SHOW OFF

(31) **Spice up your writing**

"Words ought to be a little wild, for they are the assault of thoughts on the unthinking."
(British economist John M. Keynes, 1883–1946)

We said at the start of this chapter that you had two choices when writing your business correspondence: make it short or make it entertaining (or both). This next section is about making it entertaining. By "entertaining", I mean "interesting to read". You are trying to bring your writing to life to make it:

- More memorable.
- Easier to understand.
- Less painful to read (i.e. less corporate or dry).

We will cover:

- Metaphors and similes.
- Single-word sentences.
- Deliberate repetition.
- Alliteration and rhythm.

Before we talk about these techniques, we need to discuss the potential dangers of trying to be too entertaining, especially if you're trying to be funny. Bear in mind that people work to pay mortgages, feed families etc. Let's be serious for a second. Work is serious stuff that serious people take seriously. Therefore, there is a danger that creative writing might come across as flippant. If you come across as flippant, you might as well have right-clicked on your document and selected "Delete" as opposed to "Send".

So, if you decide to use some of these techniques to spice up your business writing, you must seek the approval of someone senior (e.g. the business owner) to include it in the paper. If you are a senior person or it's your business, you should go home, go to bed, return to work the next day and check whether you think the creative technique is still appropriate. I am really talking about correspondence upwards and outwards (i.e. to your bosses or to other companies and customers). You don't need to apply the same level of constraint for correspondence going sideways or downwards (i.e. to peers or subordinates), although you don't want your subordinates thinking you're trying to be a comedian. (One of the most-used, but not overused, sayings in the military is "Familiarity breeds contempt." That is always worth bearing in mind when considering the tone of correspondence going downwards.)

With that caveat understood, let's look at each technique.

(32) Metaphors and similes are powerful

Okay, let's go back to school for a few minutes. A metaphor associates two concepts by stating that one of them is the other.

Her eyes were darting searchlights, scanning the room for her rival.

Actually, there is a little more to it than that. If something is being described (N.B. not compared but described) in a way that it literally is not, then you're looking at a metaphor. So, "an icy stare" is a metaphor, but "an icy stair" isn't. "A stare like ice" isn't one either. That's a comparison. It's a simile.

A simile compares two things by saying one is like the other, or one is as the other.

Her eyes were like darting searchlights, scanning the room for her rival.

I am as poor as a church mouse.

A couple of metaphors by famous people:

"Conscience is a man's compass."
(Dutch post-Impressionist painter Vincent van Gogh, 1853–1890)
"All religions, arts and sciences are branches of the same tree."
(Theoretical physicist Albert Einstein, 1879–1955)

A couple of witty metaphors:

Love is an exploding cigar we willingly smoke.

John and Mary had never met. They were two hummingbirds who had also never met.

A couple of similes by famous people:

"A room without books is like a body without a soul."
(Roman philosopher Marcus Tullius Cicero, 106 BC–43 BC)

"Writing about music is like dancing about architecture."
(Often attributed to English singer-songwriter Elvis Costello)

A couple of witty similes:

He was as lame as a duck. Not the metaphorical lame duck, either, but a real duck that was actually lame, maybe from stepping on a land mine or something.

Her vocabulary was as bad as like, yeah, whatever.

Below is an example from a business brochure which had just spent two paragraphs explaining the benefits of acquiring local knowledge before operating in a new environment:

"There are two ways to determine whether new waters are shark-infested: swim around to have a look or ask the locals."

This sentence is not a metaphor. It's just a statement. But it is a metaphor for the idea presented in the brochure. Be aware that a metaphor or a simile can be a standalone idea and that it's the readers' job to link it to the original idea. In fact, that's how a high proportion of metaphors and similes appear in business writing.

Metaphors and similes can make your writing interesting to read, more memorable, more efficient and more convincing. We've discussed the downside, but, if you're brave enough to use one and you're sure it's appropriate, the advantages are notable.

"Metaphors have a way of holding the most truth in the least space."
(American author Orson Scott Card)

When we get onto the chapter on biases in this book, you will see that people do not like to make decisions in a vacuum. They like to make comparisons, and they like supporting evidence. As well as making your writing more interesting to read, metaphors and similes can provide both of those things. Imagine you wrote this simile:

> "Plan A would be like throwing the pilot out of a stricken aircraft to make it lighter."

In reality, Plan A might be quite complex, and your simile might be somewhat simplistic, but your readers now know exactly where you stand on the issue. By offering a simple, memorable comparison, your readers will anchor to that simile when the time comes to consider the merits of plan A.

This is good stuff, so let's really get to the bottom of it. The idea of throwing the pilot out is madness. It's undeniable madness, and everyone agrees. If the simile is a good enough fit, lots of that agreement about the undeniable madness will bleed across onto Plan A. You are now not talking about Plan A directly, but about something far easier to explain. A good simile will "hijack" an idea. They're pretty powerful things.

But as well as possibly making you look a bit flippant, there is another danger with metaphors and similes. Your readers will not be impressed if you use an old one. Look at these similes:

> "A printer without ink is as much use as (1) a chocolate teapot (2) a handbrake on a submarine (3) an ashtray on a motorbike."

Take your pick. Actually, don't. These similes are old. You will only be showcasing your intellectual limitations if you use clichés like these. At some point (probably back in the 1980s), these similes were considered novel, but they've now been overused. They're tired. Doubtless there are a few people reading this thinking "A chocolate teapot? That's quite funny. I've never heard that before." Here's the point: if you didn't make it up yourself, ask around to test how fresh your simile (or metaphor) is.

"The first man to compare the cheeks of a young woman to a rose was obviously a poet; the first to repeat it was possibly an idiot."
(Spanish surrealist painter Salvador Dali, 1904-1989)

So, how do you write a new simile or a metaphor? Well, I'm probably the wrong person to ask. I was an intelligence officer who spent 25 years writing reports for people trying to win wars. It wasn't really the right setting for a witty metaphor. The benefits of using one would have been great, but the personal risks were too high. It was hard enough to present controversial subjects as it was. A general who has been up since 0430, is not likely to get to bed until 0100, still has to have dinner with a minister, has a meeting at 2330 to discuss the next morning's meeting and is shouldering the responsibility for half the war doesn't really want to hear that the first phase of Operation MOTORWAY in which two soldiers died was "about as much as use as a chocolate teapot". I think any person delivering that simile would be on the plane home before the general's eyes had reached the last "t" in "teapot". In truth, it would never come to that. Flippancy of that nature is weeded out way before it gets to someone important.

Remember, you don't have to use any of these creative writing techniques. They could be more damaging than beneficial, and metaphors and similes carry the most risk. But there are benefits to be had – especially if the technique suits your business environment. Don't be put off by some grumpy general (unless you're actually writing to one). Your customers might be the next tranche of revellers for Disney's Big Thunder Mountain ride. You'll instinctively know your boundaries.

So, how do you write a simile or a metaphor? Well, sometimes they just leap out at you. Other times, you have to really work at it. I have a Trivial Pursuit question card in my top drawer. The question categories are: Geography, Entertainment, History, Arts & Literature, Science & Nature, and Sports & Leisure. To assist with thinking, I consider the subject against each of these topics to see if any similes or metaphors surface. For example, let's imagine you're trying to sell a powder that kills wasps. Let's call it "Wasp Killer". But now you want a slogan. Okay, get your Trivial Pursuit card out. Here we go:

Geography: *"Wasp Killer. Sends wasps to waspital."*
(What's that got to do with Geography? I don't know. It just jumped into my head! It also suggests the powder is just going to injure the wasps. The card is just an aid to thinking. At this stage, all ideas are good. Jot them down. They might inform something else later.)

Entertainment: *"Wasp Killer. Makes wasps leave your house quicker than your 14-year-old son during a love scene on TV."*
(Too long, I know. Probably not that original either. Still, jot it down.)

History: *"Wasp Killer. Hiroshima for wasps is just one squirt away."*
(Not acceptable, I know. But, jot it down.)

Arts & Literature: *"Wasp Killer. For wasps, it's like three no's in X Factor."*
(Nah, rubbish. Not sure how I got there under Art and Literature. Still, jot it down.)

Science and Nature: *"Wasp Killer. A tsunami for wasps."*
(Mmm? Nah)

Sports and Leisure: *"Wasp Killer. Strike 3 for Wasps."*
(Mmm? Maybe)

Now, there's a lot of rubbish amongst that lot. Stuff I'd never consider using. But, it's quite easy to see connections between the ideas. "Hiroshima" has links to "tsunami", and "three no's" has links to "Strike 3". Without "three no's", I might never have got to "Strike 3 for Wasps". So, write all ideas down.

I can't teach you how to be creative. You're almost certainly already more creative than me. But, by being systematic, I've managed to come up with "Wasp Killer: Strike 3 for Wasps." It's a bit US-centric, but I quite like it.

Be aware that, quite often, metaphors and similes aren't received as enthusiastically as they're delivered. Once you've written a metaphor or simile, test it. Does it make sense to others? Is it original? Weaving creativity into business writing is not an easy thing to get right. Maybe this quote will provide you with some motivation to persevere if you think your writing needs some spice:

"A writer is a person for whom writing is more difficult than it is for other people."
(German novelist Thomas Mann, 1875–1955)

I've just tested "Wasp Killer: Strike 3 for Wasps" on my wife. Apparently, it's not "a bit US-centric". It's too US-centric and not even that good. Oh, well. Back to the drawing board. Remember, proofreaders rarely do you a disservice. And, if a proofreader says your metaphor or simile is poor or inappropriate, believe him (or her in this case).

Bottom line: Using metaphors and similes is an efficient and memorable way of getting your message across. If it's appropriate, use one. But don't use too many in business correspondence. If you're going to use one, that's great. But don't use two.

(33) ## Non-sentences can make your writing flow more naturally

A sentence is a group of words that expresses a complete thought.
[If you hate grammar, skip a whole sentence, starting from…now!]
A sentence must contain a subject and a verb, although the subject
may be implied. A non-sentence doesn't express a complete thought.
Here are some examples:

- Really?
- Worse.
- Yes.
- No.
- Possibly.

- Oh, great.
- Half dead.
- Own goal.
- Bad business.

I love non-sentences. I've used lots of them in this book. I definitely
wouldn't use this many in formal business correspondence, mind you.
So, how many should you use in formal business correspondence?
Well, that depends. Your readers will expect the level of respect
that your relationship with them dictates. Non-sentences are great
for making your writing flow naturally, so they are great for books.
They are not so good in business writing though, because they can
make you look disrespectful. That's the danger of using them. Used
occasionally, however, non-sentences can:

- Make an impact.
- Make you look confident.

Impact and confidence are big benefits. If you include a non-sentence
(e.g. "Disaster.") in the middle of a paragraph, you might achieve
some impact and look pretty confident in the mind of your readers.
However, if you then put another non-sentence (e.g. "Really?") in the
next paragraph or on the next page, you run the risk of your readers
thinking you're a bit over-familiar, and the impact and confidence you
won with your first non-sentence (i.e. "Disaster) might be lost.

(34)   Why you might want to repeat stuff

Repeating ideas in your document can be useful. Used occasionally, deliberate repetition can:

- Be used for emphasis.
- Be memorable.
- Make an impact.
- Make you look confident.

These are great benefits. But, as with all these creative techniques, there are also a few dangers. If you want to spice up your writing with deliberate repetition, you must avoid:

- **Over-cooking.** When you make your point so strongly your readers grow suspicious and start questioning it.

"The lady doth protest too much, methinks."
(From *Hamlet* by William Shakespeare, 1564–1616)

- **Redundancy.** When you waste your readers' time by telling them what you've just told them and this overrides the "spice" you'd sought with the repetition.

So, how do you do this deliberate repetition stuff? Well, there are three main ways:

- **Anaphora.** That's geek speak for repeating stuff at the start of sentences:

"We shall go on to the end. We shall fight in France, we shall fight on the seas and oceans, we shall fight with growing confidence and growing strength in the air, we shall defend our island, whatever the cost may be. We shall fight on the beaches, we shall fight on the landing grounds, we shall fight in the fields and in the streets, we shall fight in the hills; we shall never surrender."
(Sir Winston Churchill)

"<u>The future's</u> bright. <u>The future's</u> Orange."
(Telecommunication company Orange's slogan)

- **Epiphora.** Repeating stuff at the end of sentences:

"He spoke with the wisdom that can only come from experience, like a guy who went blind because he looked <u>at a solar eclipse without one of those boxes with a pinhole in it</u> and now goes around the country speaking at schools about the dangers of looking <u>at a solar eclipse without one of those boxes with a pinhole in it</u>."

"She's safe, <u>just like I promised</u>. She's all set to marry Norrington, <u>just like she promised</u>. And you get to die for her, <u>just like you promised</u>."
(Jack Sparrow)

- **Commoratio.** Repeating an idea back to back, but in different words:

"It's not pinin'. It's passed on! This parrot is no more! It has ceased to be! It's expired and gone to meet its maker! This is a late parrot! It's a stiff! Bereft of life, it rests in peace! If you hadn't nailed it to the perch, it would be pushing up the daisies! Its metabolical processes are of interest only to historians! It's hopped the twig! It's shuffled off this mortal coil! It's run down the curtain and joined the choir invisible! This is an ex-parrot!"
(Monty Python's Dead Parrot Sketch)

"Space is big. You just won't believe how vastly, hugely, mind-bogglingly big it is. I mean, you may think it's a long way down the road to the chemist's, but that's just peanuts to space."
(From *The Hitchhiker's Guide to the Galaxy* by Douglas Adams, 1952–2001)

Here are some examples that might appear in business correspondence:

It's the cheapest solution. It's within the company's control, and it's quick to implement.
(Anaphora)

In our opinion, the answer to the current situation is not making 10 people redundant. All that achieves is making 10 people redundant.
(Epiphora)

We have considered your solution and are impressed by its practicality. It looks very viable. Very viable indeed.
(Commoratio)

Also, if you look back at the last paragraph of Section 21, you will notice that I've chucked in some deliberate anaphora ("It's… ") and epiphora ("…it their own").

Generally, repetition in business writing is something to be avoided, but I think it's worth keeping these techniques in your back pocket as they can be an excellent way to emphasise something, to show confidence and to make your writing more interesting to read.

(35) **Let's get some literary variance in there**

As we're talking about repetition, it might be a good time to talk about an opposing idea: literary variance. Using literary variance in your writing just means using different words for the same thing to keep your writing interesting. Here is an example with a <u>lack</u> of literary variance:

<u>Lee</u> struggles to cast beyond 50m, so <u>Lee</u> does not catch many bass.

It will be pretty obvious to everyone reading this that the second use of "Lee" could be changed to "he". Well, making that change is applying literary variance. So, it's just a posh term for something you do already. Usually, the easiest way to achieve literary variance is with a thesaurus.

Thank you for your cooperation. The task would have failed without your cooperation.
(A lack of literary variance)

Using "cooperation" twice is a lack of literary variance. If you're using MS Office, right click on one of them and select Synonyms. Look at the options and pick one. I'd probably go for "assistance".

Thank you for your assistance. The task would have failed without your cooperation.
(Hooray, literary variance achieved)

Remember, you don't have to achieve literary variance as you're typing away. Just whack the same word in and let your thesaurus earn its living. (Make sure you know what the word you pick means, though. Sometimes, the thesaurus's synonym – i.e. the word that's supposed to mean the same as the one you're checking – is not a synonym at all.)

Here's another example with a possible lack of literary variance:

Are you happy to be alive? If you think nobody cares if you're alive, try missing a couple of payments.

The word "alive" appears twice. Is that useful repetition that achieves some emphasis, or is it a lack of literary variance? Would it be better if one of them were changed to "breathing"? Well, that's for you to decide. Personally, I like the "alive" repeated, but I'm bit of a sucker for emphasis by epiphora.

36   Weave in some alliteration or rhythm

You probably remember from school that alliteration is the repetition of the same letter (or sound) at the start of nearby words. Peter Piper picked a… blah blah. Used occasionally (and no more than once in any business document), alliteration can:

- Be memorable.
- Make an impact.
- Make you look confident.
- Be used for emphasis.

If you use alliteration in a business document, your readers will spot it, and all the benefits listed above will kick in. I judge the risks of looking disrespectful or flippant with alliteration are relatively low compared to the other creative techniques, provided you only do it once. It's definitely a one-shot-one-"kill" technique. Here are some examples:

"Smile. Speak. Serve."
(Guidelines for shop assistants)

"Veni, vidi, Visa" (I came, I saw, I spent)
(Wordplay on Julius Caesar's "Veni, vidi, vici" – I came, I saw, I conquered.)

Here's a business-letter-flavoured example:

"The second proposed solution was commercially astute, cost effective and convincing."

You can also achieve the same effect with the rhythm of your words. Rhythm is a musical quality produced by the repetition of stressed and unstressed syllables. We're not going to dissect that idea in this book. You'll know rhythm when you hear it, and you'll instinctively be able to do it if you try. Look at the last two sentences in this example:

"Level crossings protect you from one of the busiest rail networks in the world. They're not time wasters. They're life savers."
(Network Rail safety advert)

The use of rhythm in this advert makes it far more memorable. And this is a technique you can employ too.

37 A quick recap

That brings us to the end of the creative-writing bit. Here's a quick recap. You can emphasise your points, make your points more memorable, write more naturally and look more confident by using:

- Metaphors and similes.
- Non-sentences.
- Deliberate repetition.
- Alliteration and rhythm.

But, remember, these techniques can be viewed as flippant. So, use them very sparingly. They're like Tabasco sauce. Used occasionally, they'll add some welcome spice. Used routinely, they'll ruin your offerings.

Right, that's the end of Chapter 1. I should imagine you found it pretty heavy going, especially if you're new to business writing. But think back to the Kung Fu-class analogy from the foreword. Remember, most of the time, your writing will be the body of the missile that delivers the warhead. The topics covered in the next chapter are the explosives you'll pack into that warhead.

If you remember nothing else from this chapter, remember this: Make your writing as short as possible and put all the key points in a summary at the top.

Guard Against
Your Biases and
Exploit Theirs

INTRODUCTION

(38) **Biases and effects**

As you live your life, you are constantly developing little "viruses" in your mind that influence how you think. Sometimes they can be helpful, but sometimes they can really mess you up. These "viruses" are your personal biases.

Whenever you make a decision (e.g. decide to buy a TV) or adopt a point of view (e.g. believe drinking coffee causes headaches), you weigh up all the factors beforehand in your head. Quite often (and without even knowing it), you will put too much emphasis on at least one of those factors because of your personal biases.

Those who take money off the public (e.g. shopkeepers and restaurateurs) are experts at exploiting your biases, and this allows them to squeeze more money out of you.

If you look up bias in a dictionary, it will say something like this:

Bias (noun): Prejudice in favour of or against something.

So, being biased means you have a prejudiced viewpoint, and it's usually at the expense of other valid alternatives.

Try this quick test. (Don't think about it too much. If it doesn't work on you, try it on someone else.)

Quick test: There are 11 apples. You take 3. How many apples do you have?

In our tests, about 70% of people we asked answered 8. The answer, of course, is 3. (If you take 3, you have 3.)

Now, is this just verbal "sleight of hand"? The test doesn't say "You have 11 apples." It says "There are 11 apples." But, then it says "You take 3" not "Take away 3".

So, is this just a test to prove people don't listen carefully? It looks like it. And what's that got to do with bias? Well, when you substitute apples for cars, only around 30% of people are tricked. In other words, if you ask:

> **Quick test:** There are 11 cars. You take 3. How many cars do you have?

Way more people say 3.

This is because when you're at school (or when you're explaining maths to your children), apples are used in basic-arithmetic examples. Cars aren't. Therefore, a life experience has caused you to adopt an unhelpful viewpoint. That's a bias.

Here's another quick test:

> **Quick test:** There are two Jamaicans walking across London Bridge. They are related. One is the father of the other's son. What is their relationship?

The answer is on the next page...

They are man and wife.

Even though it's a simple question, lots of British people struggle to find the answer, because, in their mind's eye, the two Jamaicans were men. For many Brits, all Jamaicans look like Bob Marley.

Once again, this is an example of a bias skewing the evidence.

Those two examples are very basic, but, hopefully, they've helped to make the point about how biases developed through your life experience can affect your decision-making. Of course, some questions are far harder to answer, and, when the evidence is complex, there is even more room for bias to affect it.

The question of whether global warming is anthropogenic (manmade) is a good example. In this debate, we have thousands of the planet's top scientists forming two camps. What's interesting to note is the high proportion of scientists who adopt the viewpoint you'd expect them to. For example, those with a green agenda interpret the data to show global warming is manmade, and those with a commercial agenda interpret the data to prove it isn't. Academic rivalry is also evident as the scientists seek to undermine each other's findings. Basically, they all put different weightings on the facts and interpret them to fit the results they're looking for. Now, they're all trained to the max to avoid exactly that happening, but still, from an outsider's perspective, it looks very much like that's what is happening. Biases are powerful things with the ability to affect even our smartest scientists.

It suffices to say that your personal biases can make you isolate evidence, strengthen it, weaken it and even dismiss it. Many of your biases affect you in a very subtle way, but some affect you more noticeably, especially to external observers. All of them can be damaging to you.

As well as biases, we're also going to discuss some cognitive effects, which are really just observations about how people behave – usually to their own detriment. Understanding these biases and effects and giving them a name is the first step in defending against them. Knowing about them will also allow you to create plans to influence others' actions or, if required, to highlight their flaws using convincing language – in other words, to attack!

Over the years, I've noticed that when people are first introduced to biases and effects, the ideas often don't gel. It usually takes a few explanations and a couple of examples before they click. For that reason, we've decided to outline how each bias and effect works about five times in each section. Now that sounds like a lot of repetition, but we think it works. In broad terms, each section is structured like this:

- **Easy Definition.** A quick overview of the bias using simple words to describe the main idea (usually in the form of advice).
- **Geeky Definition.** A slightly more detailed explanation using the kind of academic words you'd find in a Critical Thinking publication.
- **Examples.** At least one example of the bias.
- **Practical Application.** At least one example of how to use the bias practically.
- **Summary.** A succinct wrap-up of the bias (from the perspective of spotting it in others).

The biases and effects have been ordered to aid understanding and for book-readability. That's why they're not in alphabetical order.

There's one more thing. If you've ever tried to learn karate or something like that, one of the first things you're taught is not to use your fighting skills on your schoolmates. Well, something similar applies here. Don't use these techniques on your friends and family, and don't use the terms you're about to learn to help you win arguments against your loved ones. There's a time and place to influence people, and there's a time and place to use geeky terms in arguments. It's never at home.

COMMON BIASES AND EFFECTS

(39) # Anchoring

Easy Definition: Don't get fixated on one piece of information when making a decision. If you do, you're anchoring.

Geeky Definition: When making decisions, anchoring is a bias which involves factoring in one piece of information too heavily. Anchoring occurs when a person overly relies on, or anchors to, a specific piece of information. Once the so-called anchor has been established, there is a bias towards the anchor.

An Example:
How many countries are there in Africa?

On a course run for intelligence analysts, the class was split into two groups, and each group was presented with two questions:

Group A:
Are there more or fewer than 25 countries in Africa?   *(2 points)*
How many countries are there in Africa?   *(5 points)*

Group B:
Are there more or fewer than 50 countries in Africa?   *(2 points)*
How many countries are there in Africa?   *(5 points)*

In fact, there are 54 countries in Africa, but those in Group A never got anywhere near the answer. This is because most British people have no idea how many countries there are in Africa, and the groups became anchored to the number in the first question. On average over a two-year period, the Group As thought there were 27 countries in Africa, whereas the Group Bs thought there were 51.

Week in week out and without fail, each group's decision was affected by the anchor. It was a simple lesson, but it stuck.

An Example:
Ensure your customers are happy with your bad service

Setting an anchor is easy. Airlines do it all the time to sugar the pill of a cancelled flight. For example, if your 10 a.m. flight is cancelled, they will quickly promise you a seat on the 4 p.m. flight. Once they've set that anchor (and your expectation), they will try to book you on an earlier flight. When you get a call an hour later saying you're on the 2 p.m. flight, you feel looked after and happy with the airline.

If they'd just bumped you from the 10 a.m. flight to the 2 p.m. flight, you'd have been disgusted with them. That's the value of their 4 p.m. anchor to them. It cost them nothing to establish that anchor, but it just moved your tick on their customer-service questionnaire from "1: Not At All satisfied" to "5: Extremely Satisfied".

Clearly, this is a tactic you can employ in a thousand contexts to win favour. Simply establish an anchor beyond what you know you can deliver, and then surprise everybody with your efficiency when you overachieve. Retailers do it all the time with the old "was £7 now £5" (see Section 115). Setting the anchor is free. It's a mind game.

Another Example:
Where's my anchor just gone?

Imagine this. You go to buy a car advertised for £10,000 and offer £5,000. The seller accepts your offer immediately and seals the deal with a handshake. You'd drive away from that deal wondering what was wrong with the car you've just bought. You'd wish you'd said £4,000. This would happen because the £10,000 anchor was destroyed by the seller's immediate acceptance. As a result, you now don't have an anchor, and you don't really know what to think about your purchase. You would actually drive off happier if you haggled like an Iraqi market-stall owner and got the car for £8,500, because you'd be making a comparison with the £10,000 anchor. You'd be £3,500 worse off, but happier. That's the power of an anchor. People like to create anchors when making decisions, because anchors provide a fixed point against which comparisons can be made.

Another Example:
"I need to hold on to something... anything!"

A version of this experiment features in Dan Ariely's book *Predictably Irrational*. You should try this with your mates. It's fascinating.

Ask a group of people to write a random two-figure number (say the last two numbers of their bank account) on a piece of paper and then place a pound sign before it. Show them an item (say a bottle of wine) and describe the wine to them using a doctored version of the words on the label. (I'll explain why you need to doctor the description in a sec.)

Next, ask your group to estimate the cost of the wine and to write their guess below the random number. Interestingly, their estimates will be proportional to the random number. In other words, those with a high random number will think the wine is more expensive than those with a low random number. In this experiment, your "guinea pigs" will anchor to the random number in guessing how much the wine was worth.

This occurs because people do not like to make decisions in a vacuum. So, when you describe the wine, doctor your description to ensure you do not say the year or something else that will give them a clue as to the value. If you do, their brains will anchor to that information immediately and make a comparison with some wine they've bought with a similar trait. In other words, try to give them no anchor whatsoever and then watch them anchor to (i.e. be influenced by) the random number.

A Practical Application:
Use anchoring to ensure a bargain

Car boot sales are a great place to use anchoring to attain a bargain. Quite often at these places, a seller will present the contents of his house on a table without having done any real research to determine the value of his wares. Of course, he'll probably know the age and how much he paid for each item, but that is likely to be his only anchor in determining the price. The great thing about anchoring is that you can override weaker anchors and make the decision-maker adopt your anchor. A quick comment, which is loud enough to be heard by the stall owner, to whomever you're with, will usually do the trick. Just say something like "Oh, my auntie bought one of these last week for £15 to put in her kitchen", and you will have set a strong anchor. You'll soon be negotiating around the £15 mark.

Do not forget the influence of a "blurt" over those who don't fully understand anchoring. A blurted offer of 80K for a 100K apartment is likely to get a "no, 90K" response. An opening offer of 95K is likely to get a "no, 98K" response. I really doubt I'm telling you anything new. But, now that you fully understand anchoring, you can attack a seller with a conscious blurt and snub a blurting buyer with more confidence. So, an "80K" blurt to you will now get a "98K" response not a "90K" response.

There is more about how Anchoring can help you coming up in Section 119.

Summary of Anchoring. If you think someone is putting too much emphasis on a particular fact or using an arbitrary value as a reference point, tell him he is anchoring.

Attentional Bias

Easy Definition: Don't think what you see is the whole story. You also need to consider the things you don't see, otherwise you're displaying Attentional Bias.

"Why is it that only trains in front of your train break down?"
(This is clearly not true, but it seems to be the case. This is because you don't factor in the trains that break down behind you or on a different route, because they don't affect you. The next time you listen to a traffic report on the radio, think about all those traffic jams you're not in.)

"How is it one careless match can start a forest fire, but it takes a whole box to start a campfire?"
(I know this is meant to be funny, but it's still worth pointing out that it's also not true. It is a mistake only to consider the forest fires that were caused by a carelessly thrown match or cigarette. To understand what it really takes to start a forest fire, you also need to consider the forest fires that weren't caused by those carelessly thrown matches or cigarettes. I'm pretty sure any arsonist would tell you that starting a forest fire is as difficult as starting a campfire.)

Geeky Definition: Attentional Bias causes people not to examine all possible outcomes when making judgements. In other words, their attention is on just one or two of the possible outcomes. The rest are ignored. A common type of Attentional Bias is one in which two conditions can be present (see the example below), meaning there are four possible outcomes. However, those displaying Attentional Bias will not consider all four.

An Example:
That seal with the white head... again?

Imagine you and your mates regularly go sea fishing in a bay near where you live, and you tend to see the same seal. Someone might say: "That seal with a white head only appears in this bay when we're fishing."

Now, that statement probably deserves a polite response. But when I said that exact thing once, my mates (also ex-intelligencers) took great delight in deriding my observation.

One quickly reminded me that I was displaying Attentional Bias. The others joined in, and it wasn't too many minutes of banter before the whole invasion of Iraq was my fault. As I rolled my eyes, he said:

"There are four possible outcomes:

1. We're fishing here, and the seal is present.
2. We're fishing here, and the seal is not present.
3. We're not here, and the seal is present.
4. We're not here, and the seal is not present.

You are only considering Outcome 1. You have ignored Outcome 2, and you don't know Outcomes 3 and 4."

He was right of course. I had displayed Attentional Bias. I had failed to examine all possible outcomes when making my observation. I was biased towards Outcome 1.

Attentional Bias is related to Confirmation Bias (see Section 47), which is when people shape the evidence (either wittingly or wittingly) to fit their theories.

Another Example:
You're safer than you think

It was 3 o'clock in the morning. I had already loaded my rucksack and holdall into the Land Rover waiting outside my house. I kissed my wife goodbye and went into my daughter's room. She was two. She was fast asleep. I looked at her in silence and wondered if this would be the last time I ever saw her. It was 1994, and I was setting off for Bosnia. What did I know about Bosnia? Nothing. This was the early days of the war. No one I knew had been before. I only knew what I'd seen on the news. Back in 1994, I was pretty terrible at speaking Serbo-Croat, but obviously not bad enough to stop me heading out to my first real war zone.

As I looked at my two-year-old daughter, I was sure this was it. I was a dead man. But it didn't turn out like that. It wasn't like the news at all. I travelled extensively up and down the country in the job I had, but I didn't see a single dead body and nobody fired a shot at me. My "I'm going to die" assessment was overly focused on the terrible events in the news. I hadn't factored in the millions of places where Bosnians were not getting shot at. My assessment had been tainted by Attentional Bias.

Insurance companies are masters at exploiting Attentional Bias. Think about this. How many house fires have there been in your town over the last decade? How many houses are there? Do the maths, and you'll soon wish you ran an insurance company. The key point is not how many house fires there were. It's how many house fires there weren't. (Don't take this as a suggestion that insurance is bad. If you're anything like me, you can afford insurance, but you can't afford to replace your house. Often with insurance, the probability of the event happening is very low, but the impact is high. That's why you need it. However, just be aware that due to Attentional Bias and because some insurance companies will actively deceive you into thinking the risk is higher than it is (see Section 105), your insurance is probably not great value for money.)

Your mind is better at processing events rather than non-events, and the news will supply plenty of events for you. To analyse a situation well, you have to train yourself to factor in the events and the non-events, else you have a false context.

A Practical Application:
Win an argument using their evidence

Accusing someone of Attentional Bias is a great way to undermine their argument. As soon as your opponent says "What about when [insert event] happened?", you can instantly counter with "What about when [insert the same event] didn't happen?" and then accuse them of displaying Attentional Bias. Here's an example:

A number of marine biologists believe that great white sharks are prevalent around the United Kingdom, and they often cite a couple of "confirmed" sightings over the past decade as evidence. Now, before you even go down the "they're basking sharks" line and attack the word "confirmed", you can use their own evidence against them. You can say "Using your evidence, there have been 3,648 out of 3,650 days when great white sharks have not been seen. That hardly makes them prevalent."

If he's smart, he'll retort with "you've not accounted for the days when there were great white sharks which weren't seen", but he probably won't, because he'll be new to Attentional Bias, and you'll be racing off with an argument-win under your belt. And that's half the point of understanding biases. It not only allows you to dissect an argument, it also gives you credible words to say which are more effective in undermining your opponent.

It will be difficult for your opponent to counter your accusation of Attentional Bias, because the accusation is usually factual (i.e. those other non-events really do need to be considered to give the statistics context).

Another Practical Application:
Persuade your mum to get on a plane

A fear of flying is Attentional Bias gone mad. If you know someone with a fear of flying, it might be possible to calm them by highlighting their Attentional Bias.

Your "patient" will have heard that flying is the safest form of transport etc., but, sometimes just the act of giving their bias a name can help them see it. Remember, it's a good practice to agree with them and then mould them (see Section 22).

Yes, planes do crash. In fact, last year, 20 planes crashed.

(At this point they'll be going nowhere near a plane.)

But focusing on those crashes is Attentional Bias. You're not considering the whole picture. Last year, about 950 people were involved in those 20 crashes, and more than two thirds of them survived.

(As we'll see later when we look at Availability Bias (Section 41), they'll find that quite a comforting statistic.)

But look at the whole picture. There are about 50,000 flights a day worldwide. That's 18.25 million flights a year.

I'm not saying they're going to book a flight with British Airways the second you say the words "Attentional Bias", but, in my experience, using (and explaining) these terms does make your argument burn a little deeper.

If naming their bias and producing those statistics don't get them on a plane, you'll have to resort to the old spiked-hamburger trick that Face used on B. A. Baracus in the A Team to drug him to a state of unconsciousness.

Oh, and when the presenters at the end of Crime Watch say "sleep tight", you should. A programme about muggings and burglaries doesn't increase the chance of it happening to you one little bit.

> **Summary of Attentional Bias.** If you think someone is not considering all the possible outcomes of a situation when making a decision, tell him his thinking is affected by Attentional Bias.

41 **Availability Bias**

Easy Definition: Don't think you'll win an argument with one prominent example. If you try that you might be showing Availability Bias.

Geeky Definition: Availability Bias is the tendency to let an example that comes to mind easily affect decision-making or reasoning. When making decisions or reasoning, the Availability Bias occurs when a story you can readily recall plays too big a role in how you reach your conclusion.

An Example:
She's been smoking since she was nine

Deciding to continue smoking because you know a smoker who lived to be 100 would be a good example of Availability Bias. In this scenario, the story you can recall plays too big a role in your decision to continue smoking. A review of medical statistics on smokers' health ought to be a weightier factor in the decision process.

Sufferers of the Availability Bias (and that's most of us) will think that the likelihood of an event is proportional to the ease with which they can recall an example of it happening.

Another Example:
Persuade your mum to get on a plane (part 2)

In the section on Attentional Bias (see Section 40), we spoke about trying to convince someone who was scared of flying to be more objective about the statistics. But, usually, it's not the statistics they have a problem with. The root of their phobia is likely to be how memorable air crashes are. Often, people who are scared of flying cannot control their Availability Bias. As they're able to recall the crash scenes they've seen on films and the news easily, the idea of crashing becomes a far weightier factor in their decision whether to fly. This is why the notion that at least 66% of passengers survive plane crashes can be a far more comforting statistic for them than saying only 0.0001% of flights crash (actually, instead of "crash", try saying "incidents classified as a crash" to reinforce the 66% survivability).

A Practical Application:
Win an argument using their evidence (part 2)

When someone cites a well-known story as an example to support their argument, you can easily and quickly undermine their position by claiming they are showing Availability Bias.

Them: *"Well, what about the great white shark that beached itself in Newquay in the 1960s?"*
You: *"That's Availability Bias. You can't put too much weight on one well-known story."*

The good thing about Availability Bias (as we've seen with the "persuading your mum to get on a plane" example) is that it's closely related to Attentional Bias (see Section 40). This means you can usually throw Attentional Bias at them too by telling them they're not considering all the times when the event they've highlighted didn't happen (e.g. when smokers didn't live to be 100). Just by being aware of these two biases, you have been able to accuse them of two biases using their evidence (and all this without expending too many calories on thinking). Even better, your statistics-flavoured "attack" will be difficult for your opponent to counter.

> **Summary of Availability Bias**. If you think someone is putting too much weight on a story because it comes to mind easily, tell him he's affected by Availability Bias.

(42)   Barnum Effect

Easy Definition: Don't be taken in by a stranger's general observations about you. If you do, you've been influenced by the Barnum Effect.

Geeky Definition: The Barnum Effect occurs when people believe that general descriptions are accurate descriptions that relate to them. This occurs most commonly when describing personality traits.

An Example:
You're a great judge of character

The Barnum Effect gets its name from the American showman and businessman Phineas Taylor Barnum (1810–1891), who earned his money in his early career by running a museum of human curiosities and hoaxes. Although probably not the originator of the quotes, he was certainly influential in promoting "There's a sucker born every minute" and "We have something for everyone."

Astrologers and mediums are masters at using the Barnum Effect. If you meet one, expect them to use words like these:

You are the quiet type, but you are a great judge of character.

You've got a bubbly personality, but you can be serious too.

You're very intuitive and naturally analytical.

The Barnum Effect works well when preceded by an observable truth. So, if you look like the quiet type, expect something like the first example. If you're wearing a "kiss me quick" hat, expect something like the second example.

Astrologers and mediums are superb at generalising and then watching for a reaction. As soon as they spot their "victim" react to something they've mentioned, they zoom in on that subject with more skilfully worded generalisations. These people have an impressive skill with words, and fair play to them for that. They don't, however, have a gift to contact the dead or read the stars.

"If you believe in astrology, you're banned from watching this show." (Stephen Fry on his TV show QI)

The Barnum Effect can be very convincing. JFK (John Fitzgerald Kennedy), the 35th President of the United States, is said to have used astrology to guide his decision-making.

Another Example:
You're a mass murderer

A few years back, a teacher in the US had a horoscope done professionally for an individual known as "Big Ed". He handed a copy of the horoscope to each of his students and told each one it was their horoscope. The students were given 30 minutes to study their "personal" horoscopes. To a man (and a woman), the students thought the horoscope was an accurate description of themselves. Upon reading Big Ed's horoscope, one student delighted "Oh, I love me" and held the pamphlet close to her heart, beaming at "her" positive traits. In fact, the horoscope was so "accurate", it caused those students who were previously sceptical about horoscopes to rethink their scepticism. When the students learnt they'd all been given the same horoscope, they were staggered. Some even looked upset by the trick, especially Ms "Oh, I love me". The worst was still to come. The horoscope they'd been given was that of Edmund Kemper III or "Big Ed". He was a 6'9" serial killer in California in the 1970s. By the age of 15, "Big Ed" had shot both his grandparents. Later, he killed and dismembered six female hitchhikers before murdering his mother and her friend. He was also a necrophile (i.e. sexually attracted to corpses). Welcome to the Barnum Effect, kids.

A Practical Application:
Flattery will get you everywhere

Either knowingly or unknowingly, lots of people use the Barnum Effect when chatting someone up. If you've ever been fed a line like any of the ones below, then you've been subjected to the Barnum Effect:

You're an independent thinker.
You seem very intuitive.
You've got a sharp sense of humour.
You're a good judge of character.
You're not living up to your full potential.

The people targeted by such flattery and suggestion are likely to fall for it. In other words, they are likely to think the lines are genuine and that they apply to them (whether they do or not). Why wouldn't they? These ideas apply to all of us, especially from our own perspectives.

You could use the Barnum Effect to chat people up if you wished or, if you're ever on the receiving end, you could recognise it to spot what might be meaningless flattery. But how can you use the Barnum Effect in business? Well, there's a well-tested idea that people do business with people they like. If you're struggling to find a specific business-related compliment to woo a potential business contact, don't worry. Just say something generic, not specific. It's likely to have the same effect. Say something like "I think first impressions count for a lot, and you guys come across as being well on top of your game". It feels like quite a cheap shot when you're saying it, but it's worth a punt, because it's not likely to be received as being a cheap shot. They'll believe you meant it, whether you did or not, and it is likely to put you on the path to being someone they like. (This is related to Appeal to Flattery Fallacy, Section 70.) And, even if they don't believe it, what crime have you committed? You can't really lose. So, am I just telling you that compliments are an effective way of improving a business relationship? No, I'm not. I know you knew that already. I am telling you that generic compliments are an effective way of improving a business relationship, and you can dish them out without expending any calories on thinking about the detail you've just been bored with.

If you're good looking (see Good Looking People Bias at Section 54) or at least better looking than those around you (see Contrast Bias at Section 48), your Barnum Effect lines will work even more effectively.

Summary of the Barnum Effect. If you think someone is generalising while pretending to be specific, tell him to stop trying to use the Barnum Effect.

One Last Thing:

Be mindful of the difference between generalising and operating at a high level. For example, a consultant who claims you have a staff-morale problem could be employing the Barnum Effect or could be right. The trick to countering Barnum Effect-style statements is to dive straight into the detail looking for evidence. This works at the executive level and the girl-at-the-gym level.

It's also worth taking a quick look at the way politicians speak. In April 2012, Prime Minister David Cameron said this:

"Everything we are doing is about helping people who work hard and do the right thing and making this country more pro-enterprise, more pro-get-up-and-go, more pro-work, more pro-effort."

Whilst this is a great example of deliberate repetition (in this case "anaphora" – see Section 34), it might also be a meaningless generalisation. I mean, who's "anti" those things? Who's anti-get-up-and-go… apart from funeral directors?

(43) **Better Than Average Bias**

Easy Definition: If you're not as good as you think you are, you are suffering from Better Than Average Bias.

"The average person thinks he isn't." (Father Larry Lorenzoni)

Geeky Definition: In decision-making and reasoning, this bias is the tendency to place too much emphasis on your own views.

An Example:
50% of people are below average

Half the people in the world are – by definition – below average, but few people classify themselves as such. Better Than Average Bias is the tendency to think you're better than you are and to afford your own views more credence than they deserve. Most people suffer from Better Than Average Bias. The obvious, egocentric explanation is that it makes us feel better about ourselves, so there is an element of vanity involved. But there is another factor at play. People are predisposed to give more weight to their own views, because they can easily appreciate the factors which got them to that position. It is always harder to see things from other people's perspectives, because they might weight the factors completely differently or have other factors you have not considered. As a consequence, their views will often look a little skewed to you, and your ideas will always seem better than average. It's part of the reason why you'll be confident in your general better-than-averageness.

Also, remember this. Your immediate peers are not the only people in your test group. Everyone else in the world is, including all the surgeons, lawyers, pilots, etc.

An Example:
We're all individuals… I'm not

There is a theory that it's easier to find favourable things about an individual than a group. (This includes when you are comparing yourself to a group.) This is quite understandable. After all, the favourable traits of a group are a difficult thing to think about. I mean, how generous were your classmates? It's hard to answer, isn't it? But, if you ask how generous was Sarah? It's easier. And, you're quite likely to judge Sarah as having above-average generosity. The problem is, you'll also do this for John, Jane, Steven and Paul. Judging people's driving ability is great example. Everyone I know is an above-average driver...definitely according to them (due to the added vanity effect) but also according to me (due to the individual-versus-group effect).

A Practical Application:
Compared to groups, the positive traits of individuals are more believable

Instead of describing how great your company is, try describing how great the individual who would work with your client is (using evidence-flavoured words – see Section 23). If you do this, your attempt to sell the excellence of your service will bore deeper into your client's conscience. (You can still weave in some stuff about your company for context.)

So, this is the usual gumpf you read in business literature and on websites:

Woodhouse Fire Safety has been providing first-class fire-safety consultancy to large corporations for over 20 years. Our bespoke solutions are cost effective and practicable.

Those kinds of write-ups are becoming tiresome and unconvincing. For extra believability, try talking about an individual:

You will be working with John Smith from Woodhouse Fire Safety. John joined our company straight from university and has progressed through our ranks to become one of our most respected specialists. With over 5 years' experience as a senior consultant to large corporations, John is a personable, straight-talking pragmatist and a good listener.

Another Practical Application:
Keep questioning your decisions

So, are you better than average? There's a fair chance you are. Unfortunately, there's an equal chance you're not. Be careful not to overestimate your abilities. Have confidence, but keep questioning your decisions.

Systematic self-auditing is always healthy. In terms of writing, remember that proofreaders rarely do you a disservice (even if you're a better writer than the proofreader and especially if you're not as good a writer as you think you are). In the intelligence arena, we've learned to systemically review all the assumptions that underpin our assessments. It's a healthy process – armed with today's knowledge, it often becomes apparent that yesterday's assumptions were flawed.

Here's a quote I came across of someone trying to be clever:

"Think how stupid the average person is and then realise that half of 'em are stupider than that."

I think it's a safe assumption that the author of this quote thinks he's smarter than average. But, is he? Is "stupider" a word? Shouldn't it be "more stupid"? Hasn't he just made himself look a bit stupid by throwing a basic grammar error into a quote berating others for their intellect? That would be a good example of irony.

But, actually, he hasn't. Stupider is a word. In fact, it's preferable to the widely used "more stupid". So, my finger pointing at "people who think they're better than they are" ought to be pointing at me. I was up for criticising the author of this quote, but I would have been wrong. Every day's a school day.

> **Summary of Better than Average Bias.** If you think someone is placing too much emphasis on his own view (because he thinks he's better than he is) or is overly praising an average individual, tell him his claim is tainted by Better than Average Bias.

44   The Broken Biscuit Effect

Easy Definition: If you make up a daft reason for doing something, you are using the Broken Biscuit Effect on yourself.

Geeky Definition: The Broken Biscuit Effect occurs when a person invents an irrational justification for their actions. Even though the person knows the justification is irrational, it still provides the impetus to carry out the action. It derives its name from the irrational notion that "broken biscuits have no calories", which a dieting person will cite before consuming a broken biscuit (or one with slightly imperfect edging) or breaking one before eating it.

An Example:
We're getting our taxes back, innit?

The first two weeks in August 2011 saw the worst rioting in London for a generation, with running street battles, widespread looting, and buildings, cars and buses being set alight.

When Sky News reporter Mark Stone stopped two 16-year-old girls coming out of an electrical store with a handful of looted electronic gadgets, he asked "Why are you doing this?" They answered "We're getting our taxes back."

To me, the girls didn't really look like employed types (based on age), but, on the assumption they were, why did they think they were owed a return of tax? Two other girls of a similar age answered the same question with "It's the government's fault. It's the conservatives. Conservatives? Er, whatever. It's the government, innit?" Another answered, "I don't know, but it's good though."

Well, at the least the last answer was rational. The other two answers (taxes and government) were examples of the Broken Biscuit Effect. This was people making up irrational justifications to do exactly what they wanted to do.

A Practical Application:
Defend against yourself

Understanding the Broken Biscuit Effect will help you combat it. For example, if you know you shouldn't eat that last cake, but you're "concerned" it'll only go to waste, you are subjecting yourself to the Broken Biscuit Effect. It's also the reason most diets start on a Monday morning. It allows the dieter to do what they want until then.

If you're aware that you're tricking yourself, it will strengthen your resolve to counter it. I'm not saying it's 100% effective. I mean, I have no broken biscuits or cakes nearing their sell-by dates in my fridge. They're all scoffed. But I probably had more of a mental tussle with myself than most people would before I did the deed.

Besides, my two Jack Russells love broken biscuits and just-in-date cakes. Crikey, that might be the Broken Biscuit Effect by proxy.

So, if you're the sort of person who at the last minute decides to have "one for the road", bear in mind that's just you subjecting yourself to the Broken Biscuit Effect.

Summary of the Broken Biscuit Effect. If you think someone has created an irrational justification to provide the impulse to act (particularly if the justification comes just moments before the deed), tell him he's tricked himself with the Broken Biscuit Effect.

45 Choice Supportive Bias

Easy Definition: Don't defend a decision or exaggerate how good it was just because you made it. Either of those would be Choice Supportive Bias

Geeky Definition: Choice Supportive Bias is the tendency for a decision-maker to defend his own decision or to later rate it better than it was simply because he made it.

An Example:
I told you it was the right decision

It's a fairly common view that George W. Bush made an early decision to have a fight with Saddam Hussein when the opportunity arose. The story of how the intelligence on Saddam's weapons of mass destruction (WMD) was handled (see Section 47) raises fair suspicion that the decision to go to war was a very risky one.

However, as soon as he was captured, the White House was not slow in using this to win support for the decision to go to war. Of course, capturing Saddam was never part of that decision. Their effort to lever it in as evidence to defend the decision to go to war was an example of Choice Supportive Bias.

A Practical Application:
Admit you got it wrong earlier and limit the damage

Choice Supportive Bias is really common, and it happens at all levels. Earlier this week, I went to a hardware store and spent a not-insignificant amount of money on some clear decking oil. I painted half the decking in the back garden with it. Now, knowing me, I probably did something wrong, but if this varnish did "exactly what it says on the tin", then there must be some small print on the tin somewhere saying "by 'clear', we mean 'milky'". The treated half of my decking is now a real mess.

I'm telling you this because it took me a while to accept it was a mess. I spent half the next day arguing that it would look okay once the rest was done, talking up the oil's wood-preservation attributes and convincing myself that it didn't look that milky. (Basically, I was looking for evidence to support my decision to fork out on a clear varnish over a cheaper coloured one.) Luckily for me, I was halfway through writing this section, so I was quite focused on Choice Supportive Bias, and it helped me to realise I was painting my decking with some expensive gunky oil. My more objective assessment of the decking situation saved me hours of work – I only had to sand half of it back to the bare wood.

This is a common theme in this chapter:

> "Being aware of a bias (including knowing its name) helps you counter it."

Another Practical Application:
Don't defend bad decisions. Keep checking whether a decision was good

So, have you ever made a decision and then regretted it? Pretty much everyone has done that. Even if it wasn't for something serious, we've probably all suffered from buyer's remorse at some point, either through guilt over extravagance or realising we've been overly influenced by a seller. However, if you find yourself actively finding positives about your choice just to defend it, then Choice Supportive Bias could be at play.

Nobody likes to be accused of poor judgement, so defending decisions is a natural thing to do. Knowing not to defend a bad decision is important, but it's only half of what is required. The decisions and assumptions that influence your work should be routinely tested. Intelligence analysts are taught to bear this in mind:

"The fatal tendency of mankind to [stop thinking about something when a decision has been made] is the cause of half their errors."
(British philosopher J.S. Mill, 1806–1873)

In other words, decisions are good. They will help you move forward, but they should not be blindly defended or assumed to be forever correct once made.

> **Summary of Choice Supportive Bias.** If you think someone is overly defending a past decision just to protect his self-esteem or trying to boost his self-esteem by exaggerating the value of a past decision, tell him he is not being objective and his actions are steeped in Choice Supportive Bias.

(46) Compromise Effect

Easy Definition: Don't always go for "the one in the middle" to avoid a decision. If you do, you've been influenced by the Compromise Effect.

Geeky Definition: When choosing something, the Compromise Effect is the tendency to avoid an extreme choice. Avoiding an extreme choice is often due to the common perception that extremes attract risk. As the middle ground feels safer, decisions which exclude extremes are made far more readily.

An Example:
A la carte menu or just a couple of choices?

Some sneaky restaurateurs deliberately include an expensive dish at the top of their menus, knowing that most customers will avoid it and select from the not-so-expensive choices. They will also include some cheap choices, knowing that people don't go for those on a special night out. Knowing the types of food people avoid (e.g. liver and stuff they could easily cook at home), the restaurateurs are able to "herd" their diners to the most profitable dishes. So, if you're the type of person who avoids the foie gras (the expensive dish), the kidneys (the horrid dish) and the tomatoes on toast (the cheap, non-special dish), you can expect the chef to knock you up a steak from the job-lot bag of steaks the restaurant just bought from the market. That example might be a little harsh and simplistic, but the point is that many restaurateurs will offer extreme choices and unpopular dishes to steer you to the dishes they want to sell you.

They also know that most people are unlikely to pick the most expensive wines or the cheapest (due to the need to maintain a classy façade or avoid embarrassment). So, the middle-ranking wines will be the ones with the highest mark-ups.

Obviously, experience will tell a restaurateur how to fine-tune this idea to the local demographic. For example, putting the highest mark-up on the second cheapest bottle of wine might work in some areas, whereas putting it on the second most expensive might work in others. Whatever the environment dictates, putting high mark-ups on the cheapest or the most expensive choices is unlikely to be as profitable because the Compromise Effect is so entrenched in us all, and people will avoid extreme choices.

A Practical Application:
Fleece the Inbetweeners

This is a simple way to make a shedload more money. If you're selling stuff (goods or services), make sure you offer at least three things with the middle choice maximised for profit.

Here's an example. If a shop sells an expensive TV and a cheap TV, the sales between the two are usually about 50/50. When a third mid-range TV is added, the sales of the other TVs drop dramatically, and the middle choice wins the lion's share of the sales (about 80%). Guess which TV earns the shop the most profit?

Now, be aware that this mass herding towards the middle ground won't happen if the prices are similar. You have to create extremes.

Let's imagine you sell widgets. At the wholesalers, Widget A costs £3, Widget B costs £4, and Widget C costs £5. You could just whack a £2 mark-up on each and put them in your shop. But that is unlikely to herd people to what you want to sell them. The trick is to optimise the selection for herding. Do something like this:

Widget A: £5
Widget B: £8
Widget C: £13

Most people will now go for Widget B, giving you £4 profit per sale.

Clearly, there are other dynamics at play. For example, if the widgets are cheaper elsewhere, your stock will be ignored. But the principle is sound. Most people will avoid extreme choices, and you can exploit that.

> **Summary of Compromise Effect.** If you think someone is taking the easy option by avoiding extreme choices, tell him he has succumbed to the Compromise Effect and selected what he perceives to be a safe option.

(47) Confirmation Bias

Easy Definition: Don't just use the evidence that fits your theory. If you do, that's Confirmation Bias.

Geeky Definition: Confirmation Bias is selective thinking where information that confirms a preconception is: (1) automatically noticed (2) actively sought (3) overvalued and (4) accepted without reservation. On the other hand, information that contradicts the preconception is: (1) automatically ignored (2) not sought (3) undervalued and (4) rejected out of hand. In summary, Confirmation Bias occurs when someone has reached a conclusion and shapes the evidence — either knowingly or unknowingly — to make it fit. Confirmation Bias will also cause people to recall memory selectively or interpret events in a way that supports their preconception.

An Example:
You're fattist – no, you're fattest

Imagine there are two applicants for a job selling medical supplies to hospitals:

Job Candidate A: *Fat 50-year-old with greasy hair and a first-class degree from Hull. 10 years' experience in the industry.*

Job Candidate B: *Fit 25-year-old with floppy hair and a GCSE Grade C in woodwork. Father worked in the industry for 10 years.*

About Candidate A. *Hull? It's not exactly Cambridge is it? And, he could be overqualified. Being 50, he probably won't integrate well into the company. I'm not sure his degree is well aligned to our business.*

About Candidate B. *I sense his potential. I think he's looking for a long-term career. It's in his blood. He could even fix that doorframe in the coffee room.*

Look at Candidate A's description. He'd lost the job at "Fat". The rest of the selection process was a farce. The panel simply interpreted or ignored the remainder of the facts to fit their opening impression of Candidate A.

In most cases, it will be quite obvious that those with Confirmation Bias are shoehorning in evidence that fits or ignoring evidence that doesn't. It's usually an active defence against being proven wrong. But, sometimes, they don't do it knowingly. They just have too much confidence in their own beliefs, which makes convincing them of their bias difficult.

Another Example:
The moon-landing conspiracy theory

On 21st July 1969, Neil Armstrong (the Commander of Apollo 11) was the first man to set foot on the moon. According to a survey by Gallup, 6% of the US population believes his moon landing was faked. In Russia, another poll states that over a quarter of the population do not believe the moon landing occurred. In fact, across the globe, this remains a particularly persistent theory. So, is there anything in it? Let's investigate.

The Apollo programme was huge. At current prices, it would have cost around $110 billion. Including the astronauts, scientists, engineers and technicians, more than 400,000 skilled workers contributed to the programme. To date, not one of them has even hinted that the landings were faked.

One of the things a career in the Intelligence Corps teaches you is "the best way to keep a secret is to tell no one". Four hundred thousand people isn't no one. It's a rock concert. In fact, it's eight huge rock concerts. Because of the way guarding a secret works (i.e. the rigour with which it's protected is reduced after each telling), the chances of keeping the Apollo crew, their wives and their families quiet about a faked landing for 50 years are very small. The chances of keeping 400,000 people quiet are infinitesimally small. This alone ought to tell us that the moon landing was not faked.

"Three may keep a secret, if two of them are dead."
(Benjamin Franklin, 1706–1790)

That aside, there is a wealth of third-party corroboration of the moon landing (not least from the Soviet Union's own space monitoring), and this ought to be enough to put beyond doubt that it took place.

I'm not going to be balanced on this one. The moon landing happened. Fact. Those who genuinely believe the moon landing was faked (i.e. not those seeking to showcase their intellect by defending a hopeless argument) are allowing Confirmation Bias to affect their reasoning. Confirmation Bias is causing them to favour information that fits their preconception of a faked landing and disregard information that doesn't fit. In essence, they want the landing to be faked, so they shape the evidence to match their theory. For example, conspiracists can easily recall the film clip of the American flag waving on the moon. As there is no atmosphere (and so no wind) on the moon, they believe the waving flag cannot be on the moon. So the moon landing must have been faked.

The more serious conspiracists will also cite space-travel experts who state that the Van Allen radiation belts, solar flares, solar wind, coronal mass ejections and cosmic rays make a trip to the moon impossible. You could almost forgive them for believing it. But they should, of course, seek a view from the scientists who overcame these issues before making a judgement. Conspiracists will also tell you that the USA had good reasons to fake the landing: they needed to win the space race against the Soviet Union; they needed to convince US citizens that NASA was a good use of their taxes; and they needed a distraction from the Vietnam War. They'll add that the USA only ever claimed to land on the moon (six times in all) during President Nixon's term, and he was a proven liar.

So, in this very quick look at the moon-landing conspiracy, we've seen the conspiracists enthuse over evidence that fits their theory and ignore that which doesn't. It's a classic example of Confirmation Bias. We've also seen the conspiracists:

- Put too much value in a story that comes to mind easily – in this case, the "flag waving in the wind" story (see Availability Bias – Section 41).
- Blindly take the word of experts (see Appeal to Authority Fallacy – Section 71).
- Adopt fallacious reasoning based on the USA's motivation and Nixon's personal qualities (see Ad Hominem Argument – Section 75).

All in all, the moon-landing conspiracy is a great example of how not to think. It's also a good example of how you can use the terms in this chapter to kill the argument of a lunatic (pun definitely intended).

Oh, after being planted, a flag suspended from a horizontal pole will continue to flap about as it settles after the planting process. And, in a vacuum, it takes much longer for the flag to settle.

Another Example:
Find the evidence to support a case for a war

In 1999, Rafid Ahmed Alwan (an Iraqi citizen who defected from Iraq to Germany) became a Western intelligence agent codenamed

"Curveball". He was of interest to the West because he claimed he had worked as a chemical engineer at a plant which manufactured mobile biological-weapon laboratories as part of Iraq's weapons of mass destruction (WMD) capability.

Many intelligence officers were unconvinced by Curveball's assertions. For example, his German handlers (those who elicited the information from him) repeatedly said he was "out of control". Also, a US official who was assigned to investigate his claims suspected he was "a lying alcoholic". Later, a CIA official described him as "a guy trying to get his green card… and playing the system for what it was worth". Despite repeated warnings from numerous intelligence analysts who questioned Rafid's claims, the US Government used his information to build a case for the 2003 invasion of Iraq. The weighting placed on Rafid's information was very apparent. President George W. Bush said in 2003: "We know that Iraq, in the late 1990s, had several mobile biological weapons labs."

The war ultimately cost 600,000 lives and trillions of dollars without uncovering a single WMD capability. So, how did the West get it so wrong?

This entire intelligence failure has its roots in one place: the political decision to invade Iraq had been made early by George Bush and supported Britain's Prime Minister Tony Blair. As a result, there was a political imperative to find facts to fit the story that Iraq had WMD. And any information that could support the story was shoe-horned in. This was Confirmation Bias at play, which – as any analyst will tell you – is the most prevalent and dangerous of all the biases. Despite all the observations by those closest to Curveball, Confirmation Bias ruled, and the information he provided was treated as "high-grade intelligence". The system (politicians, intelligence chiefs and analysts) was effectively looking for supporting evidence and ignoring non-supporting evidence.

There's a lot more to this story, so I ought to finish it by stating that there are members of the intelligence community out there who still believe there are WMD yet to be found in Iraq. They might be right. Absence of evidence is not evidence of absence. But, let's be clear on one thing: We didn't have sufficient good intelligence to go to war, and we over-played and shaped what we did have to justify the case for war. The case to go to war was riddled with Confirmation Bias.

A Practical Application:
Undermine their best evidence

There's something called a White Crow Event. It's when a single piece of evidence emerges that is absolute proof that a theory is correct. It gets its name from this idea: As soon as you see one white crow, you know for certain that "all crows are not black". That statement is 100% true as soon as you see a white one.

Here's another example. Imagine we're trying to prove it's possible to contact the dead. As soon as one person is proven to have done it once, that's a White Crow Event. All debate is over. It's possible.

Why do you need to know that? Well, most arguments are not won by presenting evidence of a White Crow Event, i.e. something that will win the argument outright. They are won by the person who presents the most convincing story involving all the facts at hand. This is really great news, because it means anything your opponent says to support his argument is going to be open to interpretation.

As soon as he presents something to support his argument, you can often jump straight in with something like: *"That's Confirmation Bias. You're making the evidence fit your theory. That could be indicative of a hundred things."*

Be aware that the most common response when telling someone they have Confirmation Bias is for them to claim you have it. There's bit of an unwritten law here. The first person to use the term "Confirmation Bias" to undermine his opponent achieves the most effect, so make sure you're first to the punch.

> **Summary of Confirmation Bias.** If you think someone is interpreting the facts to support his theory, tell him he is displaying Confirmation Bias and that he could easily infer different conclusions from the evidence.

48 Contrast Bias

Easy Definition: When ranking things, be sure to consider the whole group. You shouldn't rank something based on just one comparison.

Geeky Definition: The tendency to promote or demote something in a large grouping after a single comparison with one of its peers.

An Example:
Gather your least attractive mates together and go on the pull

Average-looking people seem more attractive when alongside those who are less easy on the eye. Imagine an average-looking man was being scored for his looks. When judged independently, he might score 5/10. But, when judged alongside a less attractive person, his score would increase if the judge were suffering from Contrast Bias. And, it's likely the judge would be. Contrast Bias is extremely common. In a bias-free world, the man would score 5/10 regardless of those around him. But we know it's not. So, if you're looking for love, it really is in your best interest to arrange a night out with a group of your not-so-aesthetically-pleasing friends. In effect, the average level of attractiveness of your group of friends is established as an anchor (see Section 39) against which observers make a relative judgement. If you're better looking than that anchor, expect a productive night.

A Practical Application:
Create a product that no one will buy and your sales will rocket

I love this technique. In his book *Predictably Irrational,* Dan Ariely offers a great example of how *The Economist* created an advert to force readers to make a comparison that influenced their buying decisions. At the start, *The Economist* presented the following advert:

Economist.com Subscription...$39
(On-line access to all articles for one year)

Print and Web Subscription..$125
(1-year subscription to the printed edition and full on-line access)
This advert saw 68% of buyers go for the $39 product and 32% go for the $125 one. Not happy with how their advert was performing, they then presented the advert below. It's the same advert but with a "decoy" added.

Economist.com Subscription..$39
(On-line access to all articles for 1 year)

PrintSubscription..$125
(1-year subscription to the printed edition)

Print and Web Subscription..$125
(1-year subscription to the printed edition and full on-line access)

What they'd done is force the reader to make a comparison between the first $125 product and the second $125 product. Clearly, the second one was a much better offer. In the minds of the readers, that comparison trumped the real comparison they should be making, i.e. the one with the $39 product. The sales then went: 16% for the $39 product, 0% for the first $125 product (obviously) and 85% for the second $125 product. In other words, the decoy (the one in the middle) had caused a rise from 32% to 85% for the $125 product.

You can use this technique too. If you're selling two things and want people to buy your more expensive one, create a decoy which costs the same (or about the same) as your most expensive product but is obviously far poorer value for money. This will cause people to make a comparison between your decoy and the most expensive product. That comparison will knock out the real comparison they should make between your cheapest and most expensive products.

> **Summary of Contrast Bias.** If you think someone is ranking something wrongly after making a largely irrelevant comparison, tell him he's suffering from Contrast Bias.

49   Moral Credential Bias

Easy Definition: Don't think it's okay to do something wrong because you normally do the right thing. Your decision to do the wrong thing would be tainted by Moral Credential Bias, if you did.

Geeky Definition: Moral Credential Bias occurs when someone's history of making fair judgements gives rise to a sense of "free licence" in the future.

An Example:
We are an equal-opportunities employer... sometimes

My mate used to work for a company that had a high turnover of staff. To combat this, they had regular recruitment rounds to maintain staff levels. They knew that women aged 35-55 were not only the most productive but also the most likely to hack the work and stay on. But, being a good, law-abiding company, they did not discriminate. They were blind to sex, ethnicity and disability during their recruitment. They displayed good morals. Well, most of the time. If time was tight and a worker was needed at short notice, the manager would tell the HR department to "find a middle-aged woman to fill that slot by Friday". Because the boss knew his previous moral stance had filled his company with the correct ratios of diversity, he felt he had done his bit and had free rein to do what he liked on such occasions.

"In institutions that do not feel the sharp wind of public criticism, an innocent corruption grows up, like a mushroom."
(German philosopher Friedrich Nietzsche, 1844–1900)

This quote captures the situation quite well. Knowing he wouldn't face public criticism (because of his previous recruitment practice), the manager felt he had licence to do what he wanted.

Another Example:
I've paid enough tax, your majesty

When I left the Army, I did an HGV driving course as part of my resettlement back into civilian life. I was rubbish at it. I didn't bother taking the test at the end of the week. I'd done enough to know I'd be lethal in charge of a lorry. Anyway, one good thing did come out of that course. On a 20-minute tea break, I was sitting in a truckers' café when I heard another instructor say to his pupil, "I just work cash in hand these days. I've paid enough tax over the years."

Half an hour later as I was daydreaming my lorry through Plymouth's narrow streets, I thought "Ah, that 'cash in hand' thing was a great example of Moral Credential Bias"… just before I slammed on the brakes for a speed bump that appeared out of nowhere. (Apparently, slamming on your brakes in a lorry is never a good thing, as my instructor, an ex-Royal Marine sergeant, told me in not so many words.)

A Practical Application:
Defend yourself and others

Understanding Moral Credential Bias is useful to help you counter it, either in yourself or in others. The idea that you're normally good is no defence for being bad.

> "If you rob a bank once, you'll go to jail. You won't be let off for the nine times you didn't rob a bank."

> **Summary of Moral Credential Bias.** If you think somebody justifies doing something wrong on the grounds that he feels he's accumulated sufficient goodwill, tell him his decision is influenced by Moral Credential Bias.

50 Distinction Bias

Easy Definition: When comparing two similar things side by side, don't put too much emphasis on small differences that would make no real difference in a wider setting. That's Distinction Bias.

Geeky Definition: Distinction Bias is the tendency to view two options as more dissimilar when assessing them together than you would if you evaluated them separately.

An Example:
Heinz Beans have got the edge

When things are compared side by side, they are often considered more dissimilar than they really are. That's Distinction Bias. Distinction Bias can magnify the near meaningless differences between two very similar things to the extent they become decisive in which one we choose. If this bias were removed, other factors (usually cost) would be far more influential in the decision.

An obvious example is the distinction between shop-brand food products and premium-brand ones. The discernible difference between the two is usually not worth the extra money. If the products were tested in isolation for taste, the difference would be negligible or undetectable for most people. However, the difference in cost is very noticeable for everyone. Therefore, the price not the difference in taste ought to be the decisive factor in which one we choose.

In 2010, *Which?* magazine asked members of the public to try 12 types of beans including supermarket and economy varieties. Branston won. Asda Baked Beans came second. Morrisons Baked Beans came third, and Heinz came fourth. The Morrisons beans were half the price of the Heinz ones. This was just one test, but it points to the fact that most people can't differentiate between premium beans and cheap ones. Lots of people claim they can tell the difference, and that's their justification for buying the expensive ones. But, even if they can tell the difference and buy the expensive ones, that's likely to be a decision steeped in Distinction Bias. In this example, the cost ought to be the decisive factor. Those who buy the expensive beans should ask themselves whether the difference they can detect is worth the extra money. So, it's now not a question of whether there is a difference. It's a question of whether that difference is worth paying double for.

When it comes to baked beans though, there is often another factor at play: the looking-like-you-can-afford-the-named-brands factor or the being-happy-you-can-afford-the-named-brands factor. That's fair enough. But we ought to be truthful with ourselves if it's one of those factors that really makes us part with the extra cash.

Another Example:
I'll teach you to drive, dear

When family members teach each other to drive, World War III nearly always breaks out between the "instructor" and the pupil. One reason for this is Distinction Bias. As the instructor (let's say it's the husband) needs to start talking like an instructor, his conversation includes far more imperative sentences (i.e. commands) than normal. The pupil (let's say it's the wife) detects the difference between the "normal husband" and the slightly bossier "instructor" husband. This difference would be unnoticeable to onlookers, but it causes the wife to respond to the perceived threat to her freedom of action (see Section 64 – Reactance Bias). In fact, other factors (e.g. the team spirit of being man and wife, the possible money saved by not using a professional instructor) ought to be bigger factors in how the pupil reacts. But it just doesn't work like that because Distinction Bias kicks in and the difference between the "two" husbands becomes overly influential. With a real driving instructor (i.e. one who's not a spouse), there are no differences to spot. He'll use command-like sentences from the outset.

A Practical Application:
Don't buy stuff you don't want

Small differences can cost you a lot of money. By understanding how

Distinction Bias works, you are better equipped to work out whether the differences you're paying for are worth it.

Imagine there are two TVs which are nearly identical in terms of functionality and look, but one has a better contrast ratio (the bit that determines how black the blacks are). The cost of the extra blackness might be an extra £200. Now, I'm not saying extra blackness isn't worth £200. I'm just saying we ought to know exactly what our £200 is buying and make a decision based on that. But TV shops don't make it that easy for you. There won't be two TVs. There will be three. Well, three price bands. Due to the Compromise Effect, which is also known as the Goldilocks Effect because it tricks us into thinking the one in the middle is "just right" (see Section 46), you will be more drawn to the middle price band. The challenge is to wash away all that Goldilocks stuff, focus on the differences between your options and then, being aware of Distinction Bias, determine whether those differences are significant enough in your life to warrant the extra cash.

If you're in the selling game, you can combine the Goldilocks Effect and Distinction Bias to herd your buyers towards your middle price band, where you can sell them marked-up goods that don't really do much more than the lower-priced stuff.

Summary of Distinction Bias. If you think somebody is making too much of a small difference when comparing things side by side, tell him he's being influenced by Distinction Bias.

51   The Dunning-Kruger Effect

Easy Definition: If you're untrained, inexperienced or don't fully understand your environment, don't trick yourself into thinking you're doing well. You might be suffering from the Dunning-Kruger Effect.

Geeky Definition: The Dunning-Kruger Effect is the tendency for unskilled people to make poor decisions or reach wrong conclusions, but their incompetence prevents them from recognising their mistakes. It links well with the old adage: "Ignorance is bliss." In uncovering this tendency, Justin Kruger and David Dunning of Cornell University were partly influenced by this observation:

"Ignorance more frequently begets confidence than does knowledge." (Charles Darwin)

An Example:
Unlike yourself, I'm a great writer

Most people are required to write stuff for some reason or other. This is one area where the Dunning-Kruger Effect is prevalent. If you don't know you can't use an apostrophe to show a plural (e.g. two solution's) or you don't know that semicolons can't be used for introductions (e.g. I like the following; A, B and C), then these mistakes don't register as mistakes when you bash out your written correspondence. To the rest of the world, you look a bit of a dunce, but, as far as you're concerned, you're a great writer. Your incompetence has stopped you seeing your incompetence. The Dunning-Kruger Effect is the reverse side of the coin to this football chant:

"You're shit, and you know you are." (Football chant)

With the Dunning-Kruger Effect, they don't know they are.

According to Dunning and Kruger, ignorance is behind a great deal of incompetence. They assert that incompetent people will:

- Overestimate their abilities.
- Fail to recognise genuine ability in others.
- Not recognise the extremity of their inadequacy.

Oh, if you didn't spot that the "Unlike Yourself" in the title of this example should be "Unlike You", you could be one of those unwittingly whacking loads of grammar errors into your work without realising it. Eeek! Solution? Use competent proofreaders.

Another Example:
Why does it keep doing that?

Microsoft Office applications (e.g. Word, PowerPoint, Excel) are at their most frustrating when they try to help you. Microsoft Word's tendency to change the font type and size after you cut and paste something is a classic example. But whose fault is that? In our office, it's always MS Word's fault when the auto-numbering kicks in without being asked or an embedded image starts choosing its own location on the page. But, in truth, it's the user's fault. Most people learn the MS office applications on the job. They become quite proficient at using the normal functions, but start losing their way around the processor when the more-out-of-the-ordinary functions are required. In my experience, very few people actually go on a course to learn how to use the MS applications. The difference in proficiency between the course-trained people and the on-the-job learners is marked.

Many people find that once they've done a course, the "gremlins" that wound them up suddenly start making sense. Document templates, style and format templates, multiple clipboards, mail merge, image manipulation and auto-numbering all transform into useful tools after training. Before training, they're just things to turn off or work around. Until the user's incompetency has been addressed by attending a course, those things that make his life a misery when using MS applications will remain the application's fault and not his.

If this sounds like how MS applications treat you, then I'm afraid you might be suffering from the Dunning-Kruger Effect.

There is some good news. The Dunning-Kruger Effect is not

permanent. People often become aware of and acknowledge their own previous lack of ability after training... or time.

A Practical Application:
Win an argument with two sentences

One of the best things about the Dunning-Kruger Effect is using the term in arguments. If you say to someone "your incompetency is preventing you from seeing your incompetency" and then add "it's a classic example of the Dunning-Kruger Effect", you might as well start a lap of honour around the room doing I'm-the-champion hands.

You'll have just bashed them hard with a tight circular argument with no chinks in its armour and underpinned it with some academic name-dropping. It will rock them back onto their heels.

> **Summary of the Dunning-Kruger Effect.** If you think somebody's lack of ability or experience is preventing him from seeing his own failings, tell him he is suffering from the Dunning-Kruger Effect.

(52) The Endowment Effect

Easy Definition: Don't overvalue your things just because they're yours. That's the Endowment Effect.

Geeky Definition: The Endowment Effect describes the tendency to place more value on something you own than something you don't.

An Example:
I love it coz it's mine

My mate's just bought a sports car. We've known each other for years, and I can't say he's really shown much interest in cars. But, now that he owns a sports car, he never shuts up about it. He's forever justifying the running costs and being dismissive of the lack of practicality. It's a great-looking car, but he never goes anywhere in it, because it's not really designed for taking things to places. For a start, it costs a fortune to fill up, and it pretty much uses a full tank to get you home and back to the petrol station. You can't transport any luggage in it. You have to empty your pockets just to get yourself in. Its primary role is to be the subject of blokes' pub chatter.

My mate was an intelligence analyst too. He understands the Endowment Effect, and he's the first to admit it's alive and well in his head. He knows if I owned the car, he'd be pretty indifferent about it. But I don't. He does. And he loves it… for that very reason. He values it because he owns it. When the water pump packed in, he paid nearly £1000 to fix it. A grand! He is fully aware that his "loss aversion" (i.e. avoiding losing the car) is causing him to accept the running costs. Nowadays, he couldn't bear to be without his rocket go-kart.

I like to think of the Endowment Effect as the reverse side of the "Fox and Grapes" coin. "The Fox and Grapes" is one of the traditional Aesop's fables. (Aesop was a slave and story-teller who lived in ancient Greece between 620 and 560 BC.) The fable goes like this:

A hungry fox tries with all his might to reach some grapes on a vine, but he fails. As the fox walks off, he remarks: "Oh, you aren't even ripe yet! I don't need any sour grapes."

Incidentally, that's the origin of the term "it's just sour grapes". Anyway, Aesop told this story to teach people not to talk disparagingly about things just because they cannot attain them. Aesop spotted that people mentally tricked themselves into disliking the things they could not have to lessen the impact of not owning them. The Endowment Effect is the opposite of that. It occurs when people trick themselves into overvaluing the things they own. This could be to justify the cost of buying it, but that's not the whole story. It seems the act of ownership forms an owner-owned relationship in the mind of the owner, who will pay to keep the relationship intact.

Hey, hang on a sec. Maybe I'm being disparaging about my mate's sports car because I can't have one. Am I Aesop's fox? Nah, I wouldn't swap it for my car in a month of Sundays.

A Practical Application:
Double your chances of a sale with real magic

The Endowment Effect causes you to overvalue the things you own. That idea is simple, but also powerful. Salesmen routinely employ it to turn your cash into their cash. It's nearly magic. Here's how it works:

The Endowment Effect can take hold before you actually own something. "Ownership" can occur as soon as you start to imagine yourself as the owner of the object. And this is how salesmen get you.

For example, when a shop states you can take the sofa home for a week to try it before buying, the salesman knows exactly what he's doing. He knows that once you've got the sofa home, you will develop an attachment to it. Once you are slouched in it at home with your feet up and with a glass of wine, you "own" it. As a result, its value will increase in your mind. This is the Endowment Effect at work. Suddenly, you're willing to pay the price of the sofa because you don't want to lose it. You are in loss-aversion mode.

In fact, the effect kicks in before you've even got the sofa home. As soon as you start to imagine taking it home, your "ownership" of it has started. Here's an example:

If a TV salesman says "Where you would put such a large TV in your living room?" or "This TV would transform any room into a modern-looking one", he's initiating your feelings of "ownership" towards the TV. You start to imagine it in your house, and you start to value it more. Once those feelings are set, you'll pay not to "lose" the TV. Suddenly, your living room without that TV is starting to look a bit drab. So, your brain is being attacked from two angles. You want the benefit of the TV. We know that. But now you also want to avoid losing the TV with which you've started to form the owner-owned relationship. With two forces working on you (push and pull), you are more likely to step over the "buy-me" line. In fact, your decision to buy the TV ought to be based on just one force: the "push" force of the

TV's benefit to you. The "pull" force you experience through fear of losing a TV you've never owned is real sales magic.

> **Summary of Endowment Effect.** If you think somebody is overvaluing something because he owns it (or is imagining himself owning it), tell him the Endowment Effect is causing an overly emotional strong bond to the object.

(53)   Hyperbolic Discounting Effect

Easy Definition: Don't judge an imminent reward to be more valuable than a future one just because it will happen soon. That's the Hyperbolic Discounting Effect.

Geeky Definition: Hyperbolic discounting is the tendency to show a preference for a reward that arrives sooner rather than later. Studies show that we are likely to discount the value of the later reward more as the length of the delay increases.

An Example:
Two sweets later or one now

You'll doubtless have seen versions of the 1972 Stanford University marshmallow experiment, in which around 600 children aged 4 to 6 were brought into a room one at a time and presented with a single marshmallow. The children were told if they could resist eating the marshmallow for 15 minutes, they'd get another one. Some of the children just wolfed the marshmallow down as soon as the experimenters left the room, but others "tortured" themselves in a bid to hang in there for the second marshmallow. Only around a third won the second marshmallow.

This was an experiment in deferred gratification. Could the future reward outmatch the immediate reward? Well, for most of the children, it couldn't, despite many worthy attempts at imposing self-discipline. Interestingly, some of those who tried to defer their gratification (i.e. wait the 15 minutes) put their hands over the eyes to remove the temptation. This is a version of the Ostrich Effect (see Section 63). It's also interesting that those who resisted the longest tended to do better in their later lives (e.g. better exam results, better jobs). The point is this. Your brain will often opt for an imminent reward over a future one, even if the future one is bigger.

Another Example:
Now-you and future-you

Hyperbolic discounting is the reason most attempts at dieting fail. It's a simple concept. The rewards of dieting are so far in the future, your brain is easily distracted from those rewards. Faced with a chocolate biscuit, your brain has no trouble whatsoever giving it a high reward score, and this blots out the distant dieting reward of being slimmer. When you're not faced with an imminent reward (or when you're stuffed to the eyes with such rewards), the brain is very good at focusing back on the distant reward.

This effect can create two personas: *now-you* and *future-you*. *Now-you* lives for the moment, whereas *future-you* invests wisely. *Future you* is the one who bought the gym membership, the exercise bike and the basket full of fruit and veg. *Now-you* is the one who watches reality TV instead of going to the gym, hangs the shirts over the exercise bike and eats crisps.

The secret to stopping *now-you* destroying *future-you*'s intentions is… God only knows. Hyperbolic discounting is a powerful effect. It gets us all, because it takes real discipline to ignore *now-you*.

In my experience, the only way to do it is to remove the temptations facing *now-you*. For example, don't keep chocolate biscuits in the house. Now, that seems pretty obvious, but how do you ensure that? Well, you need to take the battle into *future-you*'s environment. At the point when you buy the chocolate biscuits (i.e. in the shop), the reward they offer is not imminent (you can't scoff them in the shop). Therefore, your thoughts at the point of buying are partially influenced by *future-you,* not just *now-you*. However, when you're in the shop, be aware that *now-you* will often pop up with a clever little trick that plays on your sense of discipline. *Now-you* will "say" something like: "Buy the biscuits and just have one every couple of days. It's nice to have them in just in case someone else comes around." Don't be fooled. You won't be disciplined. Once the biscuits are home, their reward becomes imminent, and *now-you* gets its evil way. (Think back to the Broken Biscuit Effect, Section 44.) So, the trick is to protect *future-you* by leaving the biscuits in the shop. Because of how hyperbolic discounting works, not buying them requires far less discipline than not eating them.

Right, that was just a long way of saying don't buy chocolate biscuits if you're on a diet. But, as we've spelt out, that's far better advice than saying don't eat chocolate biscuits if you're on a diet.

"I gotta work out. I keep saying it all the time. I keep saying I gotta start working out. It's been about two months since I've worked out. And I just don't have the time. Which uh... is odd. Because I have the time to go out to dinner. And uh... and watch tv. And uh... try to figure out what my phone number spells in words."
(Ellen DeGeneres)

A Practical Application:
Sell the dream

As we've just covered, *future-you* is a buyer of things you're going to use in the future. That means *future-them* is a buyer too. *Future-them* is looking to buy a dream. This means if you're selling something because you're fed up with it or it didn't turn out how you expected (e.g. a caravan), you shouldn't price it based on your disappointment or just to get rid of it. No, have some confidence that your buyer's *future-them* is just like your *future-you* when you bought the item. You should price it based on their dream – offer them the dream as well as the caravan. It'll cost you nothing, and their *future-them* will be convinced. I mean, what do you think they're looking for?

A cramped caravan that's too much effort to hook up to your car and drive to the sea to live amongst equally miserable ant-infested self-caterers? Or a caravan that gives them the freedom to see the UK's coastlines while sitting in the shade of the awning with a cold refreshing beer, listening to the cries of the gulls and watching their steaks sizzle on the BBQ?

In all your dealings, buy "the truth" from their *now-them*, but sell "the dream" to their *future-them*.

Another Practical Application:
I want it all, and I want it now. How about half now?

Give smaller rewards now to save money in the long term.

If you are an employer, you might be able to use hyperbolic discounting to your advantage. If you are struggling to fill a position, offer a "golden handshake" (i.e. offer the employee a bonus up front as opposed to at the end of year). Potential employees will be more attracted to it than an end-of-year bonus. Another advantage is that you will probably be able to offer less with a golden handshake, because to the employee, £1,000 now is more attractive than £2,000 in a year's time.

> **Summary of the Hyperbolic Discounting Effect.** If you think somebody has failed to adhere to a long-term aim because he was "blinded" by a short-term gain, tell him he has been affected by the Hyperbolic Discounting Effect.

54   Good Looking People Bias

Easy Definition: Don't think good-looking people are cleverer or more deserving of your attention than normal-looking or ugly people. That's Good Looking People Bias.

Geeky Definition: In decision-making and reasoning, Good Looking People Bias is the tendency to place more weight on the views of good-looking people than average-looking or ugly people.

An Example:
Good policies or good looks?

From my own observations, I would estimate that close to half of any developed nation's population couldn't describe the differences between their major political parties, and this is probably quite understandable. After all, these days, the political parties are all fighting for the same middle ground. So, what does differentiate the parties? Well, it's becoming more about how the leaders look and portray themselves than their policies. Actually, I think that's understating the case. Nowadays, it's almost entirely about how the leaders look and portray themselves.

Unfortunately, politics is becoming far more of a beauty pageant than it ought to be. But that's life, because Good Looking People Bias is rife, and most of us will give more weight to the opinions of good-looking people. This is directly linked to the Halo Effect (see Section 56), which is when you judge someone positively because of a known positive trait (in this case, looks).

When it comes to politics, we probably ought to be voting based on the content of the parties' manifestos, but lots of us don't think about the policies at all. Provided we're not just voting how we always do or how our parents did, then we tend to vote based on the party leaders' personal traits, like looks, bearing and confidence. I'm not saying these things aren't important. I'm just saying that traits like looks all too often play far too big a role in how we reach decisions.

It's not just the opinions of good-looking people that carry more weight. A number of controlled studies show that good-looking people receive better grades at school, earn more money and receive better care from doctors.

Those suffering from Good Looking People Bias think the handsome and pretty are more talented, more honest and cleverer than not-so-good-looking people. It's quite a natural thing to do. Many of us suffer from this bias. But just remember, most of the smart people in history were pretty average looking... at best.

"The average woman would rather have beauty than brains, because the average man can see better than he can think."
(Anon)

Another Example:
You're too late, sir. You might still make it, lads

The check-in for my flight from Luton to Belfast was about to close. Still being two minutes away from the airport in a hire car (which I still had to hand in), I was in trouble. To give myself a chance of making the flight, I decided to park in the drop-off-only bay outside the terminal and check in before handing the hire car back. The young girl manning the check-in desk was just about to close up, and she made it pretty clear that my last-second arrival was something of an inconvenience. I quickly answered the "did you pack your own bag"-type questions and handed her my holdall. She reluctantly tagged it up and ordered me to go immediately to the boarding gate. I thanked her, nodded and sprinted outside to the hire car. Just as I was leaving the check-in desk, a fairly chubby dishevelled man skidded up behind me trying to get on the same flight. I heard the young girl say: "I'm sorry. Check-in has closed." I did not hang around for the argument that was about to ensue.

I jumped in the car, raced to the hire-car centre, handed the car in and jumped on the bus back to the terminal. While on the dawdling bus, I heard four young Irish lads worrying about whether they were going to make their flight. I asked them if they were on the same flight as me to Belfast. They were. I asked if they'd already checked in. They hadn't. I decided to put them out their misery and explained that the check-in had closed about 20 minutes ago. I told them that even the person who was just five seconds behind me had failed to make it.

When the bus finally arrived at the terminal, I hurriedly made my way to the aircraft boarding gate while the cheery Irish lads, who looked more like a boy band than the stag party they were, strolled off to find the check-in desk.

By the skin of my teeth, I made the flight. Just as I was getting comfortable in my seat, I saw the four Westlife lookalikes skipping down the aircraft aisle. "How on Earth did you get on this flight?" I asked. "A nice smile and Irish charm", answered one. He was right. That's exactly what got them on the flight.

So, the next time, you're having a spat with someone in the service industry, send your best-looking person forward to do the negotiating. Because of Good Looking People Bias, your best-looking person is likely to win more favour than anyone else in your group. Oh, and if you're ever getting grief off airline check-in staff who are dogmatically laying down the law with comments like "the rules state…", "the captain says…", etc., then the situation might be worse than you think – they probably think you're ugly to boot.

A Practical Application:
Where do I sign, gorgeous?

This is simple. Use aesthetically pleasing people as your company's frontmen (or women).

Actually, it's not quite that simple, because there might be another factor at play: jealousy of someone's good looks. This can affect your frontman in two ways:

(1) Some people are threatened by good-looking people encroaching on their "territory" (e.g. a self-obsessed or predatory boss), and they might find reasons not to invite him back.

(2) Some people will actively look for competency flaws to undermine your good-looking person. (This is a common manifestation of jealousy. It's at the root of blonde jokes, e.g. *Q. Why did the blonde lose her job in M & M factory? A. She kept rejecting all the Ws.*)

So, if you can find a competent, good-looking person who's not a threat to anyone in the target environment (e.g. he's too old, too young or just a very infrequent visitor), then your company is more likely to impress.

You might now be thinking that using a good-looking frontman is more hassle than it's worth, but I suspect it's not. Good Looking People Bias is deeply engrained in us all. Good looks are a powerful catalyst to get stuff done.

Be aware though that you can't go around recruiting people based on their good looks. That's likely to be against the law. In 2010, Prada Japan found itself in hot water after a senior retail manager announced she was asked to "eliminate any staff deemed old, fat, ugly, disgusting or not having the Prada look." The order reportedly came from Prada Japan's CEO. Of course, there's a strong argument that the fashion industry should be allowed to discriminate based on looks. But it didn't save them, so it probably won't save you. You also can't hire a pretty or handsome person because you hired an ugly one last year. That's Moral Credential Bias (see Section 49). Remember, Good Looking People Bias is a form of the Halo Effect (see Section 56), which ensures that a person's positive trait permeates throughout everything a person does, regardless of whether the trait is related to what they're doing or not.

Summary of Good Looking People Bias. If you think someone is giving more credence to someone else's views because of that latter's good looks, tell him he has been influenced by the Good Looking People Bias.

55 Groupthink

Easy Definition: Don't keep your views to yourself just to maintain harmony in the group. That leads to Groupthink.

Geeky Definition: Groupthink occurs when decisions are made due to the unified nature of decision-makers. It happens when the decision-makers strive for unanimity, and this overrides their motivation to consider alternative views. As a result, independent thinking is lost.

An Example:
So, we all agree the Japanese won't attack

There could be a number of reasons for Groupthink occurring, but, generally, it's because the decision-makers are strong-willed and dominant, and subordinates want to avoid looking foolish or annoying the decision-makers. Whatever the reason, Groupthink can cause a group to make irrational decisions, because its members are fearful of upsetting the group's cohesiveness.

The most famous and commonly cited example of Groupthink is how the US Navy treated the threat of a Japanese attack on Pearl Harbor in Hawaii. It was late 1941 and the US had not yet entered World War II. The officers of the US Pacific Fleet at Pearl Harbor had intelligence that Japan was preparing for a large-scale attack, but they succeeded in convincing themselves it would have nothing to do with them. This assessment was based on the following assumptions:

• Japan wouldn't dare mount a surprise attack on Pearl Harbor, because it would bring the US into the war, which the US would win.
• The US Pacific Fleet was too big and capable to attack.
• The US would spot an invasion force in time to destroy it.
• Torpedoes launched from enemy aircraft would be ineffective in the harbour's shallow water.

Their assessment was wrong. On 7 December 1941, Japan launched over 350 fighter aircraft, bombers and torpedo planes from six aircraft carriers. The planes sank or damaged all eight battleships, three cruisers, three destroyers, a minelayer and training ship. They destroyed 188 US aircraft and killed over 2,000 American servicemen.

Japan had a history of mounting pre-emptive military attacks, but this was not enough of a factor to override the officers' assumptions on Japan's intent. It is now known that some individuals were not comfortable with the assumptions and were more concerned about Japan's intent than others, but they felt compelled not to speak out. These individuals had succumbed to social pressures. They did not want to upset the collective view.

These two quotations capture Groupthink nicely:

"None of us is as dumb as all of us"

"Only dead fish go with the flow."

A bit more on this story: There's a oft-cited conspiracy theory out there that British signals intelligence at Bletchley Park had broken the codes of the Imperial Japanese Navy and was aware of the pending attack against the US Pacific Fleet at Pearl Harbor. The story goes that Prime Minister Winston Churchill decided not to tell the Americans. Why? Well, for two reasons supposedly: to ensure he didn't compromise the capabilities of Bletchley Park and to ensure the Americans were dragged into the war. Conspiracists claim that Churchill opted to keep quiet. If that were true, it would have been a wrongdoing equal in magnitude to ringing the Americans and telling them everything was fine (see Omissions Bias, Section 62).

How to Avoid Groupthink:
Take active measures to avoid Groupthink

Groupthink is bad. It's not something to be embraced. Groupthink is best avoided in meetings by setting rules at the start. Simply saying something like "We don't want to fall into the Groupthink trap. All questions and input are valid. Discussion is vital" will often give participants the confidence to pipe up with their individual concerns. As a group tends to be more vulnerable to Groupthink when its members have similar backgrounds, one way to overcome Groupthink is to invite outsiders to your meetings, especially ones known to be a bit outspoken. Another way is to set up a meeting specifically to challenge your assumptions or to see things from someone else's perspective (called a "red teaming" meeting – see Section 60).

I know we're hindsighted to the max with regard to Pearl Harbor, but let's think about what red teaming might have achieved back in 1941. Imagine the officers of the US Pacific Fleet had set up a red team to think like the Japanese. Very early in that meeting, one of the officers – who would all have been pretending to be Japanese (because that's what you do during red teaming) – would undoubtedly have said something like: "As events develop in Southeast Asia, war between us [Japan] and the US is inevitable. We can fight them with their Pacific Fleet or without. It's an obvious choice." That idea alone would have made the US officers challenge their assumptions, and a precautionary surveillance operation would have been mounted. As a result, the US would have had more warning, and the Japanese fleet would likely have been decisively defeated by the mighty Pacific Fleet.

Practitioners in the intelligence game are keen to hear every point of view before presenting assessments. Meetings for devil's advocacy and red teaming are common events during their normal working week. The best intelligencers have trained themselves to drag alternative perspectives from their team. As meetings are wrapped up, you can often see the chairman scanning the attendees' faces for signs of concern that was not expressed at the meeting. Many meetings end with words like "John, do you still want to say something?" It happens because the chairman recognises that Groupthink is a social condition which needs a deliberate effort to keep it at bay.

Summary of Groupthink. If you think the desire for harmony in a decision-making group is preventing the individuals from presenting alternative views, tell them the group is suffering from Groupthink.

56   The Halo Effect

Easy Definition: Don't think someone who is good at something is good at everything. Also, don't think someone's strong past performance means his latest work is good. They are both examples of the Halo Effect.

Geeky Definition: The Halo Effect is the tendency to judge someone positively because of a known positive trait. This can occur regardless of whether the judgement is related to the trait.

An Example:
One piece of work affects two grades

If a teacher marks John's first homework assignment as an A, this grade could affect the grade of John's second homework assignment regardless of its quality.

For example:

Monday's homework: A
Wednesday's homework: B+

In this scenario, John retains the "halo" he earned on Monday, and it influences the teacher's judgement of Wednesday's work, which might only have been worthy of a C+. But, now imagine a scenario where John's Monday assignment was not as good, but the Wednesday one was unchanged. The following could occur:

Monday's homework: B
Wednesday's homework: C+

In this example, the Wednesday assignment drops from B+ to C+ simply because the Monday assignment was not as good, i.e. John didn't earn a "halo" on Monday.

In the first scenario (the one with the A on the Monday), if Friday's homework were also C+ standard, the teacher might start to realise that John is not as bright as originally thought. However, at that stage, it's too late. The undeserved B+ achieved on the Wednesday has already been awarded. In effect, John scored well twice for just one piece of good work.

Another Example:
Hey, you're good at darts. Who was last year's snooker champion?

The Halo Effect can also occur when the judgement and the traits are unrelated or loosely related. For example, thinking someone is clever because he dresses smartly (unrelated trait) or thinking someone would be a good member of your quiz team to answer the sports-category questions based on his ability to play sports (loosely related trait) are examples of the Halo Effect. Good Looking People Bias (see Section 54) is a form of the Halo Effect. You shouldn't think good-looking people are more capable or more deserving of your attention than normal-looking or ugly people. That's the Halo Effect.

The Devil Effect
The other side of the coin to the Halo Effect is the Devil Effect. This is the tendency to judge someone negatively because of a known negative trait.

"The last thing I need is another podgy accountant."

"Never go to a doctor whose office plants have died."

Salesmen often fall foul of the Devil Effect when looking at potential customers. If you look like you've been sleeping next to the dustbin, some salesmen – particularly those selling luxury goods – are far less likely to engage you with any degree of enthusiasm. A few years ago, I spoke to a salesman who sold Porsches and Lotuses. Nowadays, he's a very successful car salesman, but it wasn't always like that.

Johnny, as he was called, told me it was difficult to spot a good prospective buyer. He said he had learnt that dress standards were not a good indicator of who was in the market for a posh car. Tuning his skills (or so he thought), he had taught himself to look at a person's watch and shoes as opposed to his general appearance, because these were a better indication of his wealth and buying extravagance. But, experience soon taught Johnny there was no meaningful relationship between someone's watch or shoes and his ability (or determination) to buy a Porsche. In his earlier days, Johnny was suffering from the Devil and the Halo Effect. He was virtually blanking those with a cheap watch, while expending all his energy on those with an expensive one. He said it took him 20 years of "reading" his customers' attire to learn that he should treat all prospective buyers the same. In other words, it took him two decades to counter the Halo and Devil Effects, but now that he has, his sales have rocketed.

A Practical Application:

A great service. Smiths arrived at 9 on the dot and saved me £114 (Pauline Baxter, Exeter road)

You can either walk about with a "halo" from your past activities or without a halo. If you're selling stuff, my advice is get yourself that halo. The most obvious way to do this is through testimonials from past customers. It might seem obvious, but lots of companies do not use testimonials. They should. The positivity of the testimonials – whether they're related to your pending sale or not – will help push your new customer over the "buy now" line. They're a good marketing ploy. But not all testimonials are effective. Remember, for the Halo Effect to work well, you need a really good score for your past activities. (Think back to John's "A" for his homework on Monday.)

The secret with testimonials is to publish ones that are as convincing as possible. Convincing is the key word here. If your testimonial says something like "Smiths is the best company in Plymouth by far (John, Plymouth)", the "halo" bleed-across will be far less than if you say something like "I save about £60 every time I use Smiths (John Draycott, Plymouth Sensors Ltd)". (We covered the idea of using moderation and evidence to improve messaging in Section 23.)

When people read your advertising literature, they will expect to see testimonials. For this reason, they won't notice the testimonials unless they smack them in the chops as being from real people. Ones that don't have that trait are ignored. Your readers have learnt to tune them out, just like they have the red "sale" signs in shop windows.

You might think a generic testimonial that means something to every future customer (e.g. "Smiths saved me a fortune") would be best, but that's not how it works. Specific testimonials are far more effective – even if they don't relate directly to the next customer. Remember, the Halo Effect works off the back of loosely related and even unrelated positive traits. So, a positive testimonial with believability is what you're looking for to create the biggest halo. Here's a quick guide on how to get the most out of testimonials:

• Ask a happy customer for a testimonial and coach them to use real facts and figures in their words. Don't worry if it's too specific. That's a good thing. You're looking for believability.
• Get their approval to use their real name and a photo of them.
• Try to get a collection of testimonials that speak of different traits (e.g. timeliness, reliability, value for money) and double up on a couple of ideas, but don't display too many testimonials (five or six is good).
• Make sure the benefits of doing business with you are clear, but try to avoid general statements.

Generally-worded testimonials are a waste of space. Believable testimonials are effective. They will generate that halo for you and help you to clinch the next sale.

Summary of Halo Effect. If you think someone is grading something (or someone) too highly due to an unrelated or loosely related positive trait, tell him he has been influenced by the Halo Effect.

57 Hindsight Bias

Easy Definition: After an event, don't think the event was more predictable than it was. That is Hindsight Bias.

Geeky Definition: Hindsight Bias is the tendency to think that past events were more predictable than they actually were.

An Example:
I just knew...

"I just knew this game would go to penalties and Germany would win."
"No, you didn't. You put £10 on England to win."

"I just knew I'd pass the Applied Mathematics section."
"No, you didn't. You thought you'd failed it when you spoke to me after the exam."

Another Example:
Why would anyone need a telephone?

At a demonstration of one (well, by necessity, two I suppose) of the world's first telephones, an American mayor noted: "I can see the time when every city will have one." Back in the 1870s, his statement was probably quite insightful. There is certainly no evidence that anyone around him thought it was the massive understatement it is now known to be. However, these days, the mayor's quote is often upheld for ridicule. I find that quite unfair. Any recent jibes at the mayor are heavily tainted by Hindsight Bias. In fact, for the time, the mayor was being quite astute. The following quote by another notable helps to give us some context of the era: "This 'telephone' has too many shortcomings to be seriously considered as a means of communication. The device is inherently of no value to us."

A Practical Application:
Don't hammer what might be your best team

Understanding Hindsight Bias ensures you don't label those who failed to spot the outcome as bad judges. This is important to ensure that the Devil Effect (the opposite of the Halo Effect – see Section 56) does not occur in the future. In other words, by understanding that an event was genuinely unpredictable, you do not tarnish your decision-makers as poor judges based on one "bad" performance. There is a chance their prediction was sound based on what was known at the time, and they might actually be your best team to get the next prediction right.

> "Hindsight is always twenty-twenty."

Another Practical Application:
Use the term to help you remind people what was known prior to the event

This is pretty obvious, but I've found it works. Being aware of the term "Hindsight Bias" is quite handy. It gives you something to say when your boss accuses you of failing to predict an event. You could – if your relationship allows it – suggest his accusation is based on Hindsight Bias, and then use the credibility afforded by that "scientific" wording as a platform to highlight what was known prior to the event. (Well, it's better than saying "Yeah, we know that now!")

> **Summary of Hindsight Bias.** If you think someone is using knowledge known now to slate a decision made before the knowledge was known, tell him he's displaying Hindsight Bias.

(58)   # Impact Bias

Easy Definition: Don't be overly worried about a specific bad event that might happen in the future. The future is unlikely to be disastrous if that event occurs. Similarly, don't think that if a specific good event occurs, your future will be heavenly. That's Impact Bias.

Geeky Definition: Impact Bias is the tendency to overestimate the length or the intensity of future feelings in reaction to either good or bad occurrences.

An Example:
It won't be as bad as you think

The fear of something bad happening often magnifies how bad you think it will be. Most of the time, the expectation doesn't match the reality. For example, people often say things like "I would never cope if my wife left me". One sports car, a bachelor pad and an insatiable new girlfriend later, they're wondering what they ever saw in her... or him... it works for girls too.

Before the bad event occurs, your mind envisages a life focused solely around the bad event. In reality, the bad event is likely to be overshadowed by all sorts of other events happening at the same time.

Former Vice President of the United States, Dan Quayle, is often ridiculed for this quote:

"The future will be better tomorrow."

But, given how Impact Bias works for negative events, he was right.

Charlie Brown (from "Peanuts") had a great philosophy. He said:

"I have a new philosophy. I'm only going to dread one day at a time."
(American cartoonist Charles M. Schulz, 1922-2000)

This philosophy would actually work, because your mind won't be able to discount the things that will happen in your more-distant future life.

Another Example:
It won't be as good as you think

Conversely, don't overestimate how long elation will last if something fantastic happens. For example, everyone dreams of winning the lottery and the possibilities that would unlock. However, there are countless lottery winners whose celebrations were short-lived through a realisation that they're still the same people with the same non-money-related issues.

American film director and comedian Woody Allen was joking when he said:

"Money is better than poverty, if only for financial reasons."

However, because of how Impact Bias works for positive events, he's spot on. Many other things wouldn't change if you suddenly won a truck-load of cash. You probably wouldn't be ecstatic for long.

A Practical Application:
You're damned if you do, but you only might be damned if you don't

We all know you have to take risks to succeed.

"Great deeds are usually wrought at great risks."
(The Greek historian Herodotus, circa 484 BC – 425 BC)

I can't think of a single successful person who "safed" their way to the top. However, even though we all know this, lots of people are too risk-averse.

"Most people would rather be certain they're miserable than risk being happy."
(Author of self-help books Dr Robert Anthony)

But, if you know that bad things won't be as bad as you think they'll be, you can afford to up your risk appetite. So, crack on. Ignore your brain. Take more risks.

Now, just before you go and spend all your company's cash on some risky venture, I should say this works more for personal risk than for business risk. This is because Impact Bias is something that happens in your brain about your future situation. To understand your business risk fully, you need to assess what the future environment will be like when or after the bad thing happens. There is a lesson to be learnt from personal Impact Bias when doing this: don't forget to factor in how all the elements of your environment will look in the future – not just the thing that could go wrong. There are tried and tested techniques for doing this. If you look up "scenario generation techniques" (or specifically "cone of plausibility"), you'll get a feel for how seriously businesses take this idea when working out their risks.

Summary of Impact Bias. If you think someone is acting as though a future event will be overly bad or overly good, tell him he is being affected by Impact Bias.

(59)   Isolation Effect

Easy Definition: Don't act solely on information because it stands out from the crowd. That's the Isolation Effect.

Geeky Definition: The Isolation Effect (also known as the Von Restorff Effect) is the tendency to recall something that stands out in a group and afford it more weighting than its peers. It is named after German psychologist Hedwig Von Restorff, who first documented it in 1933.

An Example:
Birthday card, carrots, LEMONADE and beer

Things which stand out are easily remembered. That's the Isolation Effect. For example, an item on a list which is a different colour or size is more likely to be remembered than the other normal-looking list items. This happens regardless of the importance of the information. Imagine you went shopping but left your shopping list at home. If "lemonade" were written in large red letters on your list, you are more likely to remember it than the other normal-looking but more important list items, like "beer". It's a pretty basic idea, but it can be employed to good effect.

Another Example:
You remember it because it's different

Remember these: 21, 17, 16, 29, 22, 18, SF, 18, 92.

If I were to ask you what the letters were tomorrow, you'd probably say "SF". If I asked what any of the numbers were, you'd be more likely to struggle. This happens because the letters stand out from the crowd. (And it happens without you imagining "Sam Fox" standing on your doorstep. I'll explain that in the next section.)

Something else quite interesting happens too, although it's not really related to the Isolation Effect. You are more likely to recall the numbers at the start (the primacy effect) and the numbers at the end (the recency effect) than those in the middle. For now, keep that idea in the back of your mind. It might just offer us a small "lever" to pull when trying to assert some influence.

A Practical Application:
Tattoo your CV on their retinas

Memory recall is often achieved through repetition to consolidate ideas in the brain. It can also be achieved through forced association. For example, if you want to remember the word "badger", imagine one sitting on your doormat. Then, to recall "badger" just think about your doormat, and there will be a badger on it. This technique is called the "method of loci". Many stand-up comedians use the method of loci to remember jokes when they're on stage. They simply do a "mind walk" around their houses recalling all the triggers to their jokes, which they previously "mind placed" in the rooms.

Repetition and forced association are great techniques for remembering things. But there is one major flaw with them: they are techniques for helping you to remember your stuff. They are not useful for getting someone else to remember your stuff, and that's why it's useful to know about the Isolation Effect. You can use it to embed memories in other people's heads.

It's a simple concept. Something that stands out from its surroundings is easily remembered and is therefore more likely to be processed in decision-making, regardless of its importance. So, to have your information remembered, there is some advantage to be snatched by presenting it differently from everyone else.

You will have to work out how this idea can be applied in your context, but here's an example we can all identify with: I see dozens of CVs for job applicants. I'll tell you this straight – I don't read them. Well, I skim-read page 1. The other pages get a five-second flash read at best. Compared to many others, I don't see that many CVs. Imagine how your CV is treated by a recruiter who sees thousands for hundreds of jobs. I reckon you have about nine seconds to make enough of an impression to survive the first sift. So, your CV needs to stand out enough to be selected and then remembered. You can't submit a CV on bright blue paper – there are etiquette guidelines you ought to operate within. But creating the Isolation Effect is still easy. Write a one-page CV. Everyone thinks you should write a one-page CV because employers are too busy to read a four-pager. That's not why. The real reason you should write a one-pager is because no one else will. Almost no one presents a one-page CV, because they haven't got the bottle to leave out detail they think might give them the edge over others. So, because of how the Isolation Effect works, your unique one-page CV will give you far more of an "edge" than can be won with any page-2-level detail. You could also try this. Highlight your best job-winning line on the CV (e.g. underline, bold). You now have the Isolation Effect (the highlighted line) nested within the Isolation Effect (the one-pager). Of course, your one-pager will make you look confident and businesslike. And, by virtue of being a one-pager, every line is likely to be meaningful. But they're just by-products of the real win. Whether they like it not, the recruiters are going to remember your CV. You might as well have tattooed it on their retinas. It's that sort of edge which will keep you in the game. (If you wanted to highlight that you've deliberately presented a one-pager, you could write "intentionally blank" on the reverse side. That smacks of confidence too.)

Here's another idea. Present your CV close to the deadline. This will increase its chances of appearing at the start or the end of their pile, and that could give you another slight advantage due to the primacy and recency effects. Hey, I know we're clutching at straws, but every point in your favour (especially for no effort) is worth having.

> **Summary of the Isolation Effect.** If you think someone is being overly influenced by a piece of information simply because it stands out, tell him he is being influenced by the Isolation Effect.

60 Mirror Imaging

Easy Definition: Don't expect others to behave like you. If you do, you are Mirror Imaging.

Geeky Definition: Mirror Imaging occurs when a person or a group is viewed through the lens of the analyst's own environment and experiences, rather than from theirs.

"I am not a vegetarian because I love animals;
I am a vegetarian because I hate plants."
(American writer and comedian A. Whitney Brown)

The quote above is obviously a joke, but it is useful to highlight that other people behave according to their own ideas, environments and cultures – and not according to yours.

An Example:
Henry the dog and Dawn's lollipop

I was about eight when I first encountered Mirror Imaging. I didn't know its name then, but I knew it when I saw it.

A young girl called Dawn was holding an ice lolly in one hand and to-ing and fro-ing on a swing. Sitting alongside her was Henry, a large, friendly dog. Henry's head was doing a "tennis crowd" as the lolly swung back and forth. "No", said Dawn, "it's not yours, Henry". But Henry's gaze was not averted.

"Okay," Dawn agreed, "just a lick". I watched as she stopped swinging and offered Henry a lick. The obvious happened. Dawn lost the whole ice lolly to Henry's immediate acceptance of the offer.

What happened? Well, Dawn thought the dog would act like her. She forgot to factor in that Henry was a big, hungry dog who was going to act like a big, hungry dog. I can now give Dawn's error a name. It was Mirror Imaging.

My Favourite Example:
We're hunting wabbits

Just 20 and newly graduated from Sandhurst (Britain's army officer-training academy), Second Lieutenant Johnny Foster was a good-looking, popular officer, who was fortunate enough to be posted to a base near the farm where he grew up. One Wednesday afternoon, he selected three of his favourite junior soldiers, packed them into his dad's reliable old Land Rover and headed off to a neighbouring farm for an afternoon of shooting rabbits. Upon arrival at his neighbour's farm, he told the private soldiers he would nip to the farmhouse to seek permission from Mr Gould to use shotguns on his land. Farmer Gould took a long time to answer the door but eventually did.

Farmer Gould hadn't seen Johnny for years, but he recognised him immediately. "Johnny!" he said excitedly. "Great to see you. My, you've grown up, lad. How can I help you?"

Johnny asked for permission to shoot rabbits, and Mr Gould granted it immediately and eagerly pointed out the areas where the rabbits congregated.

"So, what are you up to, Johnny?" Mr Gould asked.

"I'm an officer in the Army now. I've brought some of my men along to give them an afternoon off from painting the tanks."

"An officer!" he exclaimed proudly, ruffling Johnny's hair. "Well done, Johnny. Good lad. Anyway, enjoy your shooting."

Johnny started to head back towards the Land Rover. "Err, Johnny?" the farmer interrupted. "I'm sorry I was such a long time answering the door. I was actually on the phone to the vet. Do you remember our Jackie's horse? Well, it's on its last legs, and it's in serious pain. The vet can't come out until Thursday to put it down, and I can't bring myself to do it. You must be used to killing stuff in the Army. Would you mind? Please? Here, use this in your shotgun. She's in the top field." The farmer handed Johnny a special cartridge that would kill the horse instantly and showed him how to deliver the shot.

Obviously, Johnny hadn't killed anything before other than a few rabbits and pheasants, and he had to summon all his bravado to hide the overwhelming sense of trepidation and responsibility. Johnny returned to the Land Rover.

"I can't bloody believe it" said Johnny abruptly. "He said if we don't get off his land in five minutes, he's going to call the police."

"I thought you said he was a good friend."

"That's what I thought." said Johnny as he slammed the Land Rover into first gear and sped off towards the top field. "Grumpy old sod," he said repeatedly as the Land Rover grew ever nearer the horse's field. All too quickly, they were at the field. "Right!" said Johnny, slamming on the brakes. "I'm not having this. Follow me." He grabbed his shotgun, jumped the gate and loaded the slug. His confused entourage followed.

"Sir, what are you doing?" "What's going on, sir?"

Without any hesitation, Johnny headed purposefully for the horse. "This'll show the old git". At point-blank range, Johnny lifted the shotgun to his shoulder and dispatched the horse instantly with a clean loud thwack.

Now, at this point, Johnny was expecting to explain to his shocked soldiers what had just really happened. However, it didn't turn out like that. Second Lieutenant Johnny was the one who was shocked. All about him, he heard the deafening cracks of shotguns going off as his soldiers began firing at the cows in the field. He managed to stop them quickly, but Farmer Gould lost a horse and two cows that day.

Johnny's mistake was that he presumed his soldiers would react like him, i.e. like officers. He failed to factor in that they had been trained to take their lead from their officers. Johnny had mirror imaged the soldiers in his assessment of how they would react to his prank.

Another Example:
Do you want a nice phone or a robust phone?

I remember a businessman from Wigan who invested heavily in manufacturing robust mobile phones after he'd managed to break two in three months. (He stood on one and dropped the other down the loo.) He was certain that outdoor types would all go mad for a you-can't-bend-it mobile phone. They didn't. He sold almost none. As part of his research, he'd asked questions like "Would you like a mobile that you can drop or get wet?" Thousands of people said yes. Well, they would. (See Section 99 on biased questions.) Unfortunately, he'd created a meaningless survey and convinced himself that everyone was thinking like he was. They weren't. His own assuredness that robustness would trump aesthetics and functionality was not well founded, and when he produced a phone that took a backward step towards "80s house brick" instead of a forward one towards "slim-line smartphone", no one wanted it. It was an expensive error.

How to Overcome Mirror Imaging
Set up a red team

It is important to avoid Mirror Imaging, because the assumptions on which you base your decisions about someone might be way off the mark. However, avoidance is difficult, because it requires you to see the world through someone else's eyes. There are two main methods:

- Walk a mile in their shoes (i.e. experience their life to attain their perspectives).

- Set up a red team. A red team is a group of your own people who have been specifically brought together to think like the people you are examining (e.g. shoppers, business customers, a hostile military force). Once the red-team members have got themselves into the right mind-set, they either describe how they would act in their "new" role or look to challenge any decisions you've made about them that doesn't fit their "new" role. Red-teaming is good for generating alternative perspectives to help shape plans. You can use it to think like your customers, to ensure your products are of interest to them and not just you.

Summary of Mirror Imaging. If you think someone has factored in their own experience in determining how someone else will act, tell him he's Mirror Imaging.

61   Negativity Bias

Easy Definition: Don't think bad things are disastrous. If you don't keep them in perspective, you're showing Negativity Bias.

Geeky Definition: Negativity Bias is the tendency to give more weight to negative experiences or information than to positive ones.

An Example:
Good plus bad equals bad

Imagine this person:

She is athletic.
She has beautiful eyes.
She is charismatic.
She has bucked teeth.

Here, we have four bits of information about a stranger: three positive and one negative. Negativity Bias causes us to place undue emphasis on bucked teeth. This is a natural human trait, and it's difficult to counter.

Negativity Bias affects all sorts of situations. If you experience something good and something bad at approximately the same time – e.g. someone gives you an underground ticket worth £3 and you drop your ice-cream worth £3, you are likely to feel bad, not neutral. This is not about your love of ice cream… or underground tickets. It's all about negative events being more powerful. So, using the same example, you would feel bad and not neutral even if the events were reversed: i.e. someone gave you an ice-cream and you lost your underground ticket.

  Interestingly, studies show that Negativity Bias reduces as people get older. The reasons for this are unknown, but I suspect it's linked to these ideas:

"Worrying works! 90% of the things I worry about never happen."

"If you want to test your memory, try to recall what you were worrying about a year ago."

Put simply, people realise over time that they've been giving too much emphasis to negative events. Also, being more self-aware, older people tend to accept criticism more readily.

A Practical Application:
Curb those negative comments

Back in Chapter 1, we discussed the need to tread carefully when trying to influence (see Section 22). It included not slating your target's ideas but thanking him, praising him or agreeing with him, before influencing him. This idea is linked to Negativity Bias. If you throw in one overtly negative point about your target, it is likely to have far more impact than you intended, and his defences might firm up.

I've heard it said that negative comments are seven times more powerful than positive ones. I can't support that claim, but it does offer a warning to be careful about how often you make negative comments and how you word them.

My advice? Play it safe. In business interactions that rely on a warm relationship, tone down your negative comments and use them sparingly. I'm not just saying "Don't slag off your business partners". That would be too obvious. I am, however, advising you to be mindful of the extra "hidden" power that negative comments wield.

> **Summary of Negativity Bias.** If you think someone has been overly influenced by something simply because it was negative, tell him he's suffering from Negativity Bias.

62 Omissions Bias

Easy Definition: Don't think that doing something bad is any worse than keeping quiet and allowing it to happen. If you decide to let the bad thing happen by keeping quiet, your decision will probably have been affected by Omissions Bias.

Geeky Definition: Omissions Bias is the tendency to judge activity that causes damage as worse (or less moral) than inactivity that causes the same damage.

An Example:
It's a great little runner

Imagine you're selling a car, and you know the engine is on its last legs. When the prospective buyer turns up, you have a choice:

Option 1. Tell him about the engine.
Option 2. Lie about the condition of the engine.
Option 3. Say nothing and let him find out for himself.

Obviously, the right thing to do is Option 1, but what about Option 3? Surely, that's not as bad as Option 2. If that's what you believe, you're suffering from Omissions Bias. Remember, the plausible deniability afforded by Option 3 does not make it a just action.

This bias is particularly prevalent in car sales, where sellers believe the mantra "sold as seen" offers them some sort of legal protection. Let's all be clear on that — it doesn't. If you knowingly sell someone a dangerous car, you're liable for prosecution. If you knowingly sell someone a faulty car, they're entitled to a refund. Of course, you can plead innocence or ignorance, but that's not what this bias is about. It's about understanding how your brain tries to trick you on a morality issue. Not talking about the faulty engine is as bad as lying about it. You might unknowingly have suffered from Omissions Bias, but the judge won't take that into account. You would, as covered in Catholic teaching, be guilty of a "sin of omission".

Another Example:
Environmental extremists tell just half the story

I'm now going to have a pop at environmentalists. I have some difficulty with this, because they're only trying to do good. It's quite hard to dislike them. But the campaigns prosecuted by the more radical environmentalists often produce messages which are full of biases, making them interesting from a studying-biases perspective.

To avoid political and commercial interests influencing their direction, most environmentalists like to maintain financial independence from governments and corporations. Instead, they are dependent on individual donors like you and me. Well, at first glance, that policy might appear to mean the environmentalists have avoided bias infiltrating their campaigns, but, in fact, their reliance on the public's donations means the opposite is true.

The environmentalists' fundraisers know what brings in the money. They know their donors like to protect trees and save animals. Don't we all? As such, they have learned to present their version of the big story by telling small, personalised stories that their donors can empathise with. In particular, they have learned to exploit the appeal of animals, and they have become proficient at presenting statistics to influence. So, in their efforts to present scenarios that cause the public to donate, the environmentalists nearly always play some parts of the debate far too hard and deliberately omit others. As a result, their reporting is nearly always far too emotive and overly simplistic. In short, their words are designed to elicit support, not to cite facts. And they're very good at writing those words. In their messaging to the public, they almost always fail to acknowledge the other side of the story, and they never recognise any efforts towards greener practice by their targets until their targets capitulate.

The executives and the campaign managers of the green organisations fully understand the arguments, and they routinely engage behind the scenes with the heads of the corporations they attack, from a far more balanced standpoint. But, that's certainly not the standpoint the executives present to their activists and the public. Therefore, the executives' belief that the activists are performing public misdemeanours (e.g. blockading shops, throwing paint, placing stickers on products and draping banners) of their own accord is tainted by Omissions Bias. In lots of cases, the executives are deliberately omitting some of the facts so their activists feel a compulsion to act. With all the facts on the table, the activists might not be activists – they'd be plumbers, lawyers, builders, pilots, whatever. It's an understandable strategy for the environmentalists. If they told their stories impartially, they'd be toothless news organisations. I think we need environmentalists to keep some of our big corporations on the straight and narrow, but if you're about to risk arrest by tipping oil sludge over someone's foyer on behalf of some environmentalist movement, go and investigate what they're not telling you before you do.

I think the green groups would be more successful if they allowed some of the counter-argument into the debate, re-ordered the components of the arguments objectively and then sought to engage governments with intellectual rigour, rather than engaging the middle classes with emotive half-told stories. That all said, environmentalists do provide a very useful environmental "policing" service, even if they do "truncheon" millions of innocents in the course of their duties.

A Practical Application:
If it's broken, say so

Understanding Omissions Bias will help you to defend against yourself. The example about selling car with a defective engine is related to a real-life experience. When I discovered orange sludge in my car's water reservoir, I took it to a mechanic who told me the head gasket was on its last legs. The car still drove fine. I put an advert in the local paper saying "Car for sale. Drives fine. Needs a new head gasket" and adjusted the price accordingly. It was snapped up by a local car tinkerer who sold cars from his house. Three days later a young married couple rang me out of the blue and asked if I'd sold the car to a Mr Jones (that was literally his name – I lived in Wales at the time). I told them I had. It turned out he had sold them the car within 24 hours of buying it off me but had failed to tell them about the head gasket, which he had wiped over with cloth (that was nice of him). Unfortunately for him but fortunately for them, they'd chanced upon my advert in the local paper.

I had considered doing the old "sold as seen" and asking an extra £800 for the car, but understanding that would have been Omissions Bias tainting my judgement, I came clean about the head gasket. Mr Jones didn't, and he was caught out. That whole thing got quite nasty apparently, with gatherings of irate big brothers and uncles standing toe to toe. But, hey, my understanding of Omissions Bias had kept me out of the ruckus. I was the good guy.

I'm not saying you should never keep quiet to allow an event to happen. There might be times when that's exactly the right thing to do. You might want to "give someone enough rope to hang themselves". With today's employment laws, allowing people to be themselves might be the only way to get rid of them. An employee who says "They knew I was going to steal that marble and didn't stop me" is probably not going to win much sympathy. Likewise, allowing a rival for promotion to give a presentation to the directors because you know he's rubbish at presenting is probably fair play – well, it's only a yellow card. (Going next after a terrible presentation is unlikely to do you much harm either.) Allowing something to occur by inaction will also afford you plausible deniability, and that might be useful on occasion. For example, not telling your mate who is smoking behind the bike shed that a teacher is coming. You might want to apply some "tough love" but retain your friendship.

If you're a frequent eBay seller, it would be useful to understand Omissions Bias. It would allow you to make more informed decisions about how you describe your items. A mate of mine who's sold stuff on eBay for years always comes clean about the flaws in his merchandise. In the early days, he didn't, and it was quickly reflected in his online customer feedback. It nearly killed off his side-line business, and it took him a year to recover. With an understanding of Omissions Bias at the start of his enterprise, he would almost certainly have got off to a much better start.

Let's leave this topic with this thought: The term "harmful acts or omissions" is plastered throughout criminal law. If a judge thinks you had a duty to act, you definitely won't be let off if you fail to act. If this concept is new to you, be assured that it's not new to those who could come after you. So, think seriously about Omissions Bias tainting your decisions.

> **Summary of Omissions Bias.** If you think someone believes they're blameless because they allowed a bad thing to happen by keeping quiet, tell him his belief is affected by Omissions Bias and remind him he's guilty.

(63)   Ostrich Effect

Easy Definition: Don't ignore the bad things happening. That's the Ostrich Effect. It doesn't make them go away.

Geeky Definition: The Ostrich Effect is the tendency to ignore a dangerous or risky situation.

"The truth does not change according to our ability to stomach it."
(American writer Flannery O'Connor, 1925–1964)

This bias takes its name from the widely held, though completely incorrect, belief that an ostrich will bury its head in the sand when faced with danger. People will demonstrate this kind of behaviour by blotting out a problem from the mind instead of tackling the situation which threatens them. (As we will see in "Chapter 3: Reading Body Language" (Section 87), this also occurs at a subconscious level with the "eye block" body gesture.)

An Example:
Allies or enemies?

Afghans have been telling us for years that Pakistan has been backing the Afghan Taliban and housing its leaders and those of Al Qaida, including the late Osama Bin Laden. As this is the same Pakistan that the US is funding with billions of dollars each year to ensure Pakistan's nuclear weapons don't fall into the hands of extremists and to assist in the battle against Islamic extremism, the US didn't want to believe the masses of evidence being gathered by its intelligence agencies about Pakistan's duplicity.

"Denial's not just a river in Africa."
(Common joke amongst intelligence analysts)

For years, America's "denial" of Pakistan's dual strategy was the world's best example of the Ostrich Effect. And it still is to some extent, but it seems the US ostrich has finally extracted one of its eyes from the sand, leaving the Pakistanis playing the plausible deniability card about as hard as it can be played. Anyway, don't get me started on that one.

A Practical Application:
Ignore it, tackle it or manage it, but make a decision

The only real practical application for the Ostrich Effect is to understand it to improve your decision-making. Sometimes ignoring a problem is a good thing:

"No problem is so formidable that you can't walk away from it."
(American cartoonist Charles M. Schulz, 1922–2000)

Sometimes though, you have to embrace it:

"You can't run away from trouble. There ain't no place that far."
(Fictional teller of African-American folktales Uncle Remus, written by Joel Chandler Harris)

And, sometimes, there's a middle ground:

"When you can't solve the problem, manage it."
(American minister and author Robert H. Schuller)

The secret to handling problems is knowing which approach to take. If you actively embrace the Ostrich Effect, you are ignoring the problem. That's fine. It's a technique that works for certain types of problem. But if you allow the Ostrich Effect to blot out a problem that can't be handled in that way, you end up reaching for the place that Uncle Remus (see quote above) tells us is unreachable. In other words, you are just delaying the inevitable. If you know this is happening (i.e. you can say "I am being consumed by the Ostrich Effect"), you are more likely to face the demon earlier (which more often than not is beneficial). Therefore, understanding the Ostrich Effect will help you in your decision to ignore, tackle or manage the problem. Once you've picked a course of action, try not to worry about the problem. Of course, that's easier said than done. I wish I were better at following this classic Buddhist mantra:

"If you can solve your problem, don't worry about it. If you can't solve it, then what's the point in worrying about it?"
(Paraphrase of quote by 8th-century Indian Buddhist scholar Shantideva)

Here's the main point again. Understanding the Ostrich Effect will help to ensure you don't ignore the problems you should be tackling.

"Ignorance is bliss, but feigned ignorance isn't."
(Anon)

Summary of the Ostrich Effect. If you think someone is ignoring a bad situation in the hope it will go away, tell him he is embracing the Ostrich Effect.

64   Reactance Bias

Easy Definition: Don't adopt an alternative view (or do something different from what was requested) just to show you're your own boss. If you do, your decision to do that will have been affected by Reactance Bias.

Geeky Definition: Reactance Bias is the tendency to do something different from what someone wants you to do in reaction to a perceived attempt to constrain your freedom of choice. Reactance Bias can occur when you feel pressured to accept a certain view and can lead to a strengthening of resolve for an alternative view, regardless of its relative merits.

"Don't take the wrong side of an argument just because your opponent has taken the right side."
(Spanish prose writer Baltasar Gracian, 1601–1658)

An Example:
Don't tell me not to jump off a cliff.... Aaagh

During the late 90s, Britain was struck by an outburst of "mad cow disease", or Bovine Spongiform Encephalopathy (BSE). It is a disease that turns cattle's brains to mush, and we were told it could be contracted by humans, if they ate BSE-infected meat, in the form of a fatal brain disease called variant Creutzfeldt-Jakob disease (vCJD). In December 1997, the British government passed a law banning the sale of beef on the bone, because scientific research showed it carried the highest risk of being infected with BSE. One of the items outlawed was T-bone steak, which is a cut from near the cow's spinal column (where BSE tends to be found).

Now, you would think everyone would support that law, wouldn't you? But no. For lots of people, it was an unacceptable shackle on their freedom of choice, and they overtly broke the law by publicly wolfing down T-bone steaks. At the time, that didn't look like a very bright decision. It was Reactance Bias at play.

Other examples are riding motorcycles without helmets, driving your car without a seat belt and even smoking. People have pushed back against laws banning or adverts denouncing these activities, despite the benefits, because they object to having their freedom of choice curbed.

A Practical Application:
Omega 3 or starch?

Most people have heard of "reverse psychology", and this can be an effective tool to influence. Parents do it all the time. For example, if a child is being fussy at dinner, many parents have trained themselves to say something like "leave your fish fingers but eat your chips". The parents might not know it's called Reactance Bias, but they are using the child's Reactance Bias to ensure the fish fingers are eaten.

> **Summary of Reactance Bias.** If you think someone has chosen a specific action just to demonstrate his freedom of choice, tell him he's displaying Reactance Bias.

65   Self Serving Bias

Easy Definition: Don't try to snaffle all the praise for good things or overly divert blame for bad things. That would be Self Serving Bias, and those you're trying to convince will spot it easily.

Geeky Definition: Self Serving Bias is the tendency to take credit for positive outcomes or to lay blame elsewhere for failures. There are two main motivations which lead people to act in this way:

- They are trying to create a positive image of themselves.
- They are trying to preserve their self-esteem.

An Example:
I know you've been training, but I had a slower car this week

One example of Self Serving Bias would be the friend who wins at the go-kart track and says: "The karts are all the same, but I am just a better racer than you guys." His comment is designed to boost his image among his friends.

If the same friend were to lose the race, you might hear: "Hey, I would have easily won that race if my kart wasn't so lousy." This comment is designed to preserve his self-esteem.

"A bad workman blames his tools."
(well-known idiom)

Self Serving Bias is related to the Better Than Average Bias (see Section 43), in which individuals are biased to believe they perform better than the average person, particularly in areas important to their self-esteem.

A Practical Application:
Go and tell her I'm a great kisser

You might not have called it "Self Serving Bias" before reading this section, but you'll still have been pretty good at spotting it. We all are. We are naturally very suspicious of people who tell us how good they are and people who blame others or their tools for poor performance. This quote incorporates the idea that there is little benefit in praising yourself:

"Don't discuss yourself, for you are bound to lose; if you belittle yourself, you are believed; if you praise yourself, you are disbelieved."
(French writer and sceptic Michel de Montaigne, 1533–1592)

But what about if someone else praises us? That could work. And do you know what? It does!

Scenario 1:	Scenario 2:
"I am a great footballer."	*"He is a great footballer."*
"Yeah, right."	*"Is he? I would never have guessed."*

So, if you can engineer a situation whereby someone else praises you, that's going to be far more believable than praising yourself. It's why testimonials work so well (see Section 56).

This idea is a big factor in how Google's search engine works. The positioning of your website after a Google search depends largely on how many other sites have linked to you (i.e. they're praising you). The number of sites you've linked to (i.e. you internetishly gobbing off) is irrelevant to your own Google position. Google uses this because they know that others' praise is far more credible than your own. It's how they eliminate Self Serving Bias.

So, if a mistake happens on your watch, have someone else tell your boss it wasn't your fault. Not only is he more likely to believe someone who isn't you, there's a bonus: your silence on the issue will look like broad shoulders and a willingness to accept responsibility. It's a double win.

Similarly, if you do something good, have someone else tell your boss about it. The praise will fall squarely on your shoulders, and it will look like modesty on your behalf. Another double win.

Don't get caught using proxy messengers though. If you do, you're toast. The best proxy messengers are the ones who act of their own accord, i.e. without you and them being in cahoots. How do you create these doing-it-off-their-own-bat proxies? Well, it's a slow process. Just be a good honest person, and they will materialise like a chorus of fairy godmothers. All you have to do if your standing is high enough is refrain from wading in to defend or praise yourself.

Summary of Self Serving Bias. If you think someone is overly praising himself or defending himself to protect his self-esteem or to improve his social standing, tell him he's displaying Self Serving Bias.

(66) Status Quo Bias

Easy Definition: Don't think carrying on as normal is a safer or better option than introducing some change. That might be Status Quo Bias.

Geeky Definition: Status Quo Bias is the tendency to favour decisions that maintain the status quo (i.e. the existing state of affairs). Those affected by this bias choose not to divert from established behaviours unless there is compelling incentive to change.

An Example:
Sticking with your current service providers

Lots of people reading this will know there are cheaper gas, electricity, telephone, TV, internet and insurance packages out there, but they won't bother switching to them. Why? Well, for a whole range of "good" reasons. Perhaps they can't be bothered. Perhaps they don't want to be tied into a contract. Perhaps they'll have to change their email, which will affect their contacts and internet logins. Perhaps the service won't be as good, e.g. perhaps the gas or electricity supply won't be as reliable. Perhaps something will go wrong in the switchover.

For most of us, these shouldn't be big enough concerns not to save £50 a month, but that's exactly what they are when they get magnified due to Status Quo Bias.

Status Quo Bias "tells" you to keep the current state of affairs for two reasons:

- You won't have to make a decision.
- You can be sure there won't be any consequences of a bad decision. By sticking with the current state of affairs, you are in fact making a decision. But, because it's a default outcome, you don't feel as though you are. As for avoiding the consequences of a bad decision – that could be a fair point. But you might also be losing out on some benefits – and that's a fairer point. Doing nothing might be a good option, but it's not always the safest or best course of action:

"If we don't change direction soon, we'll end up where we're going."
(Professor Irwin Corey)

Status Quo Bias is linked to the Endowment Effect (see Section 52) and Negativity Bias (see Section 61), which make you place more weight on negative impacts than benefits. Those suffering from Status Quo Bias often cannot see the benefits because they are too fearful of the negative impacts.

There is another factor at play too. Humans are designed to automate processes (e.g. their work routines), and when change is pending, our brains naturally resist it to ensure the automated process is not affected.

"Nothing will kill your business quicker than the we've-always-done-it-like-that attitude."
(Anon)

A Practical Application:
Act now to avoid a tragedy

In decision-making, our brains are tuned to give negative impacts more weight than positive ones, and this is at the root of Status Quo Bias. Therefore, if you're trying to influence someone to change, it would be a good idea to plant some danger along their "status quo" path (i.e. highlight some negative things that will happen if they do nothing). This is likely to be more effective than trying to coax them off their current path just by throwing benefits at them. In other words, employ a bit of stick as well as carrot.

For example, if you can say something like "your current service provider is about to increase its prices and we're cheaper", you've given them something negative to think about... and they will. But what if you can't think of something bad to say about the competition, or if it's inappropriate? Well, you could look to target the decision-maker more directly with a negative idea. Doing nothing can often be seen as the lazy or cowardly option. If you can convince the decision-maker that doing nothing will paint him in that negative

light to others, he is far more likely to tackle his own Status Quo Bias
and be more amenable to change.

Another Practical Application:
Your inactivity suits me just fine

When I first left the Army, I worked as a consultant to the MOD for
about a year. The team leader for our small gaggle of consultants
was an MOD civilian called Mel. Mel is super proactive, but even she
couldn't weave a path through the bureaucracy, hierarchical stove-
piping, information overload and email gridlock that seems to exist
in so many public departments these days. Her constant battle was
finding someone with the authority and time to make a decision that
would allow our team to get on with its work. But, Mel being Mel,
she found a solution to overcome this problem. Whenever she had an
audience with a senior decision-maker, she would make it clear that
if he didn't intervene by a certain date, her team would start work.
In other words, she gave him an "opt out" decision to make instead
of an "opt in" one. She'd learnt how to navigate her ship through
bureaucratic treacle. Inspired.

*"Bureaucracy defends the status quo long past the time when the quo has
lost its status."*
(American educationalist Dr Laurence J. Peter, 1919–1990)

The moral of this story is simple. Whenever possible, make sure the
"do nothing" path of those you're trying to influence leads to your
goal.

> **Summary of Status Quo Bias.** If you think someone is
> showing an unfounded preference for avoiding change, tell
> him his inclination to maintain the current state of affairs is
> influenced by Status Quo Bias and is irrational.

67   News Media Bias

I'm going to end this chapter on biases with a rant about news media. This section is included to help you develop an even more suspicious eye for how some in the media portray where we live, i.e. our operating environment.

"The man who reads nothing at all is better educated than the man who reads nothing but newspapers."
(Third President of the United States Thomas Jefferson, 1743–1826)

This quote is meant to entertain, and it obviously overstates the case against the news media. However, there is a lot of truth in the old adage "don't believe everything you read."

"The biases the media has are much bigger than conservative or liberal. They're about getting ratings, about making money, about doing stories that are easy to cover."
(American writer Al Franken)

Of course, our various newspapers and other media outlets all have different reporting thresholds and levels of integrity, but be aware that the news media can be affected by some powerful biases. For example:

Commercial Bias. The first thing to remember when consuming news is that the news media is a business. It makes money from advertisers, whose payments are proportional to the number and quality of viewers it can reach. Public services (like the BBC) are not funded by advertisers, but they too need high viewing numbers to justify their existence. The bottom line is that the news media needs viewers. What attracts viewers? Interesting stories. Unfortunately, bad-news stories (e.g. conflict, crime, disaster) are far more interesting than good-news stories.

"For most folks, no news is good news; for the press, good news is not news." (American journalist Gloria Borger)

This is related to Negativity Bias (see Section 61). As a result, the world looks a worse place when viewed through a news-media lens than it really is.

Temporal Bias. It is not uncommon when a country is at war for the front pages of its newspapers to be littered with trivial gossip about celebrities. This is because the news media needs to refresh itself constantly to keep itself interesting. The news media is biased towards the present. It knows that, in terms of attracting viewers, a breaking unimportant story outperforms an on-going important story.

Visual Bias. Viewers like pictures, and the news media knows it. As a result, a filmable or photographable story will have precedence over one that isn't. Unfortunately, the things that govern our lives (e.g. politics, policy and laws) do not make interesting pictures – unlike the milk float that fell off a bridge onto someone's shed.

Narrative Bias. The news media likes stories. Ideally, a story should have some goodies, some baddies, a start, a middle and an end. If a news story doesn't have these components, journalists have a tendency to create them by forcing structure into the story or by tuning their language and coverage to demonise one of the participants. It gets worse. Once the storyline has been set, updates are forced into the narrative. After the story, the news media requires some time to lapse (what I like to call the "goldfish pause") before it can reinvent the participants in new roles. As a result, news that contradicts the storyline is less likely to be aired until after the "goldfish pause".

Fairness Bias. The act of trying not to be biased creates a bias. (No one said remaining impartial was going to be easy!) The journalistic code demands fairness in reporting, and many news media outlets manage this by trying to add balance to every story. In particular, this affects coverage on politicians and politics. To prevent being biased to one side, the media often seeks a reaction from the opposing camp. As a result, new policy always looks controversial and politics always seems contentious. New positive policies or announcements are routinely undermined by the media, who feel compelled to seek an opposing view, which might become more influential than it should by dint of its media coverage.

The BBC is so "fair", it often isn't fair, and its reporters and editors tussle with this idea constantly. For example, let's imagine that 99% of people think apartheid is inhuman and immoral and 1% think it isn't. A news programme covering this issue would present the idea as though it were a 50/50 debate (e.g. showing two street interviews with people against apartheid and two for). There is another dynamic at play: the workforce of the BBC is not representative of British society. A high proportion of the BBC's staff are way more liberal than the average person. As a consequence, the BBC's reporting tends to slant towards the views of the groupings within its workforce as opposed to the views of the country.

"The BBC is not impartial or neutral. It's a publicly funded, urban organisation with an abnormally large number of young people, ethnic minorities and gay people. It has a liberal bias, not so much a party-political bias. It is better expressed as a cultural liberal bias."
(Journalist and political commentator Andrew Marr)

Right, that's end of the sections on biases.

I suspect you knew lots of them already at some level, but what you might not have known were their names or that people are actively using them against you. It's my hope that you will now be able to apply these biases to your life to help you get your way or to defend yourself from others' attempts to influence you. Understanding these biases will also help you to win arguments. And, with regard to that last point, there's some more ammo for you coming up. Next, common fallacies.

COMMON FALLACIES

(68) **What is a fallacy?**

We all know what a fallacy is. The Earth is flat. That's a fallacy. Ostriches put their head in the sand when they're threatened. That's another fallacy. (They actually sprint off or, if you're really unlucky, kick you black and blue.) But that's just one definition of a fallacy. In dictionaries, you will see that definition recorded as something like:

> **Fallacy (noun):** a mistaken belief

But, if it's a half-decent dictionary, there will be another definition lurking below that one. It will say something like:

> **Fallacy (noun) (logic):** a failure in reasoning which renders an argument invalid

The definition we're going to talk about from now on is the second one. But, before we do, we have a problem. In researching this book, I've come to the conclusion that no one has really tied down what word goes with the second definition of fallacy.

I mean, do you present a fallacy? Make a fallacy? Do a fallacy? Commit a fallacy? Expose a fallacy? Create a fallacy? And, if the answer is amongst that lot, who does it? The person who presents the fallacy (i.e. makes the dodgy argument) or the person who believes it?

To answer this, I played some email tennis with the editors at the Oxford English Dictionary, and I pored through dozens of sites and books on Critical Thinking. It seems to me that lots of people in the logic arena are still pussy footing around with the word fallacy. They like to say "it's a fallacy", but they would rather bash their own thumbs flat with meat tenderisers than use fallacy as the direct object of a verb.

I did come to another, more useful conclusion though. Those who care about this sort of thing are starting to favour the word commit, especially in America (as confirmed by the OED researchers who scanned the 2-billion-word OED Corpus for me). And they are applying the word commit to the person who makes the argument and the person who believes it. Basically, whoever adopts the position of the fallacious argument (the dodgy argument) has committed the fallacy. That person has committed a failure in reasoning.

So, I'm going to go for commit a fallacy from now on. Commit. That's the one. Hallelujah.

Why should you care about that? Well, if you can use some of the ideas we've covered so far (e.g. the types of bias) and the ones we're about to cover (types of fallacies) in your business to-ings and fro-ings, your arguments will be far stronger. You don't want to be pussy footing around with what word to use with fallacy too. Use commit. End of chat. (Oh, and if you're ever required to submit an academic paper, then weaving in some of these ideas will score you lots of points in that arena too.)

Next, we're going to talk about the components of an argument. This is pretty academic stuff, but it's essential to know, because it will allow you to shove your head inside your opponent's argument (as if it was a big, opaque bubble) and examine all the components inside to see which ones are flawed (e.g. biased, irrelevant or illogical).

So, if a fallacy is "a failure in reasoning which renders an argument invalid", let's examine the components of an argument.

69 What is an Argument?

An argument is a series of connected propositions in support of a new
proposition. Like this:

What is a proposition? A proposition is just a statement. It can be true
or false. If you look it up in a reference book on logic, it will probably
say something like "a proposition is the meaning expressed by a
declarative sentence". Basically, a proposition is a statement. Let's stick
with that.

Unfortunately, it gets a little more complicated. The propositions
that support the final proposition are called premises. The final
proposition is called the conclusion. Like this:

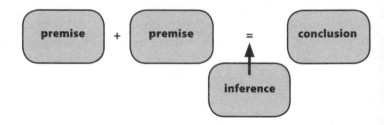

So, we can now say that an argument is a series of connected premises
in support of a conclusion.

The logic you apply to get from the premises to the conclusion
is known as the inference. Inference can also be thought of as the
reasoning behind your argument.

Remember, a fallacy is a false conclusion resulting from something
going wrong in your argument (i.e. an error in reasoning). The source
of the fallacy is not always easy to identify, but it will be one
of the following:

1) At least one of the premises is false, biased or irrelevant.

Basic example:

Words to defeat your opponent:

"You have committed a logical fallacy. Your argument is fallacious, because it is based on a false premise."
(Not all swans are white. You can get black swans.)

2) The inference is logically flawed.

Basic example:

Words to defeat your opponent:

"You have committed a logical fallacy. Your argument is fallacious, because the inference is illogical."
(You can't categorically say that Jack is white. You could say Jack is probably white.)

3) A different conclusion is possible (i.e. the argument is invalid).

Basic example:

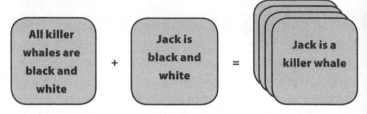

Words to defeat your opponent:

"You have committed a logical fallacy. Your argument is fallacious, because other conclusions are possible. Your conclusion is invalid."
(Jack might be a killer whale, but he could also be a zebra, a Newcastle United fan or a harlequin.)

Let's give these new words a run out.

"The US flag on the moon is flapping in the wind; therefore, there's an atmosphere. The moon landings were faked."

"What? Rubbish! There's a pole holding the flag out."

Or

"That is a fallacious argument based on a false premise. In a vacuum, a horizontally suspended flag waves a lot during, and immediately after, planting."

Now, this is a basic example, but, hopefully, it gives a sense of the value of sticking your head inside that bubble, spotting the flawed premise and then using the right words to defeat your opponent. Even if you're not convinced, external observers will be.

Remember, a fallacy is an error of reasoning. When someone adopts a position based on a bad piece of reasoning, they commit a fallacy.

Right, that's enough of the academic gumpf for now. Let's get back to the "attacking people" and "defending yourself" side of things.

70   The "Appeal to Flattery Fallacy"

Easy Definition: Don't be tricked into adopting someone's point of view after they've been nice to you. You might have committed the Appeal to Flattery Fallacy if you do.

Geeky Definition: The Appeal to Flattery Fallacy is an error in reasoning which occurs when someone adopts a position due to flattery or a compliment presented within the argument.

An Example:
Think what I think and I'll think you're great

Below are some examples of Appeal to Flattery Fallacy (flattery underlined):

<u>Someone with your intellect must know</u> *that the pay freeze was necessary.*
<u>As an expert, you must know</u> *that the pay freeze was necessary.*
<u>In your position, it should be obvious</u> *that the pay freeze was necessary.*

The person presenting these lines wants the person they're targeting to adopt a position that supports the pay freeze. The target feels some pressure to adopt that position, because he wants the first part of the argument (the flattery) to be true.

Sometimes, the "flattery" is more subtle, and it's presented in a way that pressures you into not wanting to disappoint the speaker:

<u>It was great to hear</u> *you accepted the pay freeze.*
<u>I am so pleased</u> *you have been able to accept the pay freeze.*
<u>Thank you for taking the time</u> *to consider and accept the pay freeze.*

Sometimes, they come at it from the other direction, and it's not flattery at all:

Only an idiot would think the pay freeze wasn't required.
You would have to live in a bubble to think the pay freeze wasn't required.

And, sometimes, it's not as clever as any of the above examples, i.e. there is no link between the first part of the argument and the second. Sometimes, it's just a blatant compliment to butter you up before trying to sell the position they want you to adopt.

I love your suit and those shoes. You are a real role model for me. Can we talk about this pay freeze?

A Practical Example:
Defend against flattery and attack with flattery

Don't let people use this technique on you. It is always worth bearing these two quotes in mind:

"Flattery looks like friendship — just like a wolf looks like a dog."
(Anon)

"Flattery is like cologne water, to be smelt of, not swallowed."
(American humorist Josh Billings, 1818–1885)

This next bit is a key point. Bear in mind that these arguments don't have to be played out over the time span of one or two uttered sentences. They can be played out over any time span and with great subtlety. So, if your boss suddenly starts being nicer to you or sends you on an away-day to Alton Towers, be mindful that he might have a longer-term agenda.

If you're the boss, you can do all this stuff to your workforce if there's a particularly difficult position you need them to adopt (e.g. voting for you to stay the boss). Planned and deliberate mind games can be effective.

Be aware that an appeal to flattery is often used in a work context to offload work. *"John, you're great at PowerPoint presentations. Will you put one together for me please?"* If this is aimed at you, you'll know whether it's right for you to do the presentation or not. Just recognise the flattery so you don't feel you're being made a tool of. *"Of course. Flattery will get you everywhere, boss"* or *"No chance. Flattery will get you nowhere, mate."*

Summary of Appeal to Flattery Fallacy. If you think someone has adopted a position due to a bout of flattery, tell him he's been taken in and has committed the Appeal to Flattery Fallacy.

(70) Appeal to Authority Fallacy

Easy Definition: Don't immediately adopt the same position as someone you think is an expert. Firstly, he might not be an expert in that field, and, secondly, other experts might not agree with him. If you do adopt the expert's position, you might be committing the Appeal to Authority Fallacy.

Geeky Definition: The Appeal to Authority Fallacy is an error in reasoning which occurs when someone adopts a position because that position is affirmed by a person they believe to be an authority.

An Example:
Human beings only use 10% of their brains

Learning from teachers is critical to human development, so we have a strong tendency to trust the word of perceived experts, especially if we're in unfamiliar territory. But, when someone you're arguing with cites an expert in support of his argument, you shouldn't yield straight away. The strength of his argument still depends on two things:

- Is his expert a legitimate expert?
- Do other legitimate experts agree with his expert?

Remember, it doesn't have to be true just because an authority said it. It is still worth digging into why the authority believes it to be true. Simply saying "Here's a person who's better than us – listen to what he thinks" is a meaningless premise on which to base an argument. Here are a couple of examples of world-class authority figures spouting rubbish:

- Theoretical physicist Albert Einstein, who is regarded as one of the most brilliant minds of the 20th century, stated that human beings only use 10% of their brains. This claim is widely taken as fact, because Einstein said it. However, it's nonsense. Albert Einstein was no neurobiologist.
- In the early 17th century, the world's leading astronomers (most famously Galileo) were refining Copernicus's theory that the Earth revolves around the Sun (the heliocentric model of the universe). The evidence was looking pretty good for Copernicus's theory being right, but the astronomers had to tread fairly carefully when presenting this evidence, because it contradicted the idea that God placed the Earth in the middle of the universe (the geocentric model). This whole debate placed Pope Urban VIII in a difficult situation, but, being open minded, he encouraged Galileo to publish the arguments for and the arguments against heliocentrism. Galileo did what the Pope asked, but his paper did not strike a good balance. Way too many arguments for. He also couldn't resist taking a few cheap shots at the Pope and geocentrism. That was a bad judgement. Somewhat miffed, Pope Urban put Galileo under house arrest for the last few years of Galileo's life. For a while, the Sun continued to go "dutifully" around the Earth because no one dared question the authority of the church. For that short period (before the astronomers re-mustered to champion heliocentrism again), those backing the argument that the Earth was at the centre of the universe were committing the Appeal to Authority Fallacy. The pope might have been one of the most eminent authority figures on the

planet, but he was no astronomer.

So, if someone throws an "expert" into his argument, get ready with some words like this:
"That Is a fallacIous argument. Your expert is not a legitimate expert in that field, and it is doubtful many experts would agree with him."

Another Example:
Every prison has a false bar

My favourite example of someone naively taking an expert's statement as read appeared in an episode of The Simpsons. The scene starts with Homer and all his mates (including Police Chief Wiggum) being locked up in the prison cell. It was one of those cells with no front wall but just long bars from the floor to the ceiling. The type you see in westerns.

After a few seconds, Chief Wiggum says: "During police training, I was told there's always a false bar to allow a quick escape in the case of a fire." Starting from the right, he proceeds to knock on each bar one at a time, saying "Not this one" each time. As he gets to the last one on the far left, he doesn't bother testing it. He just says "And, so, by a process of elimination, it has to be this one." Wiggum takes a step back and runs at the bar like a bull, head butting it has hard as he can. Clearly, the bar is not a fake, and he crumples to the floor, squealing loudly.

I'm describing this incident in The Simpsons because it stemmed from Chief Wiggum being told that every prison had a false bar by one of his seniors. Wiggum was so confident in what that expert had told him, he didn't think to question it one iota. In doing so, he committed the Appeal to Authority Fallacy. It's a belting example.

A Practical Example:
Who is saying that exactly?

Sometimes the people you're arguing with can't be bothered to research a genuine authority, so they just throw in a vague opening statement to make it look as though someone in authority supports their argument. Here are some common examples:

"It has been statistically proven..."
"Most people think..."
"The government has stated..."
"Experts believe..."
"Everybody knows..."
"It's widely believed that..."

Each of these is an example of an Appeal to Authority Fallacy, because a valid authority is one that can be checked and tested.

If you train yourself to spot these appeals to unnamed authorities, you can undermine a difficult interview very easily.

Interviewer: *"Mr Jones, everybody knows that..."*
Mr Jones: *[interrupts] "Who's everybody?"*
Interviewer: *"I mean, most people are saying..."*
Mr Jones: *[interrupts] "Really? Not to me they're not. Who are most people?"*
Interviewer: *"Well, research shows..."*
Mr Jones: *[interrupts] "Whose research?"*
Interviewer: *"Mr Jones, can I make my point without the constant interruption?"*
Mr Jones: *"Please do, but start with 'I think'."*
Interviewer: *"Okay, I think..."*
Mr Jones: *[interrupts] "No one gives a monkey's what you think."*

You shouldn't feel bad about smashing people who try to attack you with an appeal to unnamed authority. After all, they are looking to create an "invisible magic flaming sword" out of nothing and wield it against you. You can take it off them and hit them with it.

It's hard to avoid an appeal to an unnamed authority – it is a very natural way to start a statement. My advice? Spot 'em and bash 'em – especially if you don't want to get tied down by what they've really got to say!

72 Base Rate Fallacy

Easy Definition: Don't think "99% accurate" means a 1% failure rate. There's far more to think about before you can work out the failure rate. This idea is linked to the Base Rate Fallacy.

Geeky Definition: The Base Rate Fallacy is an error in reasoning which occurs when someone reaches a conclusion that fails to account for an earlier premise – usually a base rate, a probability or some other statistic.

(Lots of people I showed this definition to didn't understand it, so it might not make much sense. If you look at the examples below and read the definition again, hopefully it will become clearer.)

An Example:
This machine is useless because it's only 99% accurate

Imagine we have a machine that can detect whether coins are real or fake. Now, our machine is pretty good at this. In fact, when it checks a coin, it only gets it wrong 1% of the time. 99% of the time it makes the right decision. Of course, there are two types of error the machine can make. It can say that a false coin is real (a false positive), or it can say that a real coin is false (a false negative). But it will only make an error once for every 100 coins it checks.

So, our machine is 99% accurate. Now, if you ran the machine until it spurted out a coin it believed to be a fake, what would be the chance of that coin actually being a fake?

If you said 99%, that's almost certainly wrong. It could be much much lower. The truth is you just don't know. Here's why:

Imagine our machine checked 10,010 coins, 10 of which were fake.

In checking the 10,000 real coins, the machine would wrongly identify 1% of them as fakes. In other words, it would get 100 coins wrong, and place them in its fake pile. Let's imagine the machine found all 10 of the fake coins, and correctly put them in the fake pile. We would now have 110 coins in the fake pile, but only 10 of them would be actual fakes. In this example, the chance of any coin being an actual fake would be less than 10%, even though your machine is "99% accurate".

If you originally thought 99%, your answer was derived through fallacious reasoning because an earlier premise (the tiny probability of the coins being fake in the first place, i.e. the base rate) was not taken into account.

A Practical Application:
Know what those cameras will do for you

Does knowing this have a practical application? Well, it could. Face-detection software is starting to appear in all sorts of places, and you might think it's the silver bullet to your particular problem. It could well be, but don't forget it depends on what you're testing for and the percentage of those things amongst everything else you're testing.

For example, if your shop buys a "99% accurate" face-detection camera to spot known shoplifters, your store detectives might find themselves following hundreds of people around the store who have no intention of shoplifting. The usefulness of such a system depends as much on the proportion of shoplifters in our society as it does on the accuracy of the system.

What about cameras to spot terrorists? What proportion of the population are terrorists? Minuscule. There would be thousands of false arrests if face-detection cameras that weren't 100% accurate were deployed at places like airports. Of course, this doesn't mean the cameras wouldn't be useful. It just means complementary procedures would need to be introduced. And that would be useful to know before you fork out 2 million quid equipping an airport with such a capability.

Another Practical Application:
Give them 33% and tell them it's 50%

Lots of food companies exploit the Base Rate Fallacy on their packaging. When something says "50% extra free", only a third (33%) of what you're looking at is free. If you think half of what you're looking at is free, then you've committed the Base Rate Fallacy. For example, when you buy six cans of Coke labelled "50% extra free", only two of the cans are free, not three. (It's because the original pack had four cans, and 50% of the original amount is two cans.) If you thought three of the cans were free, then you failed to account for an earlier premise (i.e. there were four cans originally), and you committed the Base Rate Fallacy. There's a little more on this in the statistics chapter (see Section 105).

> **Summary of Base Rate Fallacy.** If you think someone has taken a fact at face value without factoring in a key supporting premise (like a probability or a base rate), tell him he has committed the Base Rate Fallacy.

(73) Obfuscation Fallacy (or Empty Words Fallacy)

Easy Definition: Don't make a decision after someone presents you with a load of confusing factors. If you do, you will have committed the Obfuscation Fallacy.

Geeky Definition: The Obfuscation Fallacy occurs when someone adopts a position after hearing, or presenting, an argument containing unnecessarily complex language that either impresses (when it shouldn't), confuses or deceives.

"To obfuscate: to make obscure, unclear or unintelligible"

An Example:
Black and white swans?

Earlier in the book (see Section 25), we looked at a scene from the comedy series "Yes Minister", in which the Prime Minister's aide uses obfuscation to avoid telling the Prime Minister (who's not as bright as the aide) that the IRA does not think the Prime Minister is important enough to assassinate. That's my second favourite example of obfuscation. My favourite is this:

"I cannot say that I do not disagree with you."
(American comedian Groucho Marx, 1890–1977)

It allows you to say "you're wrong" but leaves your victim thinking you said "you're right".

Deliberately clouding the facts to help press home a point or to avoid answering a difficult question means you are committing the Obfuscation Fallacy. But, falling for the argument due to a clouding of the facts means you're guilty of committing the fallacy too.

Obfuscation is not, in itself, a logical fallacy. It can only be described as a fallacy if it forms part of an argument. Here's an example. Firstly, without the obfuscation:

Lee: *"Swans can be black or white. Jack is a swan. Therefore, Jack is white."*
Mark: *"I disagree. Jack could be black."*

But what about the same argument with obfuscation:

Lee: *"Whilst the pigment particles embedded in some swans' plumage will reflect the vast majority of electromagnetic radiation from ~700 nanometers to ~400 nanometers, the plumage and structures in others' feathers will absorb a high proportion of the wavelengths perceivable as white light. Jack is a swan. Therefore, Jack is white."*
Mark: *"Yeah, whatever. Sounds like you know your onions."*

A Practical Application :
Attack with obfuscation

If it suits you, obfuscate like crazy if it's the only way to negotiate an obstacle impeding your progress. The best and easiest way to obfuscate is to present lots and lots and lots of pages of detailed work on a subject that isn't the reader's top priority. He won't read it. This means he will let the status quo endure because that's the easiest thing for him to do, and he'll think it's reasonably safe (see Section 66). This is great news if you want him to do nothing (e.g. not cancel your contract). If the status quo being maintained doesn't suit you (e.g. you need him to write you a new contract), then throw in some clear lines about the dangers of continuing without you and then obfuscate like 10 men about what you bring to the party. It's a dodgy strategy, but if the benefits you bring are not that strong, you might want to think about it.

"The secret of life is honesty... if you can fake that, you've got it made."
(Groucho Marx)

Another Practical Application :
Defend against obfuscation

I covered this in a rant at Section 25. So, there's no need for me to get back on that soap box. Here's the bottom line. If you have an important decision to make based on a long document that you don't understand or haven't got time to read, tell the author to get it all on one page. Not two pages. One.

"Nothing cuts through obfuscation cleaner than a brutal word limit."

> **Summary of Obfuscation Fallacy.** If you think someone has adopted a position without fully understanding the facts due to obfuscation (or someone is deliberately using obfuscation to cloud factors in a pending decision), tell him he has committed the Obfuscation Fallacy.

74   Gamblers' Fallacy

Easy Definition: Don't think you can predict a random event based on what's happened in the past. That's the Gamblers' Fallacy. Remember, a random event means it's random every single time.

Geeky Definition: Gamblers' Fallacy occurs when someone predicts the outcome of a pending random event based on previous random events.

An Example:
It can't be a red again

The most obvious example of Gamblers' Fallacy is predicting that the ball on a roulette table will land on red next because the previous few numbers were black. The truth is that the next number is equally likely to be black. It's a 50/50 (if you don't include the green zero) at all stages of the game. The history is irrelevant.

A Practical Example:
Don't try the old "keep betting on black" strategy

Hey, here's a plan. Let's go to the roulette table and keep betting on black. If it's red, we'll keep doubling our money until a black appears. We can't lose.

Actually, that's true. You can't. But, to make it work, you need a lot of bottle and a lot of money. I mean you need to be as brave as a lion and have a shed-load of money. This is because every time the ball spins, there's only a 50% chance of a win (actually, it's slightly less because of the green 0), and when you keep doubling a number you get to very large numbers very quickly.

Below is a legendary story which relates to that last idea.

Long, long ago, an Indian king challenged one of his subjects to a game of chess and lost. Prior to the game, the king had told his subject (who was also a good mathematician) he could have anything he wanted if he won. Having won, the subject asked for rice. More specifically, the subject wanted one grain of rice on the first square of the chessboard, two on the second, four on the third, eight on the fourth, etc. The king was a little upset at the request because he had promised his subject "anything he wanted", and he thought the request would amount to less than a sack of rice as opposed to the bags of jewels and gold he had anticipated. [No, king, it actually amounts to 18,446,744,073,709,551,615 grains of rice.] However, the king soon learned that even if he sold all his national assets, he did not have enough money to buy the rice needed to fulfil the subject's request. [In fact, he would have needed about 210 billion tons of rice, enough to cover the whole territory of India with a metre-thick layer. What happened next is disputed. Some versions of this story say the subject was punished and some say he became king. Some cultures tell this story with wheat and not rice.]

Anyway, if you're planning to go to the casino with this "great" plan, remember, it's based on a Gamblers' Fallacy that has been committed by millions of people before you. Not convinced? Imagine you started this strategy with a £1 bet on black. By the time you get to make a £16 bet, you will be staking £31 (because you'll have lost £15 at that point), and it's still just a 50/50. If it isn't a black, the total stake for the next play will be £63. And that's just a 50/50 too. But then you win. Hooray, you're £1 up. That was a lot of risk for a quid. And it's always just a quid at every stage. Like I said, you need a lot of money and a lot of bottle to make this strategy work. At a quid a time, you need a lot of time too.

Summary of Gamblers' Fallacy. If you think someone has forecast the outcome of a future random event by factoring in the results of random events in the past, tell him he has committed the Gamblers' Fallacy.

75   Ad Hominem Argument

Easy Definition: Don't attack people's personalities or beliefs to undermine their arguments. That's called an *ad hominem* argument. Stick to the facts in the argument.

Geeky Definition: An *ad hominem* argument (*ad hominem* is Latin for "to the man") occurs when someone tries to contest a claim by highlighting the negative characteristics or beliefs of the <u>person</u> making the claim rather than contesting the claim itself.

Examples:

We could dedicate a whole chapter to *ad hominem* arguments, because there are so many different types. But they all share the same idea: they're all an attack on the person and not an attack on the facts of the claim. Here are some examples:

You're fat and ugly; therefore, your claim is wrong.
You're not an expert in this subject; therefore, your claim is wrong.
It's in your interest to think that; therefore, your claim is wrong.
That's not what you said last week; therefore, your claim is wrong.
You're a proven liar; therefore, your claim is wrong.
You're a lower rank than me; therefore, your claim is wrong.

These arguments are all errors in reasoning. A person's looks, expertise, motivation, beliefs, actions and rank are not, in themselves, evidence that his argument is invalid.

In the military, we used to call arguments of this nature the "shut up" fallacy. You commit the "shut up" fallacy when you counter a claim based on *who the claimant is*. In effect, you're telling the claimant to shut up without listening to his reasoning… just because you can. This idea is best captured by the army game "paper, scissors, rank badge", which is a decision-making tool based on the game "paper, scissors, rock". In the army version, however, the highest rank badge trumps everything! *"Corporal Jones and I had a game of paper, scissors, rank badge and have ascertained that I was right."*

Of course, *ad hominem* arguments are not always wrong. There's another side to them. If someone is a known liar, there's a greater chance he's lying again. If someone is set make a wad of cash if his claim is true, you should be more suspicious. So, life's hard – you shouldn't attack a person's claim based on his characteristics or beliefs, but you must factor them in. You will do this naturally, so don't expend too many calories trying to strike the right balance.

A Practical Application:
Put 'em back in their box

Knowing about *ad hominem* arguments is far more useful when you're on the receiving end of the attack, and that's quite a likely scenario. Most people are programmed to attack the presenter of the argument rather than the argument itself. (It's far easier for a start.) Attacks with words like these are pretty common:

You don't have the experience.
What do you know about this subject anyway?
Well, you would say that, wouldn't you? (i.e. it's in your interest).

You can counter them with words like this:

"Your attack on me doesn't change what I'm saying."
(If you don't want to come across as snotty.)

"Please stick to the point. Your ad hominem attack on me is fallacious reasoning and only serves to cloud the issue."
(If you want to put your attacker back in his box and you don't mind coming across as snotty.)

> **Summary of an Ad Hominem Argument.** If you think someone has attacked a person's evidence based on that person's looks, expertise, motivation, beliefs, actions or status, tell him his ad hominem argument fails to address the pertinent issues.

Reading Body
Language

76 What is body language and how does it work?

When a chimp screams and bashes its sibling over the head to retrieve a banana, the verbal and physical actions occur at the same time. We humans, however, prefer to resolve our differences using speech first, and that's what we think we're doing most of the time. We're not. In fact, we're also performing simultaneous physical actions – even if they're not as blatant as a bash over the head.

Remember this joke?

"How do you know when a politician is lying? His lips are moving."

Whilst moving lips are clearly not an indication that someone is lying, some other body movements can be indicative of a "porky pie" being told. There are numerous examples, and we'll touch upon one later, of politicians and less illustrious individuals being found out by their body language. So, apart from picking out which political leaders are lying (or choosing to omit the truth, which is most of them at some point, I suspect), how can reading someone's body language help you?

Well, scientists will tell you that speech only conveys about 7% of your message. That seems a bit low to me, but it's a fairly consistent figure in the world of those who look at this stuff. They also say that 38% of the message is in the pitch, speed, volume and tone of voice, leaving a massive 55% of the message conveyed by body language. Even if that figure is four times as high as reality, it still stands to reason that reading people's "non-verbal communication" will provide a valuable insight into what they are thinking. Sometimes it will confirm what they're saying, but sometimes it will contradict their words and give you clues as to what's really going on.

When people talk, they complement their words with various body movements (e.g. nose touching). Some of these body movements are known as cues. Everyone transmits these cues unconsciously, and, if you miss them, it can be like trying to read a book with loads of the pages torn out.

"What you do speaks so loud that I cannot hear what you say."
(American essayist Ralph Waldo Emerson, 1803–1882)

Knowledge of non-verbal communication will assist you in all aspects of life. It would certainly improve your success with dating (but this is not that sort of book, I'm afraid). It will strengthen your position during all manner of negotiations, from an argument in a pub to the purchase of your next house. Without a word being said, it can tell you when your spouse, boss or colleagues are annoyed at you.

Most people decide within 30 seconds of meeting people whether they like them, and much of that decision is based on body language. What if you could modify your body language to ensure you present the best impression? That would be pretty useful. It would also be valuable to know when people are faking theirs. The ability to read non-verbal communication will also help you to gauge how your messages or arguments are being received and how your opponents think they're doing in countering them.

77 The basics – what's it all about?

Body language is a legacy from when we were less developed as a species, and speech was not the primary means of communication. As man developed from early hominids (a primate of the family Hominidae), speech as the means of passing information about well-being, food and group interaction overtook body language. This probably occurred between 100,000 and 2.3 million years ago with the emergence of the homo series of pre-humans. There is still much debate whether this occurred through the evolution of social gestures (i.e. as an extension of body language) or through the increased complexity of brain function. Whatever the case, evidence of the origins of our body language can still be seen in apes (our nearest relatives), which exhibit a range of expressions remarkably similar to our own.

Right, that's the history out of the way. We now need to look at the basics of body language. To do this, we will divide the body into discrete segments and look at the cues (known in poker as "tells") from each segment. The tells are the behaviours which you exhibit unconsciously that reveal the inner you. For example, if your arms are crossed close to your body, it can indicate you are unhappy or being defensive.

We're only looking at individual body areas and their associated tells because it is the easiest way to study them. However, Lesson 1 (and the most important point about reading body language) is that you usually need to read several tells that indicate the same inner emotional state to gain an insight into what is going on – you cannot rely on just one tell. When a cluster of tells points to the same inner emotional state, they are said to be in "congruence". It is then your job to determine whether the cluster of tells is congruent with what your target is saying.

"The human body is the best picture of the human soul."
(Austrian-British philosopher Ludwig Wittgenstein, 1889–1951)

78 Turn on your active observation

Before we look at the tells, we need to talk quickly about seeing.

"One may have good eyes and yet see nothing."
(Italian proverb)

If you're a driver, you will know that you can eat up miles of motorway with the active part of the brain disengaged from driving while you daydream. When you snap out of this state of "autopilot", you don't actually remember driving or any details of what you've passed. However, this mind state doesn't occur at junctions or town driving. That type of driving needs more mental effort.

Something similar happens with your routine day-to-day view of the world. Most people travel through life looking but not seeing. Their minds go lazy on them. They adopt "looking autopilot". However, you can change that by turning on your "active observation". Just as you don't let yourself negotiate a difficult driving manoeuvre with your brain in neutral, so you can put your brain in gear when it comes to looking. While it requires effort, like most things that do, it yields rewards.

To put it another way, "active observation" is like "active listening". When you're listening actively, you don't just let the sounds wash over you, you concentrate on them to extract as much as you can. When talking face to face, most people let the images wash over them, but it is possible to concentrate on what you're seeing to extract as much as you can – you might just discover the ability to read people in a way that you didn't think possible. Before we get into the detail, here's a top tip. You must be very subtle with active observation. Be careful not to stare unnaturally at your target and certainly not as if you are auditioning for the part of Count Dracula, because this will definitely alter their behaviour towards you (and not in a good way).

(79) Posture

Your posture (the way you carry yourself) can be indicative of your emotional state. Think of a football team which has just won the FA Cup. They stand with their backs straight, and their heads and hands held high. They maintain eye contact, and they look at the world like the champions they are. On the other hand, the defeated players look down at the ground, their shoulders are slumped, and their arms are by their sides. Their heads are withdrawn into their shoulders like a tortoise into its shell. That's all pretty obvious. But more subtle postures can be revealing too.

Standing tall and walking with one hand clasped in the other behind your back exposes the stomach, chest and neck. These are your vulnerable areas, and showing them off without protection is a sign of confidence. Members of the British royal family, head teachers, senior army officers and others in positions of authority can often be seen holding this posture. This hand-clasped-in-the-other-behind-the-back gesture should not be confused with the wrist-gripping gesture (a sign of frustration) or the gripping-of-the-upper-arm-behind-the-back gesture (a sign of trying to gain self-control).

Expect people to read your posture. If you wander into a car showroom looking as if you are on the losing side before you've said a word, expect to pay more for your vehicle. So, get in there like the champion you are. If the salesman comes at you looking a bit meek, then see it and act on it. Use your bare-chested confidence to set the anchor (see Section 39) for the price negotiations.

(80)   Feet and legs

Leg and foot movements, like much of your body language, are a legacy linked to the "fight or flight" decisions that animals, pre-humans and humans have been making since time immemorial. In other words, your legs and feet still react to events without conscious thought.

In times of danger, our brains instinctively tell us to either freeze or, if required, run to safety. Freezing might not seem like a sensible response in times of danger, especially given that humans aren't exactly masters at blending with their environments and the old dinosaurs-can-only-detect-movement idea must be well out of our system by now. But it can be. When on a patrol in Northern Iraq, our man on point (the person leading the way) suddenly froze. We all did the same. It seemed like a very natural response, and, on this occasion, it was a potentially life-saving one. Our point man had seen a group of Kurdish separatists patrolling towards us. Like us, they froze when they saw our patrol. A somewhat awkward pause followed, before both patrols moved off in different directions. Freezing makes you feel like you're reducing your profile (noise, visibility, movement, aggressiveness) and allows you to take stock of the situation. It sometimes feels right. If either patrol had run, the chances of that encounter escalating into a fire fight would have increased markedly. Our instincts and their instincts caused us both to behave in our best interests.

This freeze or run instinct is at the heart of why our legs and feet reflect our feelings. If the eyes are a window to the soul, then the legs are the signposts to what you are thinking. People are far less guarded about how they position their legs during a conversation than they are with other parts of the body, so leg and feet positioning is usually a good cue that you can add to the cluster of cues you're trying to build up.

When you're having a conversation with someone, if his feet point towards you, then there's a fair chance he likes you, is interested in what you're saying or agrees with you. If, on the other hand, his legs and feet point away from you, it is often an indicator he wants to be somewhere else. It's almost as if he's already walking away from the conversation. If he does this with just one foot, it should also be added to the mix of cues suggesting he doesn't want to be there. Similarly, if he's seated with his hands on his knees with his weight shifted forward, he is mentally already standing up and preparing to be somewhere else.

The trick is to see this happening and to use it to your advantage. For example, if your boss is adopting these types of positions, get to the point quickly and exit. Remember, he's probably not that interested in what you've got to say (see Section 3). Just accept that, and stop yourself being a bore.

When commanding soldiers, I was not good at hiding when people were boring me, but lots of them were equally bad at realising they were boring me, despite my fairly unsubtle body language (like reading emails while they were talking). Those close to me actually presented me with a table-tennis bat with "1 minute" written on one side and "Now go away" written on the other. The plan was I held it up mid-conversation when people had outstayed their welcome. Obviously, I never used it – that would have been far too rude. But, for the sake of retaining their own credibility, those people ought to have read my signals before I started blatantly ignoring them. If your boss rolls his eyes and shakes his head as you leave his office, you've probably not done yourself many favours. See the signs and get out early. You'll look businesslike, and he'll appreciate it.

This can also apply to things like job interviews when you're trying to impress. If the interviewer's feet are pointed towards you, there's a good chance he's interested in you and you're making a good impression. Keep it up. If his feet turn away, you might need to start improving your answers or change tack. (But don't stare at his feet throughout the interview.)

It's not all about fight or flight. Feet can also reflect happy emotions, which they usually do by springing up and down. It's the root of the term "jump for joy". As an adult, you are more socially restrained, but children, like dogs, will literally jump up and down with happiness (just tell a six-year-old he's off to Disney World to meet Mickey Mouse and watch), and there remains an inner child in all of us. As a result, we may not bounce up and down in our seats, but our legs will jiggle up and down (not to be confused with nervous or restless bouncing), and we will point our toes upwards when happy or excited.

Remember, most body-language movements don't just mean one thing. Many (like leg jiggling) are indicative of differing emotions. It's all about context. For example, nervous leg jiggling will probably occur at a time when you would expect it to (e.g. during a briefing or a reprimand), and it will probably coincide with another body-language movement which manifests itself when people are nervous, like neck touching. You're looking for a congruence of indicators that all point to the same thing.

81 Hands and arms... and thumbs

Hand and arm positioning is one of the biggest giveaways to someone's thoughts and emotions. For example, when someone is happy (e.g. in an interesting conversation), he will move his hands and arms in an animated manner. A happy person will even have animated arm movements when walking. Conversely, if a person is feeling down, his arm movements become more suppressed as if his arms have suddenly become heavier, and they sink, reflecting his mood.

We all use our hands and arms to gesticulate when we speak. Again, just watch a child. Children tend to gesticulate far more freely than adults. As we grow up, we learn to conceal our emotions, and this includes limiting how much we gesticulate. But if you watch an adult who is arguing to the point of losing his temper or getting excited, his arm movements become far more animated. Arm gesticulation usually indicates a flood of emotion, either positive or negative. It is a sign of the adult constraints on emotion failing, and the adult reverting to more child-like mannerisms. Even when suppressed, there is usually sufficient hand and arm activity for you to interpret. But again, remember – it's all part of an overall picture. It's not just a case of animated arms meaning happy or angry, and suppressed arms meaning sad or controlled.

Hand movements are also used to mime or partially mime the words being said (called self-mirroring), and care must be taken not to confuse these mimes with body-language cues. For example, if a person is talking about pushing a car, he might imitate the push with his palms down. That's not a palms-down gesture (covered later). It's just a mime. Similarly, if a person is talking about opening a magazine, he might rotate one of his hands from palm down to palm up. Again, that's not a body-language cue. It's a mime, or, in this case, a partial mime. Presenting mimes and partial mimes is the main reason people consciously move their arms and hands when speaking. However, the way in which the mimes are performed (e.g. in an animated or sluggish manner) can offer a clue about their thoughts and emotions. The mimes themselves don't. Eliminating them from your "reading" takes real practice. There is also a cultural influence to consider. The Mediterranean peoples use far more gesticulation to accompany talking than northern Europeans. (Picture the Italian gesticulating wildly at the scene of an accident.) It has also been observed that people who have a limited vocabulary use their hands and arms far more than eloquent individuals as a way of compensating. So, you could be dealing with an inarticulate person as opposed to a happy or an angry one. These are all factors which could confuse your interpretation of someone's hand and arm movements. And, as ever, never forget that you are looking for clusters of cues, not just isolated ones.

But this doesn't mean it's not worth observing hand and arm movements. There are some very definite signals which are worth keeping an eye out for. For example, when people are told something they disagree with or dislike, they tend to pull their hands closer to their bodies. It is believed this happens because the subconscious tries to give reassurance – almost as though it's trying to get them to hug themselves. (In extreme examples of stress, full-on self-hugging can actually occur.)

Arm movements also become less pronounced in those trying to avoid detection. In Iraq during the hostilities, one of the tells for spotting a suicide bomber was that the bomber exhibited far less arm movement than those around him. This is because the bomber subconsciously thinks that by not moving his body as much, he is making himself less noticeable. (It's a microcosm of the freeze response.) Similarly, a shoplifter will often have non-animated arms as he tries to make himself inconspicuous. Also, an individual caught in a lie will momentarily stop his arm movements as he tries to steer around that part of the conversation.

Numerous experimental studies show that palms-up behaviours portray positivity, whereas palms-down ones can portray negativity or, more often than not, neutrality. Palms-up movements are also presented as a sign of honesty and welcoming. This is a well-reported trait, and anyone worth his salt who is trying to convince you of his idea or sell you something will do so with lots of palms-up gestures. You might not know you're reading his body language, but you will be.

Now, at this point, it starts to get a little complicated. Don't forget, we said palms-up gestures are presented as a sign of honesty. They do not always mean the person is being honest. It just means the person wants you to think he's being honest.

Joe Navarro, an ex-FBI interrogator, in his book *What Every Body is Saying* actually shows that palm-down displays are often associated with truthful declarations, e.g. "I did not rob that bank". If the accused believes he has nothing to hide and the truth will stand on its own merits, he might not feel the need to throw in some "convincing" palms-up gestures. So, palms-up gestures only really tell you that the person wants to be believed and not that he's telling the truth. It also doesn't mean he's telling a lie. So, life's not simple unfortunately. But, all of these ideas add to the mix that you are trying to interpret.

If you are negotiating to buy a car and the salesman is exhibiting palms-up behaviour while stating that he cannot go any lower on the price, he wants you to believe him, and thinks he's exhibiting open and honest behaviour. If his palms are down (for example, resting or pressing on a desk), his statement is likely to be more emphatic in its delivery. In the first instance, keep negotiating, because you might be able to push the price down further. In the second, he's probably at his limit, and you won't get further concessions from him. So, if you can get him from flailing around the showroom floor with lots of palms-up gestures to crying at his desk with his hands flat on its surface, you should probably take that as a sign you've won the negotiation. Clearly, it won't be as obvious as that. It's for you to read the shades between those two positions to understand how you're faring.

There's also a widely held theory out there that people who don't gesticulate with their hands when talking are considered less trustworthy than those who do. Politicians know this only too well, and they tend to be more animated than most. In particular, they like to use lots of open-arm gestures to convey honesty. They also tend to avoid pointing, which is seen as rude, opting instead for straight-hand indicating to produce a more authoritative yet less rude point.

Staying on the theme of being rude, next we'll look at handshakes. This is a well-worn subject, and much has been written about handshakes and how to perform the perfect shake. My advice would be not to expend too many mental calories thinking about this. Just shake the person's hand naturally and smile a bit. Your grip should be firmish, but it should not maim the recipient. Any actions that are too contrived (e.g. staring, hand crushing, being too happy, being too enthusiastic) will just be disturbing.

Back in the 1980s, "handshakeologists" would have told you that, as well as a manly grip, you should also be the one with your palm facing downwards during a handshake (i.e. you should make sure your hand is on top). This, according to them, would establish a lasting dominance. (I have actually seen two people trying to achieve this in a handshake. It was the most cringe-worthy, two-second arm-wrestling competition I've ever witnessed.) I'm totally unconvinced it has any effect whatsoever. I also think telling someone to ensure a "strong manly handshake" is another poor piece of advice. I am never charmed by individuals who try to assert their masculinity or dominance by crushing the life out of my metacarpals. For a man, you can avoid an annoyingly strong handshake by pushing the web of your hand (the skin between forefinger and thumb) hard into theirs, as this makes it difficult for them to grip tightly. If you are a women and some ill-mannered "baboon" is crushing your hand, simply state in a just-too-loud-but-confident manner "you're hurting my hand". The individual will look foolish, and you'll have taught him a life-long etiquette lesson. In fact, you could say this even if he's not hurting your hand and you wanted to take him down a peg or two before a meeting. Now, that's manipulation!

If you're a hand-crusher, my advice would be to quit it. It leaves a negative rather than positive impression. Conversely, the dead-fish handshake (limp and cold) should also be avoided. However, if you do encounter a limp handshake, just remember there could be a good explanation for it. The shaker might have a hand injury, be a musician or simply be a tradesman who needs his hands.

Next, a quick story on handholding that might help readers who do business outside Europe. In the West, handholding between heterosexual males is simply not done, but it is common in other cultures. During the war in Iraq, I was working with a colonel from an Iraqi Army intelligence unit. Mohammed was very professional and very personable, and we seemed to get on well. After a couple of months, we were walking outside discussing the day's work when he reached out and held my hand. I'd seen Iraqi officers holding hands before, and this flashed into my head just in time to stop me ripping my hand from his. However, my discomfort must have been written all over my face. Within a few seconds, the interpreter said: "He is holding your hand because he trusts you". If I had pulled my hand away, it would have been culturally extremely rude, and our professional relationship would have been damaged. So, if you're a man operating in a country where males are more tactile than in Europe, such as the Middle East, and your male host wants to hold your hand during a coffee break, go with it – you're doing well.

Steepling shows confidence

Steepling conveys confidence. (Steepling is when the fingers of both hands are touching but not the palms.) As it is quite an easy gesture to spot, it is useful for revealing a person's state of mind. When a person is confident in what he's saying, he will steeple. However, when the conversation starts to make him feel uneasy, he will move from the steeple position to interlocking fingers. This is a subconscious pacifying gesture designed to reassure himself. It's a form of self-hugging. If his confidence increases, he is likely to return to a steeple. Interestingly, men tend to steeple above the waist, whereas women generally do it at waist level or below. So, if the person is sitting behind a desk, this important indicator about their confidence level could be lost. Therefore, when interviewing people, it is best not to use a table so the full range of non-verbal cues (including feet, legs and hands on knees) can be observed.

Neck-touching is another subconscious gesture designed to reassure. It also shows that a person is feeling uneasy. A woman will tend to touch or cover her superstitial notch (at the base of her throat), whereas a man will usually touch the side of his neck or run his fingers around his collar as if it's just become too tight or his tie has just become a noose. These are all common forms of the self-hug. I once worked with a woman who was a senior manager. She had a tell of stroking her eyebrow whenever she was unhappy or concerned. She did it unconsciously as a pacifying manoeuvre. Beware though. Neck-touching can also be a flirt designed to encourage the target's eyes to the neck and further down the décolleté. This type of touch looks more like a downward caress rather than a straight touch, so you should be able to spot the difference. Both men and woman do it. This, in turn, should not be confused with a woman hiding her cleavage from letches. Oh, it's a minefield.

82   Facial expressions

From the smile of a parent to the frown of a teacher, we've all
been trained to respond to people's facial expressions since birth,
and the face is usually the first place we look when establishing
communications with someone. People make snap judgements based
on facial expression, and this judgement affects whatever is being
said, especially in terms of its gravity and believability. This is related
to the Halo Effect (see Section 56), which ensures that a person's
positive or negative traits bleed across onto other things. It's also
the reason why attractive people receive more attention than others
(see Good Looking People Bias, Section 54). Suffice to say that facial
expressions can underpin or undermine whatever is being said and
give strong clues as to what the person is thinking. The very good
news is that you're probably already excellent at reading the signs.
(You will instinctively know that tension and nervousness are shown
by furrowing the forehead, squinting the eyes and lip compressions.
You will instinctively know that disagreement and aversion are shown
by pursing the lips, crinkling the nose and rolling the eyes.) The very
bad news, however, is that you're probably not great at masking these
signs. When you're in autopilot mode, your face will give you away. It
takes real practice to spot when your autopilot mode will let you down
and when you should engage in a bit of acting or facial-expression
suppression. That might be harder than you think though, because of
micro-gestures.

*"The face is the mirror of the mind, and eyes without speaking confess the
secrets of the heart."*
(Saint Jerome, 347 AD (approx.)–420 AD)

Micro-gestures are the small twitches that flash across your face.
They are extremely difficult to mimic or prevent consciously, but they
can be read if you keep an eye out for them. The trick is not to be
blinded by larger gestures. When a smile is genuine, it will usually
be accompanied by a micro-gesture around the eyes (crinkling of the
skin around the eye area). This "smiling with your eyes" is difficult to

mimic, so the absence of this micro-gesture could offer a clue that the smile was faked. Disdain is another feeling that can be detected with the micro-gesture of a lightning-fast smirk.

"Your mouth is saying yes, but your eyes are saying no."
(A line that a Russian teacher used on me as she was checking whether I'd followed a particular grammar point. I was obviously in auto-pilot mode as I was saying yes. Either that or she could read the micro-gestures I failed to mask.)

83 It's all in the eyes

Your first judgement about a person will often occur during initial eye contact, and, until you are in eye contact with someone, you are not communicating effectively. It's difficult to put a finger on why it happens, but some people make us feel at ease, while others make us feel uncomfortable. Clues to a person's trustworthiness, friendliness and dominance are all partially conveyed through microgestures of the eyes, and you have already developed the instincts to read them.

Other traits are conveyed not so much through the eyes but more through how a person uses his eyes. For example, a person who is nervous or has something to fear is less likely to look you straight in the eye. (There's more on that coming up. Please don't take it too literally.) Someone who has something to hide will generally only look at you for a third of the time during your conversation. On the other hand, someone who holds your gaze for more than two-thirds of the time could either like you (or be interested in what you're saying) or dislike you (or be uninterested). With the latter, the gaze-holding is a non-verbal challenge. As ever, context is key, and a person's tendency to stare or to avoid eye contact must be thrown into the mix for interpretation alongside the other cues.

The type of gaze is also important. There are three main types of gaze.

The Business Gaze. Gazing into a person's eyes and then his forehead is known as the business gaze. In a meeting which has no other interactions going on other than business, most people will be gazing at each other in this way. It is useful to know this, because it might be possible to maintain a business-like bearing if someone starts gazing at you in an inappropriate way. In other words, flicking your gaze to deflect someone's amorous intentions by looking at their forehead in between eye contacts might be a way of saying "I'm just here to seal the deal".

The Social Friend's Gaze. Gazing into a person's eyes and then his chin is known as the friend's gaze. This might be useful to spot when a meeting is moving from a business footing to social one. Throughout my Army career, I learned that you could sometimes get more done with beer and a chat than you could with a hundred staff papers. If you think you're in that situation, you might want to start thinking about flicking your gaze at your target's chin in between eye contacts.

The Intimate Gaze. Gazing into a person's eyes and then at the chest and lower is known as the intimate gaze. You will notice this gaze when a person is interested in you sexually. (People who are expressing sexual interest also flick between eyes and lips, but as we covered earlier, this is not that kind of book.)

(Be aware that these are Western gazes. Other cultures have their own. The Japanese, for example, will gaze at your neck rather than your face because they prefer to avoid eye contact. With that as the backdrop, it's quite important you don't mistake Japanese neck-gazing as a European intimate gaze.)

84   Eye Access Cueing

Eye access cueing is done by watching how a person's eyes move
in their sockets. When someone tries to recall information from the
past or to think about the future, his eyes will move in a particular
way. (For example, both of his eyes might move to the top left in their
sockets.) Whilst you cannot tell whether someone is lying from these
eye movements, you are able to tell whether the person is recalling
information or constructing information (i.e. imagining something).
For most people, it works like this:

• **Eyes Go Top Left.** Recalling information, e.g. a childhood
memory.
(Try it on yourself: What was the colour of your childhood bedroom?)

• **Eyes Go Top Right.** Constructing a mental picture.
(Try it on yourself: What would you do if you won the lottery?)

• **Eyes Go Middle Left.** Recalling a sound.
(Try it on yourself: Can you remember the sound of a dropped glass
shattering?)

• **Eyes Go Middle Right.** Imagining what a sound might be.
(Try it on yourself: Imagine the sound of stepping on a squeaky dog
toy.)

• **Eyes Go Down Right.** Accessing an emotion.
(Try it on yourself: Where's your first pet now?)

• **Eyes Go Down Left.** Talking to yourself.
(Try it on yourself: So, how are you today?)

These eye movements are quite easy to spot. Unfortunately though,
they're difficult to interpret. If a person is telling you a lie, he could
be remembering what he's said previously (eyes generally go top left),
or he could be constructing the lie (eyes generally go top right), or a

bit of both. If he's telling you the truth, he will recall the truth (eyes top left) or might be deciding how it affects him (eyes top right), or a bit of both. And there will probably be some emotion accessing (eyes bottom right) thrown in the mix too. On its own, an eye movement is inconclusive, but it ought to be added to the equation along with the other tells.

85   Social and Business Uses

As we've covered, a person will unwittingly communicate lots of free and sometimes secret (from his point of view) information about how he thinks your interaction is going. And, as we've also touched on, the person you're interacting with will respond subconsciously to your body language. So, reading body language can both improve your understanding and allow you to exert some influence. Whilst these benefits could be crucial to a business or social success, more often than not they just give you an edge that might otherwise be lost.

You will, of course, read information and exert influence using your body language naturally, so the margins to be won by doing it deliberately could be very fine. This benefit must be balanced with the risk of being caught applying body language deliberately or just looking weird through over-observing or staring.

With that caveat out the way, there is a technique which is relatively easy to carry out and which could help you to develop a harmonious and productive relationship, business or social. It's called mirroring.

Mirroring is a subconscious copying of gestures. At the most basic level, if someone smiles at you, you smile back. If a colleague across the desk yawns, you might yawn. This happens more than you might think. If you watch a newly dating couple in a restaurant, their body movements and postures are often mirrored, if they're getting on. This happens naturally, but you can fake it. In both social and business contexts, you can use mirroring to achieve a positive effect. For example, if you copy your target's movements (e.g. chair positioning, hand positioning, enthusiasm, yawns, coffee drinking, biscuit eating) and your mirroring looks natural with a delay which is sufficient to mask your game (usually 10-15 seconds), then your target could subconsciously develop an affinity with you which might develop into added respect for your views. Warning: if you mimic the movements exactly and immediately, your target might think you're mocking him. If you're caught mirroring (and lots of people are aware of this technique so be careful), you're toast. The best bet is to do it very subtly, leaving enough room for plausible deniability. The mirroring game will also keep you awake at a boring meeting, and you might end up being the only person looking at the talker. At the very least, he'll take that as a sign of your interest, and that in itself will do you no harm whatsoever. It's a win-win – provided you're not caught.

A bit nervous about the mirroring game? Don't worry. There are some very safe things you can do to improve your effectiveness. For example, if you are in a discussion with someone and his eyes are showing signs of lots of recalling (eyes top left) or imagining (eyes top right), then take this as an indicator to stop talking. While your target is in "eyes up" mode, he will not be paying full attention to what you're saying. As a result, the communication could be slowed or ineffective. Let him finish his thought process, so you can throw your words at a more receptive brain.

You'll be getting the idea by now that you can read a specific body gesture to attain information or apply that body gesture to exert some influence. For me, it brings to mind Newton's third law: "For every action, there is an equal and opposite reaction." Unfortunately, this does not apply to all the gestures and tips outlined. For example, you cannot deliberately look up lots to shut the speaker up. I know. I tried it for a few days with my co-author. It just gets you a dead arm.

86 Proxemics (don't stand so close to me)

"Personal space" is the area surrounding a person into which any encroachment feels threatening or uncomfortable. The size of someone's "personal space" varies from person to person and from culture to culture. It is different in urban environments than in rural ones, and it varies according to the situation. As a general guideline though, "personal space" with strangers is about 1.2m, with work colleagues is about 45 cm, with friends is 15-45cm, and with a partner is 0-15cm. (The branch of knowledge that deals with the amount of space people want for themselves is known as proxemics.)

When you're on a crowded tube, others are forced into the personal space you would normally reserve for your nearest and dearest. As a result, you seek to distance yourself mentally from the fat tourist breathing in your ear by avoiding eye contact. (Next time you're on a busy tube at rush hour, check out how many people are looking at everything except each other.) This is all to maintain the illusion of personal space.

People like their personal space, and you can exploit that. If it suits you to intimidate someone or to make them feel uncomfortable (perhaps you need them out of the room for whatever reason), you can attack his personal space to achieve your aim. In my days as a young officer, we used to play a fairly mischievous game at parties. It started by picking a wallflower (someone who looks socially ill at ease) and talking to him. The aim of the game was to engage him in conversation while encroaching on his personal space. The trick was to do it in a way that he didn't really notice at a conscious level. However, subconsciously he would be aware and, as a result, would move backwards to re-establish his personal space. The winner of this (admittedly childish) game was the one who got the wallflower to do a complete backwards lap of the room without being rumbled. Of course, I'm no longer proud of my still-unbeaten record for a backwards lap of the bar by an unsuspecting fellow cadet, but this game does demonstrate how we can be influenced at a subconscious level to act. This can of course be applied to those who are trying to intimidate you. As they encroach into your personal space, understand what they are doing and stand your ground. It will feel uncomfortable at first but, because it is no longer happening unconsciously, you will be better able to deal with the encroachment. I have even seen people deliberately lean towards an intimidator to give them a taste of their own medicine.

87 Body language liars (how to spot people faking it)

As we've already discussed, interpreting body language is difficult. So, straight off the bat, it is worth saying that spotting a liar is not going to be easy. Even trained professionals such as policemen and customs officers who regularly encounter people being deceptive can only spot about 50% of the lies told to them.

"Behaviour in the human being is sometimes a defence, a way of concealing motives and thoughts, as language can be a way of hiding your thoughts and preventing communication."
(American psychologist Abraham Maslow, 1908–1970)

Throughout the previous sections, we repeatedly highlighted the need to accumulate a congruence of body cues before making a judgement. Well, when trying to sniff out a liar, you're looking for a lack of congruence of body cues. This is because liars tend to fake some of their non-verbal communications but are not skilled enough to fake all of them. They also tend to exaggerate the ones they can fake.

Lies work because the clues that give them away are extremely subtle. In fact, they are almost invisible to the untrained eye. This is because the "training course" for liars is pretty comprehensive. We are all taught to lie from an early age, predominantly for social convention. At six, we put on that fake smile for the auntie who smells of cats. Just a few years later, we're all experts at showing surprise and delight at presents as the buyer watches us unwrap. Then, we're pretending to like food we'd rather not eat to appease the cook. And, a few years after that, we're telling our boss that his suit doesn't make him look like a pimp. They're just the white lies. We'll have woven dozens of "black" ones into our lives too by then. However, the cards aren't stacked wholly in favour of the liars. There's one key point in the detectors' favour. The severity of the lie is directly proportional to the strength of the signals given off. This means that if a person is delivering, or being quizzed about, a serious lie (i.e. one leading to severe consequences if detected), he is far more likely to exhibit observable signs, particularly of the flight or fight response.

When a person is involved in serious deception, he will feel as though his mouth has suddenly become dry. As a result, his voice may waver or crack, and he will swallow more. It is a common misconception that people who do not hold eye contact are being deceptive or those who look you in the eye are telling the truth. This is not the case. Liars, con-artists and sociopaths learn very quickly to look you in the eye while being deceptive. Also, people might look away for a number of other reasons, including cultural sensitivities, social inferiority and stress. So, it's far too simplistic to say a liar won't look you in the eye.

"Experience teaches you that the man who looks you straight in the eye, particularly if he adds a firm handshake, is hiding something."
(American author Clifton Fadiman, 1904–1999)

A person who is being deceptive or who is stressed (and that "or" is important) might also engage in eye-blocking (deliberately preventing himself from seeing, usually with his hands) as he subconsciously wills himself out of the situation. In other words, he will try to escape the awkward questioning or the stressful situation by metaphorically sticking his head in the sand. This is clearly the Ostrich Effect (see Section 63) at play. It's more common than you might think. Imagine being in a pub during an England versus Argentina match when the referee awards Argentina a penalty. From the instant the referee makes his decision, a high proportion of those around you will put their hands over their eyes. But an even higher proportion will probably put their hands over their mouths.

Mouth-blocking (covering or even just rubbing the mouth) is another activity a liar might do. Young children exhibit this behaviour most clearly. They will often cover their mouths completely with their hands after lying. It's like they're trying to keep the whopper inside. As you get older, you get more proficient at lying, but even an adult liar will give himself away by shortened versions of the mouth-block. A person who rests his chin on his hands, touching the corner of his mouth might also be performing a mouth-block. Interestingly, these traits also occur in someone who is withholding information as opposed to lying. He might think withholding information is not as serious as telling an outright porky (that would be Omissions Bias, see Section 62), but his subconscious won't feel the same way, and it will throw in some cues (which is quite fortunate for those trying to determine whether a person knows something or not). A liar might also touch his nose more. That's another common tell to be thrown in the mix.

As we have covered and will touch upon again, these are not just signs of lying. A mouth-guard gesture by someone listening to you could just imply they don't believe you or don't like you. It can be most disconcerting for a speaker to see his audience displaying mouth-guard gestures. If you're that speaker, and it's possible to do so, it would be advisable to stop and ask for feedback on what's been said so far. This can kill the issue they have with you, making them more receptive to the remainder of your presentation. If you're briefing dozens of people, they won't all be stroking their mouths in front of you, but the odd person might be. If that person is important enough to warrant it, a quick "Is everything okay, Jack? You're looking a little concerned" is a safe way to get him back on side or to ensure you're not digging yourself a deeper hole.

Quite often, a person being deceptive will try to distance himself from the lie by getting away from those questioning him or by building a physical barrier between him and his accuser. Moving a cup of tea between him and the accuser is one way. But, if you're the accuser and you're sitting opposite him, he's almost certainly going to put the cup of tea between you and him. I mean, where else is he going to put it? For this reason, a smart "interrogator" will move around to test whether the cup of tea is being placed naturally for convenience or subconsciously as a barrier. I once interviewed a soldier who we suspected belonged to a banned radical group. He denied any knowledge of the group. However, when I placed some of the group's propaganda found secreted in his room on the table, he subconsciously placed the glass of water he'd been toying with between me and the leaflets. Placing the glass between him and the leaflets would have been far more natural. It was such a clear example of barricading which, added to the mix of the other traits he was displaying, it gave me added confidence he was lying. And he was.

As discussed earlier, legs can be a good indicator of inner emotions, and they can add to the body-language "evidence" that someone is lying. Legs locked at the ankles or legs locked around chair legs (with the person sat as though braced for a crash) can show that an individual is withholding information. However, leg-crossing can mean other things. For example, a woman who crosses her knees and wraps one leg around the other in an ankle lock might just be showing signs of vulnerability or shyness rather than withholding information.

The main tells outlined above can indicate that a person is attempting to deceive. However, they might just be indicators that the person is stressed. I have spoken to numerous soldiers over the course of my career either on matters of a disciplinary nature or during security investigations, and most of them exhibit some or all of these behaviours. Some were lying, but the majority were not. They were just experiencing stress. Why? Quite simply, they would rather not be in front of an officer being given a grilling. You might be completely innocent, but the environment makes you feel uncomfortable nonetheless. That discomfort manifests itself as stress, and stress behaviours and lying behaviours are very similar. The trick is to link the behaviours to the questions you've asked and try to isolate the subjects that are causing the observable behaviours. To do this, it might be necessary to put your subject at ease or to wait a while before questioning him. This could reduce the stress signals.

When a military is at war, putting your accused at ease is not the done thing. Experience has taught soldiers that their enemy is far less guarded about withholding information while in a state of confusion or stress. So, soldiers don't want their captors to be stress free. They want them to blurt information while they're still in "shock of capture" (as it's called). Obviously, that's no setting for reducing stress signals, which means that detecting lying signals becomes virtually impossible in someone who's just been taken prisoner of war. (What the captors are attempting is to ensure the prisoner is too flustered to do anything more complex than tell the truth.) An occasion could arise when you might find it useful to question someone while they're still flustered (e.g. questioning a recently caught shoplifter or questioning an employee who's just delivered a pitch that went against your express direction). That's fine. Just don't expect to glean too much information from that person's body language other than him being stressed to the max.

88   Is he plotting against you?

There are no signals in body language that specifically indicate a person is plotting against you. It all happens at a far more basic level than that. For example, if someone is plotting against you, he is likely to show signs of dislike or contempt. Not looking at you while you're talking or looking at others while you're talking is a common indicator of dislike. Microgestures like flash sneering or sighing are also signs of dislike or contempt. Much like a liar's, a plotter's key gestures are unlikely to be congruent with his words. He might be able to fake some of his body language, but he's unlikely to be able to fake all of it. If his social veneer is friendly and these indicators are present and he would have something to gain by "throwing you under the bus", then you might have a plotter on your hands. We used to say that when someone like that pats you on the back, he's just conducting a reconnaissance for a knife.

(89) Can you make your body language lie?

Yes, but it's very difficult. Remember, you are programmed at a subconscious level to perform the cues that will give you away. A famous example of someone trying to hide their body language and failing is Richard Nixon. When the later-disgraced US president gave a well-rehearsed speech in front of the world about the reasons for the military incursions into Cambodia during the US-Vietnam War, the tone of his voice was smooth, and his body cues were all congruent with telling the truth. Well nearly. Some sharp-eyed cameraman spotted that Nixon had his fist clenched so tight his knuckles were white. Nixon was trying to keep a tight hold of his lie so no one else would detect it.

The biggest thing in your favour is not your ability to suppress the tells or deliver false ones, but the observer's inability to read them accurately. That will give you a lot of "plausible deniability" space to play in. He will never be sure from your body language alone that you're lying. You must keep your confidence in that idea.

The biggest danger you face is when someone knows just one or two body-language signals and takes them as gospel. For example, if you were to look top right just before telling your boss you're late because you ran over a cat, he might say: "That's a lie. You looked top right." As we've repeatedly covered, *one tell does not a fact make*. But, if your boss thinks it does, you've got quite a job on your hands to undermine his confidence (albeit unfounded confidence) in his own assessment.

90   A Final Word on Body Language

Reading body language is a useful skill once you have mastered it, but it is only one of the clubs in your golf bag of skills to help you read a situation. While a high proportion of our messages are non-verbal, as we've seen, reading that non-verbal part of the message accurately can be challenging. There are definitely advantages to be seized and influence to be exerted by reading and presenting body language, but do not expect it to be the silver bullet for all your problems. And it might seem an obvious point, but do not forget to concentrate on what is being said. You also need to analyse any arguments made for their logical and intellectual merits. There's a lot to be thinking about, but, if it were easy, everyone would be doing it.

See Through Statistics

91 An introduction to statistics

"A statistician can have his head in an oven and his feet in ice, and he will say that on the average he feels fine."
(Anon)

Statistics is the science that deals with collecting, classifying, analysing and interpreting numerical information. The findings from all that activity are also called *statistics*. So, *statistics* (the science) creates *statistics* (the results). In the next few sections, we're going to be talking about how the former can be tweaked to ensure the latter supports a specific claim.

Statistics are the lifeblood of private companies, politicians and governments. They all use statistics to influence you and to manipulate your actions. For example, they will use them to persuade you to make investment decisions, to encourage you to buy their products, or to show you they are tough on crime or skilled at managing the economy. From their perspectives, statistics are great, because they look like irrefutable evidence. However, just like words, numbers can be used to show whatever the author wants them to show. Manipulative companies and individuals have become highly adept at spinning statistics to make the "facts" look more favourable to them. The next sections will show the key techniques they use (and which you can use if you're prepared to be a baddy in the statistics game) to spin numbers to support their arguments. If you're only prepared to be a goody, the next sections will offer an insight into how to present numbers safely and, more importantly, how to unpick others' statistics.

92 **You can't trust the experts**

We all use statistics to simplify and summarise our world. I ran 6 miles yesterday. My car does 16 mpg. I live 2.5 miles from a train station. I earn the company average of £29,000 a year. These are all statistics. If we were close friends, you might question some of the statistics I've just given you. "Do you mean the woods run? That is not 6 miles. It's about 4.5", you might say. But, because we're not close, you cannot challenge my statistics. That's a pretty obvious point I've just made, but there was a reason. You are far less likely to challenge statistics on a subject you know little about, especially if the person presenting them seems like an authority on it. If someone who sounds pretty authoritative (e.g. a political analyst, an MP, a doctor, a professor) makes a point on a subject that is not well known to the general population (e.g. a scientific research study, a medical breakthrough) or on a complex subject (e.g. the economy, global warming), we tend to be far less critical of their assertions than we should be. This is related to the idea that people stop thinking when they're told something by someone in authority (see Section 71). Those authoritative types know this, and, boy, are they milking it. Lots and lots of them are manipulating their statistics to suit their aims.

"I gather, young man, that you wish to be a Member of Parliament. The first lesson that you must learn is, when I call for statistics about the rate of infant mortality, what I want is proof that fewer babies died when I was Prime Minister than when anyone else was Prime Minister. That is a political statistic."
(Sir Winston Churchill 1874–1965)

"Statistics: The only science that enables different experts using the same figures to draw different conclusions."
(American humorist Evan Esar, 1899–1995)

93   Telling just half the story

Before we look at the techniques used to manipulate statistics, let's remind ourselves of how an argument is composed.

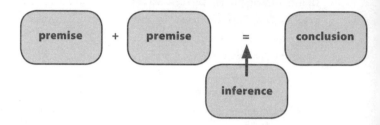

All too often, a company presenting a statistic will omit (either deliberately or unknowingly) at least one premise that ought to be included in its argument. As a result of leaving out this premise, the inference (i.e. how the company got to its conclusion) is likely to be meaningless and its conclusion is very likely to be false.

Here's a simple example:

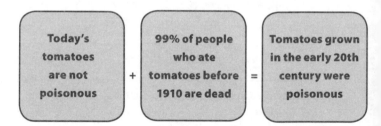

Clearly this is nonsense. Common sense (and a basic grasp of maths and human mortality) tells you that old age killed off the pre-1910 tomato eaters, not the tomatoes. The premise "Most humans don't live beyond 100" has been omitted from this argument. That missing premise is known as a "confounding variable". A confounding variable is one that distorts the relationship between two other variables. Put simply, when people present statistics, they don't always consider everything they should. There are often hidden influencers. Let's look at another argument with an obvious hidden influencer.

"Men who have survived two or more heart attacks almost never die from lung cancer. Therefore, heart attacks improve your lung health."

In this case, there is another confounding variable that derails the "multiple heart attacks improve your lungs" conclusion. Clearly, most of those men die of another heart attack.

Sometimes, however, the confounding variables are harder to spot:

"During the summer holidays, one in three drivers involved in traffic accidents tested positive for marijuana. Therefore, marijuana is causing people to drive recklessly."

There are several significant confounding variables in this example, but here is a key one: People will test positive for marijuana for 30 days after taking it. So, if I took marijuana three weeks ago and had an accident, I would be one of those drivers who tested positive, but the marijuana would almost certainly have had nothing to do with the accident. However, if an upstanding member of society (let's call him "Outraged of Tunbridge Wells") believes marijuana is a pernicious influence on today's youth, he can use this statistic to blame marijuana for a high percentage of car crashes and to support his argument for stiffer sentencing. If this were a real example, we would have cause and effect linked not by scientifically supported evidence but by an illusion of evidence using statistics. As we will see, this is a common use of statistics.

Of course, I would not argue against the notion that driving under the influence of marijuana is an issue that needs to be addressed, but the point to be made here is that simple statistics in support of a bold conclusion are easily challenged. You can almost go on forever challenging statistics like these. I bet almost 90% of those involved in the traffic accidents would have proved positive for coffee. What are we supposed to conclude from that? Coffee causes more accidents than marijuana? What about the reverse logic? Two thirds of those involved in the accidents did not prove positive for marijuana. Therefore, logically, these statistics could show it is twice as safe to drive under the influence of marijuana than not. That's nonsense of course. To understand the significance of the statistics presented, we would need to know a few baseline figures like the percentage of the driving population which would test positive for marijuana routinely (i.e. before having a crash).

This is a simple example, and, already, we've rubbished the inference and the conclusion by identifying other confounding variables or by highlighting why the inference is biased (e.g. marijuana is a cause when 33% proved positive, but coffee isn't a cause when 90% proved positive).

The point here is that statistics can be attacked easily, and one of the best ways to do it is to identify the confounding variables that the originator left out.

One last example. There's a theory out there that more crimes are committed during a full moon than during other phases of the moon. It's certainly a statistic that is believed by lots of policemen on the beat, and it's been backed up on more than one occasion by crime-database analysis. Surely, there can only be one explanation: it's the inner werewolf in us all. A full moon obviously makes us all go a little bit crazy. It is, after all, where the word lunatic comes from. Well, can a full moon make us all go a bit mad?

As an ex-soldier, I know that going on night-time patrol during a full moon is a bad thing. Well, it's good a thing to see where you are going, but it's a bad thing for remaining undetected. Statisticians who have studied this lunar effect (or the Transylvanian effect as it's also known) are divided as to whether the rise in crime rate during a full moon is a statistical anomaly (probably caused by a small dataset – more on that later) or because more criminals are seen plying their trade in the increased moonlight.

Now, if someone stood up publicly and presented the "inner werewolf" idea and backed it up with some very comprehensive statistics collected across every police force on the planet for the last hundred years, his presentation would be debunked instantly as soon as you raised the better-light-conditions idea. That's the power of finding confounding variables in others' statistics. It's also one of the dangers of spinning statistics to support your arguments.

94 They're not lies. They're bullshit

"Lots of the statistics you see every day are bullshit."

They're not my words. In his essay "On bullshit", the eminent Professor Harry G. Frankfurt of Harvard states: *"Bullshitters aim primarily to impress and persuade their audiences, and in general don't care if their statements are true. While those deliberately lying need to know the truth in order to hide it, bullshitters, interested solely in advancing their own agendas, are uninterested in the truth of a statement."* He concludes: *"Bullshit is a greater enemy of the truth than lies are"*. In a nutshell, Professor Frankfurt is saying that bullshit is designed to convince you of a point, regardless of the truth. If you think about it, being a bullshitter is quite convenient, especially if you can't bear to think of yourself as a liar. As a bullshitter, you're not a liar, because you need to be sure of the truth to lie. As a bullshitter, you're just trying to get others to adopt your position, and what's so wrong with that? And you don't even have to call yourself a bullshitter. You can call yourself something else, like a marketeer or a public-relations executive. But definitely not a liar.

This has a serious and somewhat sinister side, as this careless or deliberate omission of facts to influence statistics has been used to sell all manner of drugs, potions and talismans. And, to put it in the words of Professor Frankfurt, *"It's all bullshit."*

95 Using the law of large numbers

"The National Lottery is a tax on people who don't understand statistics."
(Anon)

Most British adults have been in a bookmaker's at some point. For most of us, it was just the annual flutter on a horse at the Grand National or a quick bet on who'll win this year's Six Nations Rugby. However, lots of us like to bet more seriously, be it on horses or dogs or at casinos. So, can you beat the bookies if you keep going to the betting shop and get really good at it? In a word, no. Returning to the bookies day after day is just a sure way to turn your money into their money.

Let's have a quick look at how the bookies are faring. In the first half of 2012, the British bookmakers William Hill made nearly £70 million in profits from online operations alone. Since it started in 1994, the National Lottery has taken in over £100 billion and raised over £28 billion for good causes, which is a gigantic sum. These figures tell us that betting is a hugely profitable enterprise for those that run it. But, given that lots of people win huge amounts on games of chance like the National Lottery and in casinos, how can gambling companies ensure they make money in the midst of all this randomness and apparent good fortune? Aren't they just gamblers too? Well, not really. The reason they're not is the Law of Large Numbers.

"The gambling known as business looks with austere disfavour upon the business known as gambling."
(American satirist Ambrose Bierce, 1842–1914)

The Law of Large Numbers states: "The result will revert to the mean value in the long run". More simply put, as you keep playing a game of chance, any good or bad luck you've had is slowly cancelled out, and you will move closer to an average amount of luck (the mean). Here's an example. When you toss a coin, each toss has a 50% chance of being heads. Over three tosses, it is possible they will all come up heads. This is less likely but still possible over five tosses… or ten. It's still possible but extremely unlikely over 100 tosses. The more times you flip, the closer your result will be to the expected value of 50% heads and 50% tails. Casinos know this, and weight their games by a small margin in their favour. For example, in roulette, the house profit margin is only between 2.7 and 5.3%. That might not sound a lot, but, in the long term (and remember we could be talking about millions of individual bets), the Law of Large Numbers will prevail, and the casino will come out on top. Provided they can keep us playing, it's guaranteed cash for them. The gambling business doesn't gamble any more than any other business.

Let's take this opportunity to say a few words about lotteries. In our National Lottery (where your selection of six numbers must match the six drawn from a pool of 49 to win the jackpot), the odds of winning the jackpot are about 1 in 14 million. So, if you bought a lottery ticket every week, you should only expect to win the jackpot once every 269,000 years. Good luck with that – you'll need it. To put this in perspective, you currently have about a 1 in 30,000 chance of being killed in a road accident. Looking at those odds, I would probably spend my lottery stake on a crash helmet. Most of us know the odds of winning the lottery are infinitesimal, but it doesn't stop us playing. Well, we can thank our Availability Bias (see Section 41) for that. We've all seen stories about lottery winners, and they play a far more significant role in our decision-making than they should. (Personally, I like to think of it as a way of giving money to good causes and funding national-level sport initiatives, and that provides enough impetus for me to yield to my Availability Bias and have a pop at the lottery.)

96 It's all relative

Unfortunately, statistical data is a bit like play dough.

"Facts are stubborn things, but statistics are more pliable."
(American author and humorist Mark Twain, 1835–1910)

Statistics can be moulded into many shapes depending on the whim of the user. And, unless you're looking carefully, it's often difficult to spot the manipulation.

Let's imagine there's a new cancer drug out that, if taken every day, will reduce the risk of stomach cancer by 50%. Fantastic, sign me up you'd say. But, unfortunately and as usual, that's not the whole story. If the cancer rate is 1 in 50 of the population (2 in 100), then the drug will only work for 1 in 100 people. Suddenly, that doesn't sound so impressive. The "50%" describes the situation in relative terms, whereas the "1 in a 100" describes it in absolute terms.

Let's look at another one. "CT scans on children triple the risk of cancer". What? That sounds terrible. I will admit it doesn't look great, but it's the relative increase. Let's say the risk of cancer is 1 in 10,000. The risk after a CT scan is therefore 3 in 10,000. When described in absolute terms, it sounds far less of a problem, especially when you consider that the CT scan is probably being done to detect something eminently more serious like a tumour, a haemorrhage or bone trauma.

Remember, when it comes to increases in risk, you could be talking about very small increases indeed despite words like "a 300% increase". Often, the headlines are not there to inform you but to shock you into an action, like buying insurance or a newspaper. And, it's for that last reason that journalists in particular like relative comparisons.

Journalists also like trimming their headlines for effect. I once saw a newspaper heading which read: "Bacon increases the risk of dying by 20%". Now, I like bacon, so I read the article. Quite early on, it wandered into other areas of a "typical" bacon-eater's life and

– from the perspective of the title – it quickly started hinting at some confounding variables (see Section 93). With all the padding removed, the article basically offered a comparison for the mortality rate of someone who has a penchant for bacon sarnies, drinks too much, smokes too much and does no exercise with that of a Royal Marine Commando. The headline "fat lazy smoker likely to die earlier than non-smoking fitness fanatic" doesn't quite have the same selling power. What's probably more interesting is that the relative difference between the two was only 20%. Hang on, isn't the risk of dying 100% for everyone? What does that figure even mean? Do they mean dying before the age of 40? 60? 70? Of a heart attack? Of food poisoning? Of a tape worm? Remember, as soon as you present some statistics, be ready to have them scrutinised.

Back to winning the lottery. A 1-in-14-million chance. That's really quite depressing. Never mind. Think of it like this: if you've been having two goes every week since it started, then so far you've been nearly 2,000 times more likely to win it than someone who just had a quick one-pound flutter during the first week. And, that number is going up every week!

(Unfortunately, this does not mean your chances are improving. (See Gamblers' Fallacy, Section 74.) It just means you've had nearly 2,000 1-in-14-million chances.)

97 Cherry picking

Another technique employed by statisticians is cherry-picking. This is Confirmation Bias (see Section 47) at its best... er, worst. Cherry-picking occurs when a person makes a claim about a subject and then selects only the tests which support the claim or ignores any translation of the data which could refute the claim. This technique is particularly prevalent in the world of nutritional supplements, where commercially driven scientists have become adept at finding evidence to support the marketeers who peddle potions and supplements designed, or – more correctly – marketed, to cure all ills.

"A common cold if given proper treatment will be cured in seven days but left untreated it will hang around for a week."
(Common saying)

Marketeers have been using cherry-picked tests for years to sell us stuff, ranging from the notion that Vitamin C prevents the common cold (in spite of the numerous medical studies proving that it doesn't) to the notion that root vegetables and lemon rind prevent HIV. I'm always up for a bit of blackcurrant-flavoured "Lemsip" on the off chance that Vitamin C does actually help a cold, but clearly not all the marketeers' assertions are so harmless. The root-vegetables-and-lemon-rind "cure" and other similar quack "remedies" have been responsible for hundreds of thousands of deaths from AIDS in South Africa over the last 10 years. When I say "quack", don't imagine some backstreet snake-oil merchant. It seems some of the big drug companies have been cherry-picking too. GlaxoSmithKline (one of the world's largest pharmaceutical companies) was fined a whopping $1.9 billion in July 2012 for misselling drugs, and numerous pharmaceutical companies have been caught bending or outright falsifying statistical data in an attempt to prise your cash from your grasp.

Some of the tricks employed in spinning statistics are blatantly underhand. An obvious one is only reporting test results that support your claim. That's pretty bad, but companies have also been caught duplicating positive data in different scientific papers to make it look as if several studies have reached the same conclusion. Another ploy they use is to stop a study as soon as they've gained sufficient positive data. In other words, they're not letting the Law of Large Numbers kick in. They know that by continuing the trial, the likelihood of their positive result being down to chance would increase.

This stuff is all pretty dishonest, but the worst manipulation of all is suppressing negative data on drugs shown to be harmful – even to the point of suing doctors attempting to highlight a problem.

So, how prevalent is Confirmation Bias? Well, back in 2003, it was found that trials run by drug companies were four times more likely to give a favourable outcome than a study carried out independently.

Globally, pharmaceutical industries are worth £150 billion a year. And some of that is because they've been looking at the data from their trials through their profit-first goggles.

98   Saying it with pictures

We all know that a picture is worth a thousand words. We all know that graphs are a great way to portray complex information, and we all know that graphs are a powerful way to deliver a message. We tend to be more trusting of graphs than words. After all, seeing is believing. But don't think you're in safe territory when you're presented with a graph. There are tricks to spin those too.

Changing the baseline

A common trick to make a result look more favourable is to change the baseline when presenting the data graphically. Let's imagine someone were making a case that Brits are not ripped off at the petrol pumps compared to Americans. In support of his argument, he might present a graphic like this:

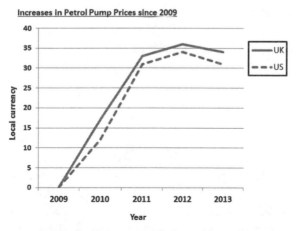

Statistics from US Department of Labour and petrolprices.com

Now, this graph doesn't tell the whole story. Far from it. For a start, the US line and the UK line are plotted against different baselines. The term "local currency" means that one is plotted against pence while the other is plotted against cents. In fact, over the period 2009-2013, the value of a British penny hovered around 1.6 cents. So, if both lines were plotted against the same currency, the US line would be about a third lower on the y axis than it is at the moment. Now, that graph would be far more likely to enrage Brits. But that's only half the story with this graph. This real underhandedness of this graph is that it leads you to assume that prices in the UK and US have been generally equal, but that too is way off the mark. In fact, over the period shown, there was never a time when the UK price per litre was not considerably more than double the US price per litre. But this graph looks to hide that fact too by showing just the "Increases in petrol pump prices". This graph tells you nothing other than US and UK prices tend to follow the same trend, which is of course the price of oil. But, unless you're prepared to scrutinise it, it could easily make you think we're all paying about the same for our petrol. And look at the sources of these statistics. They are very credible indeed. Of course, they're not the ones at fault here. It's the devious git who decided to change the baselines on us.

Truncating the axis

Truncating the axis of a graph is another way to improve the impact of a statistic. By doing this, a 1% difference can be made to look colossal.

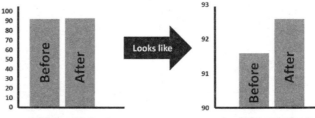

Without truncating the axis   With truncating the axis

Of course, truncating the axis could be a genuine act to make a graph more useable or simply to save space on the page. However, be aware that this technique is routinely used to exaggerate an effect. So, if you spot a truncated axis, put your "suspicion glasses" on and give yourself an extra second to scrutinise the figures more closely. (Conversely, expanding an axis is a good way of lessening the impact of a statistic.)

Using 3D and perspective

In a similar vein, it is possible to change the impact of a pie chart by showing it in 3D as opposed to 2D and by exploiting perspective (the closer something is, the bigger it looks) to make a thin slice of pie look like a veritable feast

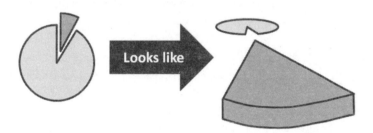

Now, you might think no one would fall for such a blatant trick and that those presenting such a graphic would be running the risk of exposing their biases if they used this technique. Well, that's a fair thought, but it's not accurate, I'm afraid. If you keep an eye out for this method of making something look more substantial than it is, you'll encounter it far more than you might have imagined. People will do anything to strengthen their messaging, especially when the raw figures don't really say too much in their favour.

99 Using unfair questions

Answer this question with either "yes" or "no":

"Have you stopped shoplifting these days?"

It doesn't matter how you answer that question, you're condemned as either an active shoplifter or an ex-shoplifter. (Next time you're at the pub, shout across the bar and ask your mate if he's all clear at the clinic. It's an old one, but it's still a fairly useful line to have in your back pocket during a round of banter.)

Now, the shoplifting and clinic questions were obviously biased, but some trials and polls feature questions which are far more subtly biased. Asking biased questions is another way to twist a result. Look at these questions:

"Do you think the UK should leave the European Union?"
"Do you think the UK should remain part of the European Union?"

Because of an inner desire to avoid confrontation, we are far more inclined to "agree" than "disagree" when presented with questions of this nature. In other words, we are more likely to answer "yes" to these questions. With regard to any potential referendum, this is going to be a real issue, and I suspect the debate about which question is to be asked will become a heated issue as any referendum draws nearer. I personally think the human desire to "agree" with such questions is so strong it will trump the British people's thoughts on whether they want to be in or out not. In other words, the result of the referendum will depend on which question is asked. Why do I think that? Well, on balance, I think I want the UK to remain part of the EU, but I also really want to answer "yes" to the first question. Of course, the bias could be negated by posing both questions, requiring people to answer "yes" to one and "no" to the other. But that's just messy. It's one to watch.

(100) # What does "average" mean?

The use of averages to beguile and confound is another common trick
with statistics. Do you remember "mean", "median" and "mode" from
school Mathematics classes? Most people will take the word "average"
to represent the "mean average". That's when you add up all the
numbers and divide by how many numbers there are.

Here's a set of numbers:

1, 7, 2, 1, 3

With this set, the mean average is 2.8 (the sum 14 divided by 5).

But the word "average" could also be used to represent the median
average. That's the middle-ranked value in the series. To get the
median average, you line them all up in order and pick the middle
one. Here, it's 2 (which is the middle value in the ordered list of 1, 1,
2, 3, 7). (If there is an even number of numbers in the set and so no
obvious middle one, add the middle two, and then divide by two.)

   Lastly, the word "average" could be referring to the mode average.
That's the most frequently seen number in the set. In this case, it's 1
(which features twice).

   When we're talking about a normal distribution of values (or "bell
shaped" distribution as it's known; e.g. a typical school test, where
a couple of people do really well, a couple do really badly, some do
pretty well or badly, and most are somewhere in the middle), then the
mean, median and modes averages will be approximately the same.
However, when we're talking about a random distribution of values,
the type of average chosen can dramatically affect the value that is
presented as the "average".

Look at these test results:

**8%, 8%, 9%, 41%, 70%, 71%, 72%, 74%, 78%, 81%, 82%,
87%, 88%, 89%, 90%, 92%**

With the 9% score, I could claim that my score was above average. (I would, of course, be using the mode average when making this claim.)

And what about this claim:

"Half of all doctors are below average in competence."

With this claim, the mean average is being used. It's a true statement, but it's a meaningless one. Half of any normally distributed group you choose is below the mean average. But it still sounds bad. There's more fun you can have with this idea. For example, you can disguise the group you're talking about.

"Don't fly with Trower Airlines. It has been statistically proven that half of its pilots are below average."

Now, as we're talking about the mean average of all the pilots in Trower Airlines, that's a true but meaningless statistic. But, the connotation here is that a test has been done with every pilot of every airline. If that were actually true, it would not be a meaningless statistic. It would mean Trower Airlines employs below-average pilots when compared with other airlines.

So, why do we need three different kinds of average? Let's take a quick look at each one.

Mean is the most common average, and it's the one that people will think you're talking about if you don't specify which average you're using. Mean average is useful when a central tendency or middle figure is needed, but its weakness is that is can be badly skewed by outliers. For example, it would be useful in measuring the average salary of a group of metal workers in a factory, but it would be less useful in measuring the average salary of everyone in the factory, because the factory owner's and executives' salaries would skew the mean figure. As a result, a senior manager could find himself on a "below average" wage.

Median is useful when the distribution has outliers. These are numbers outside the normal set that will skew the mean but will not affect the median. For example, if we were to look at the average age of a school class, the mean will be skewed by the age of the teacher. The median, however, would give us a better idea of the age of the children.

Mode is useful when the things being compared do not have numeric values. If we wished to look at the average bank account held by a group, we could use the mode.

Don't forget the word "average" could have vastly different values for the same group depending on which average the author chooses. Don't think others won't spin this idea to their advantage. It will be used against you, so be on your guard.

Finally, before we leave averages, here's a quick word about ordinal sets (that's when data has been ranked in an order). When a newspaper publishes a list of the 10 best films, you cannot say that number 5 is the average "best film". You cannot create a mean from an ordinal set. Similarly, the top film is not three times better than the third film. There's no relationship between the numbers on the list other than how they're ordered. That seems like an obvious point, but as half the people reading this book are below average (compared to the other half of people reading this book), I thought I'd better spell it out.

(101) Ignoring facts and telling stories

After the London riots in 2011, a number of political commentators asserted that the youth of today were less law-abiding than the youth of 20 years ago and linked it to a general decline in morals across the country. Well, what does less law-abiding mean? Is this comment just referring to London or does it apply to the whole of England, or the whole of Britain? Terms like law-abiding and morality are difficult to put numbers against. How do you measure them? Well, a starting point might be to determine what is meant by youth (e.g. under 18) and to check whether the youth crime rate has increased in the last 20 years per head of population. However, that would take some real investigation, and a journalist with a looming deadline linked to tomorrow's print-run may not have the time to do the work. Instead, a generic statement (or news bite) that the journalist feels is right gets woven into the article. News bites based on intuition can trump research. For me, this idea always brings to mind a TV interview during which a senior police officer was getting a grilling for a recent spate of stabbings in London. The officer – who had clearly done his homework – repeatedly told the reporter that, in spite of the recent events, knife crime had been trending downwards for years and continued to do so (which the officer attributed to a range of police initiatives). The reporter wasn't listening, and he repeatedly harangued the officer for a lack of police action. To me, it looked obvious that the news bites on knife crime which had been circulating in recent weeks had trumped all research. At that time, if you'd asked anyone whether knife crime in London was up or down, it would have been hard to find anyone who thought it was reducing. In the public's mind, the easy-to-recall news headlines were trumping the real figures (see Availability Bias, Section 41). The point is this: Be pretty suspicious of the statistics you see in the papers, and don't believe everything you read. There are some notable biases in the news media (see Section 67 for a reminder).

"Trying to determine what is going on in the world by reading newspapers is like trying to tell the time by watching the second hand of a clock."
(American novelist Ben Hecht, 1893–1964)

Newspapers love news bites, and they can skew the truth. But, actually, I think we can live with that. Most people have learned to take the sensationalism presented in newspapers with a healthy degree of scepticism. However, there's something else going on which is far less palatable.

On slow news days, papers will sometimes use articles that have been spoon fed by companies' public relations departments. So, a headline like "70% increase in ice-cream sales over the heat wave" will probably have originated with a phone call from the ice-cream sellers' corporation. A 2001 study in Australia found that over 40% of the "news" in their newspapers was fed by PR departments. It's not news. It's advertising.

Also, there is a need to be wary of "independent reviews". It is a fairly common practice for product reviews to use company-delivered prose to pad out an article. I use online newspaper sites, and they often feature reviews on things like holidays, cars and houses. Even though these articles are not presented as adverts, they are often lifted directly from the vendor's advertisements and might even have a link to the vendor's website. Such articles are lazy journalism. It's far easier to cut and paste someone else's blurb about a product than to invest time and money on proper research for a proper review. And who's going to complain? Certainly not the paper's editor. He gets to fill column inches for next to nothing. And certainly not the vendor. He gets free advertising. And certainly not the reader. We're too trusting. It's a win-win-lose situation, and we're the losers.

Another thing to be wary of is news articles that give an overtly one-sided view. Sometimes news is not news but an agenda. There are plenty of pernicious journalists and columnists out there with an obvious bias towards an objective. Environmentalists are a great example. One of the broadsheets uses a senior member of Greenpeace to write articles. "Excellent", I hear you cry – someone who has a good grasp of the issues. Well, that's undoubtedly true, but it in no way translates to unbiased journalism. Anything such people write will be tainted with all the biases and preconceptions that environmentalists bring to the argument. It will also dampen, if not omit entirely, the counter argument. The same applies to business leaders and anyone else with an agenda to push. It is fine to express an opinion, but when this is presented as fact, it's not journalism – it's manipulation.

"People everywhere confuse what they read in newspapers with news."
(American journalist A. J. Liebling, 1904–1963)

So, apart from statistically dodgy news bites and advertising, what else do we wrap our fish and chips in? The answer to that is speculation. Most newspapers are not averse to just making stuff up. My personal favourite dates back to 2002. It was a double-page feature about Al Qaida and Osama Bin Laden's secret lair in Afghanistan. Bin Laden's headquarters were presented as a command centre that any James Bond villain would have been proud of. They stopped just short of including a shark tank and a huge laser. Now, if you've ever been to Eastern Afghanistan, you'll know that their report was devoid of any link to reality. For a while, Bin Laden was hiding in a cave complex, with some natural caves and some caves tunnelled out during the Russian occupation. However, his very rudimentary hideout was about as far from a 5-star "Dr Evil" HQ as it's possible to get. However, it's easy to understand why the article was printed. After all, the subject was topical, and something needed to be said. What was the alternative? An article describing the caves accurately? That would have been far harder to research from a central-London Starbucks and would have done almost nothing for the sales figures.

Lots of the defence- and terrorism-related stories in the news are riddled with speculation and outright fabrication, making many closer to fiction than fact. As it was my job for about 20 years, I'm quite comfortable with that assertion and lots of us in that arena can cite numerous examples. What worries me though is this. If you extrapolate those inaccuracies into the areas I don't know much about (e.g. economics or domestic politics), we're probably reading articles about those subjects that have been written with an equally cavalier approach to the truth.

We all know that today's papers will be tomorrow's fish-and-chips wrappers, but some of them don't deserve the delay. They would serve more purpose as today's fish-and-chips wrappers.

102 Ignoring the baseline

If you look up "baseline" in a dictionary, it will say something like "a starting point for a comparison" or, if it's a slightly posher dictionary, "a measurement, calculation or location used as a basis for comparison".

I like to think of the baseline as the <u>context</u> for a comparison. Things have to be compared in similar contexts, otherwise the comparison might be meaningless. For example, you can't claim the side wall of a building is taller than the rear wall if you measure one from the floor and the other from the foundations; you can't claim your village is safer than the town because there are fewer burglaries in the village each year; and you can't claim the residents of Nevada look after their cars better than those from Alaska because their cars last longer.

The elements being compared in each of these scenarios have different baselines. They cannot be compared accurately until the baselines are made similar or accounted for. So, to perform meaningful comparisons, you would have to measure both walls from the same point; do something like determine the number of burglaries in the village and town per household; and make some adjustments for the environmental effects on cars. Only then could useful comparisons be made. Ignoring the baseline is a common error when presenting statistics. Sometimes it's done accidentally, but often it's done intentionally. If you ignore the baseline, you can't really offer a true comparison.

"Ignoring the baseline is like comparing apples with motorbikes and Wednesdays."
(Wing Commander Alex Hicks, Ministry of Defence)

So, if you compare raw numbers without adjusting for baseline differences, you will not get a meaningful result. (If that suits your purposes, you could go for it – just make sure you have a plan for when your statistics are ridiculed.) Look at this example:

"Fewer policeman on the beat in Edinburgh than London shows the Government favours the South over the North in the fight against crime."

It's not going to surprise many people that London has more police officers than Edinburgh, given that London has a much greater population. Of course, a more reasonable comparison would be the number of policemen per head of population (and perhaps the originator of this statement meant that), but even that would be open to scrutiny as visitor numbers probably ought to be a consideration too. (With about 30 million overnight visitors a year, London gets approximately 10 times as many as Edinburgh.) Statistical comparisons are offered all the time using raw numbers or inappropriate baselines.

(103) # Making emotive comparisons

Some environmental groups have become highly proficient at spinning data to make their assertions more emotive. A common tendency is to present statistics that cover a long period of time to derive figures that fit what they want to say. For example, in 2010, Greenpeace attacked the Indonesian conglomerate Sinar Mas with the claim: *"an area one third the size of Belgium has been deforested since the 80s."* In the same attack, Greenpeace stated: *"...over the next 150 years, the company's plantations on peat land will emit twice the annual Greenhouse Gases (GHG) emissions of Germany"*. Without the time spans, these two statistics are far less emotive. The first could read: *"Each year across Indonesia, 1% of the area of Belgium is deforested."* The second could read: *"Each year, the peat lands will emit 1.3% of Germany's GHG emissions."* (It must be said the time span of "150 years" is not a random number. It is the number of years deforested peat land will emit GHG if left to dry out.)

When someone presents a statistic that looks as though it's designed to influence, I would advise closer scrutiny. You may find that the underlying facts themselves are questionable. In the case of this argument, Greenpeace suggests the GHG impact by deforestation is 18–24%, but others – with no apparent agenda – assess it as 6–8%. And why did they choose Belgium? This is also part of the emotive reporting. Belgium covers 30,528 sq km, but Indonesia covers 1,904,569 sq km. If they had used something the same size as Indonesia, the result would have been less "impressive". Belgium is small but well known. It sounds bigger than it is. And why Germany? Well, that was also carefully selected in this statistic. Germany is big, and it's renowned for being industrially active, but its GHG emissions are impressively low.

It's a good idea when presenting statistics to use values that people can understand. Telling people sizes in "football pitches" as opposed to hectares is useful, or, for big areas, using a comparison like "the size of Wales" is also useful for British people. However, when those presenting statistics start using seemingly random descriptors (like

Belgium and Germany), be mindful that you're very likely looking at statistics that are designed to be emotive. They're meant to influence not to inform.

Of course, this is a technique you can use to add impact too. For most of us who don't live there, Middlesex and Sussex sound like they're about the same size. However, Middlesex is about 600 sq km and Sussex is about 3,800 sq km. So, if you needed to offer a comparison on a 3,600 sq km area, you could (depending on who you're presenting it to) achieve more impact by saying "an area six times the size of Middlesex" as opposed to "an area nearly the size of Sussex". The trick is find something that creates the impact you want due to public perception as opposed to fact. Here's another example. Wembley Arena can seat about 12,500 people. However, Wembley Stadium houses 105,000 people (seating and standing). So, if you were to say *"Each month, our visitors could fill Wembley Arena twice"*, you're saying you get 25,000 visitors a month. However, lots of Brits' minds would flash to an image of Wembley Stadium, and your boast would seem far more impressive. In Britain, the M1, M2, M3 and M4 motorways are 194 miles, 26 miles, 59 miles and 190 miles respectively. It's easy to see how using the M2 in a comparison might be more effective, especially for people who live near the M1 or the M4 and who don't know much about the M2. They'll just assume it's a comparable size to their local motorway. Even if they don't, I doubt they'll realise it's about an eighth as long. It's not lying. It's just a careful selection of comparators for impact. Spot these comparators or employ them… whatever works for you.

(104) Using data from a biased sample pool

A couple of years ago, I underwent physiotherapy for an injury sustained while running. The military physio told me that the majority of the injuries treated by physios were sports-related. Now, if you were conducting a survey on injuries treated by physiotherapists across the UK, you'd quickly spot that her assertion was biased as she worked on a generally younger, more active slice of the population. By itself, her data would not be useful in determining the types of injuries that physiotherapists treat across the UK. That might seem pretty obvious, but sometimes bias in the sample population is a little harder to spot.

A study of street fights in which someone was killed found that 90% of the fights were started by the person who died. Can you see an issue with sampling here? Here's a clue. If a person kills someone in a fight that he started (i.e. it was not self-defence), he would be charged with either manslaughter or murder. Therefore, any lawyer who doesn't advise or drop hints to the survivor that he needs to claim self-defence probably isn't the sort of lawyer you'd want representing you in such a case. So, to determine the percentage of fatal fights started by the person who died, you can't ask the survivors of fatal street brawls who started their fight. That's a biased sample. If you removed the bias from the sample by trawling through court records to determine how many of the fight instigators were the ones killed, I suspect the figure would be considerably lower than 90%. (Common sense alone tells you that people tend not to start fights with those who could kill them.)

Sometimes, the bias in a sample population is even harder to spot. One to keep an eye out for is online polls and phone-in surveys. They are usually biased because those taking part are self-selected. They usually have an interest (and therefore a bias) in the questions being asked. I can remember a few years ago David Beckham being named Britain's best-dressed man in an online poll. That seems fair enough. What's interesting though is that he was also ranked as Britain's worst-dressed man in the same poll. The polls just confirmed that Beckham was the most-talked-about celebrity on the lists. I can also remember Donald Duck winning a "who should be the next Prime Minister" on a pre-election online poll. Those taking part clearly found the funny answer more attractive than the sensible options.

It's common for the silent majority not to cast a vote or to pick up the phone, because the subject simply doesn't bother them that much. Just before the Queen's Golden Jubilee in the summer of 2002, there were a number of newspaper polls which suggested that a large proportion of the population didn't want a Royal Family. The papers started to believe their own polls and predicted the Jubilee would be a non-event. What they'd failed to account for was the silent majority who didn't bother with the polls. (They had been influenced by looking at figures deriving largely from those anti-monarchists with a strong enough interest in the issue to complete the poll). The Golden Jubilee was a massive event. It was marked with large-scale events and widespread public displays of affection for the Queen across the country. I can remember the scene along The Mall. It was a turbulent sea of waving flags from Buckingham Palace to Admiralty Arch. Clearly, this was a self-selected pool of millions of monarchists. But there were so many on The Mall and so much country-wide activity, it definitely raised my suspicions that the participants in the pre-Jubilee polls had been self-selected, making the sample pool biased. So, even though the pre-event polls predicted a damp squib, it was the silent majority that was shouting on the day.

(105) Making deceptive claims

Sometimes, it's not the figures that have been doctored to manipulate you. It's the words presented with the figures. Let's have a quick look at how some motor insurers present their statistics. One particular gem I found online showed a picture of a severe car crash with the title "The dangers of driving". The advert stated that car crashes cause 2,538 deaths per year and that "1 in 200 people are killed in car crashes". (I'm now definitely off to buy that crash helmet and to hide under my bed.) Unfortunately, fear sells and, like all commercially driven statisticians, the people who presented these figures know it.

I thought that "200" figure looked a bit low, so I went trawling for some statistics to back it up. I couldn't find any. So, did they just make up that "1 in 200 people are killed in car crashes"? Possibly. But, in my experience, these people are usually a little bit more conscientious than just inventing figures. So, were they spinning the truth with their language? Probably, and this is my suspicion.

Let's look at those words again: "1 in 200 people are killed in car crashes." What does that mean? Does it mean the cause of death for 1 in 200 of us will be a car crash? Well, it could mean that. But, it could also mean that 1 in 200 of us will die if we're in a car crash. The English is ambiguous.

I fully suspect the marketeers for this insurance company know that most people won't take their words to mean "in modern life, there is a 1 in 200 chance that your cause of death will be a car crash". They know that most people will take those words to mean that "In 21st century life, you have 1 in 200 chance of your life ending as a result of a car crash". They also know that most people will just take their statistics as read without questioning what they really mean. These statisticians almost certainly didn't lie. They just gave us enough room with their words to let us make up our own meaning.

Here's another example. Over 90% of consumers think that "50% extra free" means half of what they're buying is free. It doesn't. "50% extra free" means 33% of what you're buying is free. Do you remember the Coke-cans example from Section 72 (Base Rate

Fallacy)? If you buy six cans of Coke labelled as "50% extra free", only two of the cans are free, not three. (It's because the original pack had four cans, and 50% of the original amount is two cans.) The marketeers are not lying to you. If you look at a bag of sweets which has "50% extra free", the small print will say something like "300g for the price of 200g". However, they know what they're doing. They know you're not going to read the small print. They know that you'll think "50%..." means half. Figures can easily be presented to influence.

Incidentally, "buy one, get one free" equates to 100% extra free. That means you pay half price for both the items. Hang on, half price means 100% free? For many of us, that looks counter-intuitive at first glance because the word "half" goes with 50% not 100%, and that's the space the marketeers play in.

As well as deliberately using words to deceive you, marketeers will also employ some of the methods we covered in Chapter 2. Look out for words like these:

- *"Scientists have proven it will make your skin smoother."*
 (This is an appeal to an unnamed authority. It makes the claim seem more believable. Buyers should ask "Whose scientists?" See Appeal to Authority Fallacy, Section 71.)

- *"It contains polypeptides which help the cells communicate."*
(This is obfuscation. It makes the claim more believable because the buyers trust that the writer knows what he's talking about. See Obfuscation Fallacy, Section 73.)

- *"Formulated with active Dead Sea minerals, our vitamin E-infused nourishing cream is enriched with ivory-coloured Shea butter and organic jojoba oil for continuous hydration."*
(Descriptions like this and a high-price tag play to the expectation effect. See Expectation Effect, Section 113.)

106 Spinning statistics with a small sampling pool

"8 out of 10 cats preferred it". That looks pretty conclusive, but what if the sample was only 10 cats, and it was just a statistical anomaly? (Small samples creating errors is the key point here – it's the opposite side of the coin to the Law of Large Numbers (see Section 95). But, what did those cats prefer the touted cat food to? How many other options were offered? What if they were hungry cats who would eat the first thing plonked in front of them? How did they even measure preference?) However it was done, it looks like a manipulated figure to me.

Using small sampling pools is a common way to achieve the results you need. Let's imagine I was trying to sell you a potion that guaranteed heads every time you tossed a coin:

"Guaranteed head every time you toss.
Watch.
See, a head.
Right, who wants some of this potion?"

Clearly, you wouldn't buy that potion until you'd seen the vendor flick at least a two dozen heads back to back. (Even then, you'd start questioning whether it was sleight of hand.) In this scenario, you wouldn't trust such a small sample because you fully understand the situation. However, we're far less likely to question a statistic when we're in unfamiliar ground, and lots of companies know this and are prepared to present statistics from small samples. A number of beauty companies selling products to make you look younger have been caught using this ploy, as have companies in the homeopathy circus. In fact, beauty-product marketing is riddled with claims that have been drawn from tiny sample sizes. The evidence supporting my "heads-every-time potion" is really no different from that supporting many of the other big-name beauty products being peddled. The difference is that buyers are usually not aware of the sample size, they trust the scientists' claims, they want their claims to be true, and they don't have a good grasp of what the components in the product are.

If you read a scientific paper describing intellectually rigorous and repeatable (a key point) tests, you might come across something called a P-value. A P-value gives a percentage chance of the answer being arrived at by chance alone (at least, that's a good enough definition for our purposes). Obviously, the lower the percentage, the better. Quite simply, a P-value of 1% means there is a 1 in a 100 chance that the result was "luck". Because of the way the Law of Large Numbers works (see Section 95), the larger the sample size, the lower the P-value.

(107) A final word on statistics

Every day you are bombarded with statistics. Don't forget that lots of them are presented not to inform you but to influence you to buy something or to adopt someone else's point of view. And never forget that some of the worst offenders are the respectably titled experts who operate in fields you know nothing about. These people are actively spinning statistics to influence you. It's their job. So, we all need to be far more sceptical about statistics. Even if the statistics are not outright lies or obviously biased, there's a fair chance they're being presented by people ignorant of or indifferent to their accuracy, i.e. bullshitters. Also, remain mindful that when you use statistics (and often your audience will expect objective empirical evidence to back your arguments), you expose your reasoning to attack. Don't be afraid to use statistics, just make sure they've been properly researched and are intellectually defensible. The challenge is to have factored in all the variables before you present your statistics. It's quite hard for someone to check your underlying data. It's far easier for them to find a confounding variable. (Think back to all the data supporting the lunar effect. It's great data. It just has nothing to do with our inner werewolves.) And don't forget to examine the reverse logic and be prepared to explain it. (Think back to two thirds of people in car crashes not testing positive for marijuana – Section 93.) Also, use as many samples as you can (to lower the P-value), and make sure they're not from a biased pool.

"The individual source of the statistics may easily be the weakest link."
(British statistician and banker Josiah Stamp, 1880–1941)

It's worth knowing that the Office of National Statistics (in the UK) is a goldmine of rigorously collected and wide-ranging statistics. Well, that's nearly it on statistics – just one last word from Sir Winston Churchill:

"I only believe in statistics that I doctored myself."
(Sir Winston Churchill 1874–1965)

Shop Smarter

(108) **Introduction**

From cradle to grave, you are being bombarded by retailers with messages and images designed to influence your buying decisions. Not only do they exploit the personal biases you've developed throughout your life, they also have a range of neat tricks designed to push you over that "buy now" line. The insidious point about some of these tricks is that they're used to create biases which the retailers can exploit at a later date. Many of these retailers are playing the long game, and some of them start on you even before you're born. In this chapter, we will cover some of the tricks they use, and this will help you counter them. We will also discuss some tricks you can use to turn the advantage to you.

Scientists have long known that babies can hear in the womb, and experiments at Belfast University have shown that children at birth can recognise TV themes and advert jingles that they heard before birth and are pacified by them. Other research has shown babies respond to tastes and smells encountered in the uterus and show a preference for them that lasts into later life. The marketeer Martin Lindstrom in his book *Brandwashed* demonstrates that a person's preferences for brands acquired in childhood continue to influence them into adulthood.

It reminds me of the Jesuits' famous claim:

"Give me the child for seven years, and I will give you the man."

Well, much like the Jesuits, savvy marketeers know that if you give them a child, they will give you a man… who is programmed to buy their goods forever.

Evidence of influence by companies trying to alter and subvert your buying decisions is everywhere. All supermarkets are engaged in two battles: one overt against their competitors, and one covert against you, the shopper.

Particularly in times of austerity, you can't move in your local supermarket without spotting a two-for-one or a multi-buy offer or some other "special" deal. However, quite often, you are not getting the good deal the supermarket chain would have you believe. Using a combination of psychological ploys, the stores are duping you.

In 2012, the consumer magazine *Which?* confirmed that stores are continuing to trick us using the old "was £10 now £6" ploy. All too often, the item was never £10 in the store you're in but rather in some obscure store miles from anywhere, and only for a short period of time. This allows the store legally to claim the item "was £10" and make you feel as though you've saved £4.

This technique causes you to establish an anchor (see Section 39) at the artificially high price, making the lower one seem like a better deal. It's a pretty underhand trick, but it isn't the best-kept secret in the world. I should imagine a fair proportion of the people reading this book know it goes on. But, regardless of whether you know it not, the technique still probably works on you – because it provides the impetus to buy. If you want the item, you want the bargain to be real. And as you probably don't track the price of every item across the store, you can't be certain it's not a bargain. Perhaps it is. At this point, your Confirmation Bias (see Section 47) will be telling you it is a bargain and blotting out any contradictory thoughts. And that's usually enough to tip you over the "buy now" line.

So, how can you make sure you don't fall for their tricks? You could try buying some of your shopping in budget supermarkets such as Lidl or Aldi, which often stock the same stuff. Quite simply, their prices tend to be lower because their overheads are less. How? Well, they offer less choice, which cuts back on transport and infra-structure costs. They use "hire" trolleys, which cuts back on trolley teams. They tend to stack their goods high and leave them on pallets in the shop, which cuts back on the staff needed to make every shelf look untouched by earlier customers. They will often think nothing of letting you queue five or six deep before opening another checkout. They don't offer you loyalty cards, and they will charge you for their carrier bags. They're also usually quite demanding employers, and they tend to get their money's worth from their staff. (For example, checkout staff are expected to put 35–40 items a minute through the till. Their average speed is recorded by the till and checked each night.)

So, if you're the sort of person who likes his can of baked beans to have been lined up at the front of the shelf before he takes it home, or the sort of person who doesn't want to be seen by the neighbours carrying Lidl bags from his car to his front door, or who doesn't want to have to remember to keep a "trolley pound coin" with him, then you will have to throw yourself at the mercy of the higher-end shops. These guys are far more likely to play mind games on you to cover all those extra costs of creating a more pleasurable shopping experience.

An obvious way to save money at the higher-end shops is to switch to the supermarket-own or budget brands, which are often made in the same factories as premium brands. The difference in quality between premium and budget brands, if discernible at all, is usually not worth the extra money (see Distinction Bias, Section 50). For those of you who use these higher-end stores, we will now cover some of the ways they're trying to influence you so you can be on your guard.

(109) You're being herded around the store

Supermarkets have become masters of influencing you with their displays and shop layout. At the most basic level, they put the items they most want to sell at eye level and at "junctions", like the ends of aisles. They then start getting a little sneakier by positioning daily necessities such as bread and milk towards the back of the store, forcing you through an Aladdin's cave of tempting treats to reach what you really need. It's a common story. You only went in for some milk, and you came out with crisps, dips and some "half priced" blueberries. In fact, as soon as we enter a shop, we are unknowingly driven like geese around the store. They will entice you in with flowers and fresh fruit, and then it's for you to navigate yourself through their maze of temptation before you find the exit. They also place a lot of the junk food, sweets and sugary cereals lower down on the shelves. It's not convenient for you, but it's quite convenient for your children. (We will look at how kids influence their parents' buying decisions later.)

The stalls that hand out free samples are not only designed to sell specific products, they are also designed to slow you down to improve the chances of you making an impulse purchase. The checkout queue is also a profitable place for a supermarket as it's the one place you're relatively static. A few years ago, this used to be where impulse purchases or "children bait" like chocolate bars were stocked, but that ploy was too overt. Customers saw straight through that trick. (Given the number of Veruca Salt-style tantrums witnessed at the tills, it was almost impossible for shoppers not to see what was going on.) So, supermarkets did us all a favour when some removed the sweets from the checkout areas (usually to end of a nearby aisle... at kid-eye level). Most switched targets from children to adults. They soon realised that the tills were the best place for you to assimilate more complex information, and they started placing adverts and leaflets for car insurance, mortgages, holidays and banks for you to consider during your "static" time.

110   Loyalty cards, coupons and vouchers

When you arrive at the till, you hand over your loyalty card to claim the bonus points for your latest purchases. Later these points will be turned into money-off vouchers for your future shopping trips. That seems great. Something for nothing. But what's really happening?

What you are really doing is giving them free rein to look through your shopping and buying decisions. This is called data mining, and it is the biggest growth area in marketing. Stores amass huge amounts of data about you and your buying habits. This information is then used by them and other third parties (often without your knowledge, because who reads the pages of small print that accompany the store card?) to target you and persuade you to shop there more often.

Users of the online retailer Amazon will be familiar with this type of targeting. Every time you visit the website, you are shown recommended purchases based on previous purchases and browsing. Loyalty cards operate in the same way. They allow the supermarket to present you with tailor-made offers by post or email or with your receipt. For example, if you regularly buy dog food, you might receive some dog-food coupons with your receipt. So now you can either buy your next stack of dog food at a discounted price (at that store) or at full price elsewhere. The store relies on this decision being a no-brainer. From their perspective, that coupon almost guarantees your return custom in the near future. If it does fail to get you, or you haven't used their stores for a while, expect a time-limited discount voucher in the post or by email enticing you back. Once these guys have got their hooks into you, they're reluctant to let you go. This isn't all bad for you as it might be cheaper to shop using the vouchers. You just need to be aware that you are being manipulated, so check that the offer is worth accepting (rather than sleepwalking into it as the store would have you do). More specifically, the "20p off dog food" voucher that got you back into the store might have just cost you £5 if you compared the whole shopping basket with a similar shopping basket in another store. (In doing this comparison, you shouldn't just be on the lookout for higher prices but also for items you wouldn't have bought in the other store.)

The emails tempting you to do your food shopping online are also very persistent. I haven't used online grocery shopping for over five years, but I still get regular email offers to tempt me back. This is because once you have become familiar with using a particular store's website, and once it shows you that it can speed up your online shopping by remembering your usual buys, you are highly likely to stick with it rather than learning to navigate around someone else's website. So, it's worth their time to pester you. These bonus points and vouchers are all presented in a way that makes you feel like you're getting a free lunch, but really these schemes incur a cost. And guess who pays for that in the long run?

Oh, it gets way sneakier. Insurance is another area where your loyalty cards are starting to have an impact. Some insurance companies are allegedly using the data collected by supermarkets to look at your buying decisions – a window to your soul or, more accurately, a detailed insight into your lifestyle, enabling them to tune their tariffs and offers to you. It would make good sense for them to do this as it allows them to assess the risk of insuring you. If your loyalty card says you buy four bottles of whiskey and 100 cigarettes every week, then it's a fair assumption that you're a drinker and smoker. From this data, they assess that you're likely to be a higher motor- and life-insurance risk than someone who buys lots of vegetables and fruit every week. And, this would be useful information to help them build your insurance quote. It doesn't even have to be that complicated. A buyer of cat food is a good target for a pet-insurance email, while consistent buyers of nappies and baby food are more likely to consider life assurance or child-trust funds.

So, how can you use this information? Well, you could get at least two cards per store. Buy your cakes, whisky and beer on one card and your celery, hummus and prawns on another, and watch as the different offers come in for the different cards. Here's the rationale. If you do your shopping on just one card, you might get two vouchers: one for cakes and one for celery. If you do it on two cards, you'll get one for cakes and one for whisky on one card, but also one for celery and one for hummus on the other. Oh, and make sure the person who insures the family car is the owner of the "celery" loyalty card. This isn't really about saving money. It's more about you manipulating them instead of them manipulating you. Even if running two store cards is too much hassle for you, which I fully suspect it is, it's still nice to know that you could, if you were minded, use their spying on you against them.

Vouchers are an incredible marketing tool. The power of that piece of paper should not be underestimated. About 50% of the UK population use savings vouchers from newspapers, magazines or online. When we find a saving voucher that's relevant to us, we feel as though we've found something special – as if we've uncovered a secret passport to a good deal.

In researching this book, I looked at 30 vouchers from a mix of those in newspapers and magazines and from websites. I then spent some time reading the small print or hunting for comparable deals. Over a third of the vouchers (12) did not offer a substantial discount on prices offered by other retailers. In effect, these were advertising rather than discount tickets. Another third (10) had strings attached.

They required you to buy more products than you would normally buy, sometimes through contracts. The remaining ones (8) were real offers. They were from companies who were confident enough in their products to let you test them at a genuinely discounted rate.

30 vouchers is only a small sample, but, for me, it was enough of a test to know that we need to keep our guard up when using vouchers. They might just be giving us the impetus to buy products, rather than providing a genuine discount.

If you could use vouchers to improve your business and you don't, you should probably consider it. Of course, it's up to you what type of voucher you offer (i.e. one that's just an advertising ploy, one that's a bulk-buy trap, or one that encourages people to try your product), but whichever one you choose, it needs to make the potential users feel as if they've just discovered something that's as good as real money.

111 The pester power of kids

Adverts aimed at children and teenagers are the bane of most parents' lives. The marketeers want your children to pester you for a toy or sweets when they are at their most expensive, normally just in time for Christmas. The launch of toys is frequently timed to coincide with Christmas shopping and, on occasion, deliberately limited in number to encourage panic buying.

Linking toys to films is another tactic the marketeers use to create hype. Creating a film about a long-existing toy, such as Barbie Doll, seems like a fair marketing ploy, but marketeers are capable of being far more callous than that. A number of children's films are specifically created with toy sales in mind. The film Teenage Mutant Ninja Turtles was an example. Initially a comic, the TV and film spinoffs were produced as an "advert" for the toys. That seems far more underhand to me. It's a deliberate attack on your wallet by marketeers who are using your kids as their proxies.

These days, they're getting at you through your kids more than ever. Promotion methods are becoming more sophisticated as technology races on. Now there are other ways that little Timmy can be singled out and tempted. This is done not only with a relentless bombardment of adverts on the TV at specific times of day (e.g. just after school), but also with adverts tailored to his internet surfing, particularly by social-media websites like Facebook, which use things like cookies (small pieces of data from websites which are stored on your computer) to place adverts that he will be susceptible to. This is all before he starts playing his video game, which is likely to be littered with product placement (see Section 112).

One parent told me that the only way to reduce the pester power would be to forbid all children's TV and games with adverts and never take your children to the supermarket. The alternative is to teach your children early that adverts are a way of stopping people thinking for themselves.

(112) Product placement

Do you watch Coronation Street? Have you noticed a white "P" by the title? That means the programme contains product placement.

Whenever a product appears in a book, a film, a computer game or on TV, there's a fair chance you're looking at deliberate product placement. The marketeers' intention is to promote the product through association. During a film, for example, when we see the hero using a placed product, in our minds, the product has been endorsed by the hero. At this point, the Halo Effect (see Section 56) kicks in. The way we feel about the hero of bleeds across to the product. For example, the Cornetto he's holding suddenly seems a more high-class ice-cream or the aftershave he's just applied appears more manly and heroic. We register that the hero had a good experience with the product, and we seek to create that experience for ourselves.

This is not a modern-day phenomenon. Since the early days of cinema, recognisable brands have appeared in films. The Christmas classic *It's a Wonderful Life* (1946), which features a young boy who wants to be a famous explorer, prominently shows a copy of *National Geographic* magazine, suggesting it's compulsory reading for every young adventurer.

Retailers like product placement. The opportunity to target a specific audience is highly sought after, and they invest millions in product placement to influence your decisions in the shop. As you'd expect, the products chosen depend on the film's intended audience. Famously and pretty indiscreetly, James Bond ensures that men continue to drool over Aston Martins. For women, the most obvious example is *Sex in the City*'s association with Manolo Blahnik and Jimmy Choo, which has caused women everywhere to hanker for the wares of two very expensive shoe designers. However, product placement is usually far more subtle than those examples. James Bond's glance down at his Sony Ericsson mobile phone in *Quantum of Solace* is a little less conspicuous. If you're looking for it, you'll notice that quite often the camera lingers just a smidgen too long on a brand name. That's no accident. You're looking at product placement. It can be as subtle as a can of beer on the window ledge during an inconsequential scene or a glance at the time on a wrist-watch. It all registers with you whether you know it or not.

(113) **Expectation is a powerful influence**

We all buy things we can't afford. We all buy things we don't need. We buy things because we want them. Often, we do this not out of necessity, but because we think they will make us or our lives better.

Companies know this, and much of their marketing revolves around the feel-good factor that buyers expect to get from their purchases. And a feel-good factor is actually what most buyers get, meaning their purchases have the desired effect. However, this might have very little to do with the benefits the item brought them. Often the buyer experiences the feel-good factor because he expects to experience the feel-good factor. The idea that someone's expectation is responsible for the outcome is related to the placebo effect.

The placebo effect (from the Latin "to please") is a trick your brain performs on you. It was first linked to the use of pain-reducing medicines. It was found that patients who thought they'd been given drugs to reduce pain still reported less pain even though they'd been given a harmless substitute for real pain-relieving drugs. Needless to say, the practice of giving patients what were effectively sweets instead of painkillers caused quite an upset. But, even so, since then, hundreds of studies have shown that the placebo effect works in areas other than pain relief. One of those areas is shopping. If you expect something to do you good, it does.

Actually, expectation can be even more powerful than that. It can even make you feel good before you've bought your item. Expectation can create a Pavlovian response. (Remember Pavlov's experiment with dogs? He rang a bell every time he fed his dogs. Before long, the sound of the bell alone would cause his dogs to salivate.) As a result of the brain linking the feel-good factor with the pending purchase, buyers – rather like Pavlov's dogs – feel good even at the prospect of buying their item (hopefully, with less drool).

Another series of experiments showed that people thought non-branded pain-relief tablets were less effective than their more expensive branded counterparts, even though the active ingredients were identical. This is also the placebo effect in action.

The makers of Stella Artois beer ran with this idea as a basis for their marketing campaign. They used the phrase "reassuringly expensive" to suggest that Stella Artois used more expensive ingredients and was therefore better than its cheaper competitors. Lots of beer drinkers thought so, and the successful ad campaign ran for 23 years. Numerous products, from watches to cars, are sold this way. They want us to believe they are more expensive because they are better. Sometimes this is obviously true, but sometimes it isn't, and many of us fall for it regardless.

Of course, it's not always that simple. We've just said that lots of things that cost more money are better than their cheaper counterparts. What we often fail to do though is determine whether the difference between the expensive one and the cheap one is worth paying for.

One of my friends recently wanted to buy a new car. He was eyeing up a bright shiny sports car to replace the older bright shiny sports car he already owned. The new car was three times more expensive than his current car. In rationalising his pending purchase, he initially focused on the new car's features: xenon lights (awesome), a sports exhaust (also awesome, unless you live next door) and an iPod-compatible mp3 stereo (again, awesome). He thought about how great it would be to drive, and he reached for the telephone to call his bank manager. At that moment, his focus switched to the money, and the call was postponed to allow some more thinking time.

Was the new car going to be three times better than the old one? Was he likely to get three times as much pleasure from driving it? Unsurprisingly, the answer to both questions was no. The call was never made.

Remember, product placement (see Section 112), Distinction Bias (see Section 50), the Endowment Effect (see Section 52), and *future-you* (see Section 53) are all leaping about in your brain to get you to act irrationally or impulsively. With a bit of thought, you can actively suppress those influencers and make a more rational decision. If you're sure you've taken yourself to that more sober place in your head and considered all these factors influencing your decision-making, and you still want the car or whatever, buy it.

(114) **Eating out. It's not all about the food**

Your expectations also affect what you taste. A Frenchman, Fredric Brouchet, carried out an ingeniously simple experiment in 2001 with wine experts, which cast doubt on what people can really tell about the quality of wine. He gathered 57 well-respected oenophiles (wine-lovers) and got them to take part in a series of taste tests. The first involved swapping a high-quality *Grand Cru* (premium vintage wine) and a stock bottle of table "plonk" by switching bottles. The majority of the experts tasted what they expected to taste from looking at the bottle, describing the so-called high-quality cru as "woody and complex" and the so-called "cheap" bottle as "light and faulty".

Brouchet then tried a taste test with a bottle of white wine and a bottle of red. Again, the descriptions matched what the experts expected to taste. The red was described as "full of jamminess" and "crushed red fruit". Not one person noticed that the red and the white were exactly the same bottle of wine. (Brouchet had just added red food colouring to the white wine.) As Brouchet himself stated, our taste expectations of a wine *"can be much more powerful in determining how we taste a wine than the actual physical qualities of the wine".*

This is an example of Expectancy Theory. It is a point to note when you are debating whether to plump for an expensive vintage or a more modest offering. Even if you are super clued up on wine, it is pretty hard to tell the difference between a £7 and a £17 bottle (especially after a couple of glasses). However, because of how Expectancy Theory works, you are likely to prefer the £17 bottle if you know it's the £17 bottle. If you can train yourself to suppress Expectancy Theory, you'll be able to go with what tastes nice for you rather than being overly influenced by price or "expert" reviews. And you might just save yourself a tenner per bottle as well as having the satisfaction of knowing that you, not they, decided what you should buy.

Another recent study by Heriot-Watt University in Scotland showed that perceptions of taste can be altered by listening to music. While listening to "O Fortuna" from the opera *Carmina Burana* (which featured in *The Omen*), the test group described a wine as "powerful and heavy". With lighter music like Tchaikovsky's *Nutcracker Suite* in the background, they rated the same wine as "subtle and refined".

This is why expensive food in an expensive restaurant is normally accompanied with fine cutlery, starched table cloths and music to suit the food. They all combine to make us think the food tastes better. These things shape our gastronomic experience, and restaurateurs know it. They understand how influential Expectancy Theory and the Halo Effect (see Section 56) are to your enjoyment of their food. If it's expensive, you will be inclined to think it tastes better than a cheaper version. (In another study, 75%-fat-free meat was perceived as tasting better than meat with 25% fat content.) Expectation plays a key role in what we taste.

Look at the following dishes. A long-aged, slow-cooked shin of

Ayrshire beef with a mushroom and port reduction accompanied by a petit-pois mousse, and pot-roast beef shin with mushroom gravy and mushy peas? This is, of course, the same dish described to meet your expectations. Restaurants know how to describe food to appeal to your expectation and improve your dining experience. Of course, it isn't all bad. Hopefully, these things will add to your dining experience. However, to remain in the driving seat, it is always worth remembering you're paying for the product and the setting, but the product is the reason you are there. The setting (décor, lighting, music, price, etc.) is meant to complement the product not mask it or transform it into something that it isn't.

How food looks is also important to how people perceive its taste. An artistically presented piece of sea bass on fine china will probably be enjoyed more than an equally well-cooked fillet of sea bass on a chipped plate. But, it affects us at an even more basic level than that. In the early 90s, Coca-Cola marketed a clear cola-flavoured drink called Tab Clear. It failed to make an impression on consumers. One of the reasons was its colour. People didn't think Tab Clear tasted very "colary". But, with their eyes shut, they couldn't tell the difference between Tab Clear and normal Coca-Cola. Coca-Cola conceded: *"Clearly you can't please some people."*

115 Scrutinising the bargain tags

When shopping, make an effort to check what you're being led to believe is a bargain is a bargain. Recently, I noticed a boldly advertised £1 deal on some own-brand breadcrumbs. Next to them was a premium-brand product, which was more expensive per packet. On closer inspection, however, I noticed that the more expensive packet contained twice the quantity of breadcrumbs and was actually cheaper by weight. If you buy a multi-pack of beans, you would expect it to be cheaper per can than buying the cans individually or cheaper per can than a smaller multi-pack. But that's not always a sound assumption. It can be financially worthwhile to compare unit price or weight price as you shop. This is especially true for packed or bagged fruit. Often, something like a bag of apples that looks like a budget buy (especially given the big, red "Only £2" sticker) is more expensive per apple than if you selected the apples individually. I'm not talking about those posh-looking packs of four perfect-looking apples in a cardboard carton versus four apples out of the basket. I'm talking about a bag of apples packed like a bag of spuds versus the same number of apples out of the basket. Supermarkets lead you believe it's a bargain and then sting you for a few extra pence per apple. They justify this by claiming that their customers do not mind paying for the convenience of pre-packed items. That's fine, but they package it in a way that leads the customer to think it's a budget pack, and that's sly. So, check the unit price or weight price.

Nowadays, many supermarkets do this for you on their shelving price tags. They'll happily tell you the price per kg, per lb or per item. Be aware though that sometimes they mix them up to cloud the issue. For example, it's not uncommon to see onions expressed as price per kg next to onions expressed as price per lb. When they're not "clouding" by mixing baselines (see Section 102) in this way, those tags are very helpful, but they're also doing something else to you. They're giving you long-term confidence in your bigger-pack-cheaper-items assumption. If you keep shopping with that assumption, they'll get you in the end. I'm sure this is not news to you, but we can all get out of the habit of questioning something when the answer is already given to us (even if that answer may not be completely accurate). Of course it might be possible to take the value-for-money checks too far. I once witnessed a mother and daughter checking whether they were getting value for money on toilet paper by comparing the price per sheet... Yes, I said sheet.

And this is the main point. The supermarket relies on you being mentally lazy and letting them do your shopping for you. As we shall see later, this is also prevalent in places like bookshops. For example, a lot of the signage (like the one on the breadcrumbs) implies a bargain where there isn't one to be had. The supermarkets know this, and they are actively toying with you. The BBC current affairs programme *Panorama* found that some supermarkets had used labels saying "Now £2.99!" when the price had actually risen. They're not lying. If you want to make the assumption that the previous price was higher, that's your error. They know that you will scan quickly for the brightly coloured signs and make an assumption. If you can imagine the manager behind that "Now £2.99!" sign laughing at you as he issues the instruction across the supermarket chain, it'll help focus your mind on the "bargain tags" hanging off the other products throughout the store. If you want to see this in action, monitor the price of those two-minute microwave rice packs for a few months. They fluctuate enormously, but even when the price goes up, it's always billed as a saving (e.g. "2 for £3!", when they were only £1.25 each the week before). Other issues with multi-buy offers are that they persuade you to buy more than normal, thereby maintaining the shop's profits. If the food is perishable (bread and fruit being the classic examples), you are likely to end up throwing some of it away. Indeed, recent studies by the UN, amongst others, state that over a third of all food purchased in the UK is discarded without being used (particularly bread and salad). For perishable products, "Buy One Get One Free" appears to be a hugely wasteful way of increasing supermarket profits.

And don't shop when you're hungry. Research has shown you spend more and buy more junk food than if you shop on a full stomach. Your hunger pangs catalyse those effects (hyperbolic discounting and irrational justification, see Section 53 and Section 44) that make you buy junk.

In summary, stores know the overwhelming majority of their customers are either too lazy or too busy to invest time doing the maths or research to determine whether a bargain is really a bargain. And, boy, do they exploit it. This idea is taken to the extreme at my local pizza takeaway. (The worst thing is, the store staff have also become blind to the real value of the "offer".) Below is a genuine conversation I had with them while writing this book:

Me: *Can I order a pepperoni pizza please?*
Them: *That'll be £9.85*
Me: *Thanks*

Them: *It's "buy one get one free" Tuesday. Would you like a free one?*
Me: *Errr, yeah, go on then. Thanks.*
Them: *That'll be £17.85*
Me: *I thought it was free.*
Them: *It is. It's "buy one get one free" Tuesday.*
Me: *So, one pizza without "buy one get one free" is £9.85, but with the free one, it's £17.85.*
Them: *That's right. It's "buy one get one free" Tuesday.*

[Repeat the last two lines three times]
[Repeat the first three lines once]

(116) Relative pricing and fractional pricing

Relative pricing

Another common way for retailers to play mind games with you is with relative pricing. Imagine you need a new computer. You have two choices: one at £400 and one at £900. They have quite different specifications and are not really comparable. One is notably better than the other. Retailers know that shoppers find it difficult to choose between two products but easy to choose between three or more. This happens for a couple of reasons:

(1) Two of the three laptops are likely to be close matches and so comparable. Once a buyer makes that comparison between the two closely matched ones, the winner will trump all other laptops, even the ones not included in the comparison. This effect is so strong, shops will include a laptop whose sole raison d'etre is to lose such a comparison by the buyer. It's known as the decoy. (This is covered in the section on Contrast Bias. See Section 48.)

(2) With three choices, buyers are offered a middle ground, which is where most of us feel safest. The shop knows the majority of its customers will buy the middle model, so it builds in a higher profit margin for the middle choice. (This is also covered in the section on the Compromise Effect. See Section 46.)

Clearly, these two ideas could clash; for example, if the middle-ground model loses the comparison with the top model. Stores understand this, and they avoid that clash through product selection and pricing. In the examples below, the model underlined is the one they want you to buy (and the one which offers them the most profit):

- **Middle ground wins**:
  Model A (£290); Model B (£390); Model C (£520)
- **Middle ground loses comparison (meaning Model A is never considered)**:
  Model A (£290); Model B (£520); Model C (£550)

Fractional pricing

Why are products priced at 99p rather than £1 far more appealing? This pricing technique is known as fractional pricing. We're programmed to give precedence to numbers as we read them from left to right. Therefore, £1795 feels closer to £1700 than £1800. But, that's not the real magic behind fractional pricing. It works by making the buyer feel there has been a concerted effort to drive the price down as low as possible.

A similar effect occurs with seemingly random prices. Imagine a car priced at £14,579. This is more appealing to the buyer than £14,500 because he believes the price has been set in relation to something else, such as the cost of the construction. £14,500 just looks like an arbitrary number. The truth is they're both arbitrary, and you should not be influenced by fractional pricing. You beat their mind games by doing your research and getting your own realistic anchor on which to base your purchasing decision.

This quote neatly captures the value of making numbers look more precise:

"71.62% of statistics have extra decimal points added, just to look a bit more believable." (Anon)

Interesting snippet: There's a theory out there that originally the 1p reduction from £1 to 99p was to ensure the till had to be opened and the transaction recorded. The "ding" of the till as the assistant fetched the 1p change would alert the owner at the back of shop to the sale. This ensured the till assistant didn't pocket the buyer's pound and allow the bought item to be written off as stolen. So, it appears the benefits of fractional pricing might have been a by-product of an anti-theft measure. This story smacks of an urban myth, and it's now so widely promulgated that, if it isn't true, it's become impossible to untangle it from the origins of fractional pricing.

117   Shopping in the "sales"

End-of-season sales are another ploy used by shops to weave their mind magic on you. When you're looking around the end-of-season stock, be aware that retailers sometimes deliberately purchase too much stock just so it can be reduced in the sale where they know they will still make a margin on it. This means that you should not be influenced into buying something you don't really want or need just because you think it's a bargain. The trick with sales is to compare the price with what other shops are offering. It's often a mistake to focus on the discount being claimed. Sometimes though, this is harder than you might think. Recently, I saw some "bin ends" wine which was 50% off. Great! However, before I restocked my wine rack, I thought I'd better check it really was 50% off compared to other merchants' prices. It was at this point my research hit a brick wall. Lots of supermarkets have exclusive deals with vineyards, meaning the prices could not be compared. And, we already know we can't trust "was £9.98 now £4.99"-style labels. All you can really do is look at the wine type, grape and vintage and try to gauge whether it's really a 50%-off deal. Frankly, that's all a bit of a hassle, and it assumes you are reasonably knowledgeable about wine – supermarkets know this and know that most people won't bother. So, unless you are really up on your wines, just stick with what you know. If you want to try a new wine, that's great, but make that the reason and not because you've found a bargain, since it will be really difficult to tell if you have.

Buying a new sofa is also an experience fraught with non-existent sales. In stores like DFS, it's hard to find a time when they don't have a sale. Their sales are marketing ploys designed to make you feel you're getting a better deal than you are. It's a common practice at the end of the "sale" for them to change the name and pattern of the sofa, and put it back on "sale". Shops like DFS and SWS also offer interest-free credit deals. This is a fallacy – the price of the interest-free credit is built into the price of the sofa, i.e. by making the sofa slightly more expensive, the "free" credit can be offered as an incentive.

I doubt I'm telling you anything new, and when you're not in the market for a new sofa, you're probably making fun of DFS's TV ads about their massive bank-holiday sales too. But attitudes change when you actually need a new sofa. Suddenly, these deals start to look a lot more attractive. At the point of buying, you want the savings and the interest-free deals to be true. And if you want them to be, they are. That's how it really works. So, when you need a new sofa, it is hard to treat their "deal" as the marketing tool you know it to be. But show some mettle, shake it off and shop around. If you have the cash, you know there are retailers that will do you a discount for a convenient sale, so go for it. And, if it does suit you to buy your sofa on credit, recognise that you might find better deals on sofas with shops that charge some interest. We all know these "special event" sales routinely trick other people – just make sure you're not "other people" when it's your turn to buy a sofa.

118 Research is the key to cheap holidays

Travel and leisure is another area where sellers employ psychological tricks to create the impression you're getting the deal of the century. You're not. I mean, how can such a high proportion of offers be such great deals? (Again, in some places, it is more difficult to find something that isn't on sale.) The "three days for the price of two" or "kids go free" deals are all tempting, but less so when you realise that the "deal" is already factored into an elevated price (e.g. the day-rate for the two days is higher or the parents pay extra).

With holidays in particular, there is a lot of overt competition, especially on the internet, and there are good deals to be had. The use of web-aggregator sites that pick deals from other travel websites can reduce the work of finding a bargain. The best deals, unsurprisingly, are outside the school holidays. If you're just booking flights, don't forget to look at the airlines themselves (the websites may make money by collecting a fee from the airlines, so cutting them out of the middle may improve the price). It might also be possible to snatch a deal by travelling to a country when it has a national holiday. On these days, there are fewer businessmen travelling, and this can increase seat availability on aircraft and lower prices. It's something to look out for.

If you can, be flexible about when you're holidaying as last-minute bookings can be a good way to get a better deal. Often tour companies have pre-bought flights and hotel rooms which need to be filled, and this is something you can exploit. The challenge here is finding a last-minute booking that is actually a last-minute booking and not something just calling itself a last-minute booking. Be aware that there are tour operators out there who are trying to sell you something that looks like a last-minute-holiday deal for a normal price. These companies have learnt to prey on those of us who are looking for a last-minute deal (either because we've failed to get our acts together or are trying to beat the system). But there are also companies out there that are under genuine pressure to fill the seats they haven't been able to fill. The challenge for you is to see past the "50% off" blurb of the company preying on last-minute shoppers and to buy the places that will otherwise go begging from the company that is trying to cut its losses. There's only one sure way to know whether you're buying a "discounted" holiday or a genuinely discounted holiday: you have to do price comparisons for the following week or with other sites. If the holiday is priced like something you could get the following week or with someone else, then you're being preyed upon. If, however, the holiday is priced notably lower than a similar holiday for the following week or with someone else, then you've hit the jackpot. It seems an obvious point, but don't forget, the tour operators know you'll be looking around for a last-minute deal, so that'll be the story they'll spout to get their hooks into you.

Haggling can be a way to knock the price down. Obviously, you can't negotiate with a travel website, so if you want to get a better deal than advertised, phone the tour operator or travel agent and ask. The same goes for hotel rooms. Start by checking room costs online (including website aggregators). Next, visit the hotel website to check prices, as some hotels guarantee their online rates will be the lowest available. And, if all prices are the same, book directly with the hotel to avoid website service charges. Finally, give the hotel a call directly and negotiate. This is often the best way to get a discount or an upgrade. When a hotel isn't fully booked, reservation managers are frequently given the discretion to beat any other rate – even the hotel's own online rate. However, to haggle effectively, you must be armed with the information from online. Just being audacious on the phone won't cut it. It's all about prior research. *Manui Dat Cognitio Vires* (Knowledge gives strength to the arm).

119   Timing is the key to buying a cheap car

The single most expensive purchase most people make (apart from their own home) is their car. If you're in the market for a brand-new car, then be aware that most sales staff will have a certain number of extras or discounts they expect to throw in to make you feel you're getting a good deal. You shouldn't be wowed by superficial nonsense like a set of free mats or even alloy wheels. They cost a fraction of the car's value. Take them out of the equation, haggle harder and then buy them as aftermarket items (those offered for sale by manufacturers other than the original car maker), which will be cheaper.

If you are prepared to wait for your new car, you can get a better deal at certain times of the year. If you time your purchase for the end of the quarter (i.e. March, June, September and December), the sales team will be trying to meet their targets and, possibly, to keep their jobs. You are also in a stronger position to negotiate harder in the weeks before new registration plates are issued (September and March) or when new models have been announced, as most retailers want to clear their showrooms to make way for new stock. If you buy a car in these time windows, you are actually doing the showroom a favour, and you should tell them as much in your negotiating. It's a similar situation to the last-minute holidays. At certain times, retailers have pressure on them to sell, giving you a real "lever" to pull to get a bargain, so make sure you pull it. Don't let them trick you into thinking you've pulled it by giving you a free tank of fuel.

There's also a lot going on when you purchase a second-hand car. Car dealers' initial prices are all inflated. So, the 10% discount you've just negotiated might not be such a deal. Don't let the screen price be the anchor (see Section 39). The only way to know whether you're getting a deal is to use industry-standard guides like Glass's Guide or CAP. The price these guides set is a much better anchor that you should use, not some arbitrary value assigned by a dealer. A few years ago, Glass's was an industry-only volume, but nowadays it is available to the general public. You can adjust prices for condition, age and mileage. Expect the dealer to come up with some nonsense about how Glass's is no longer used, why this particular model is rare, how it's in better condition than the guide caters for or why the first full moon makes cars more expensive. He'll be talking rubbish. Dealers have to use an industry standard for valuing cars, and these guides are it. You must use the right anchor, not his anchor. He does this for a living, and he understands how anchors work. If he is any good at his job, he would have set a low one when he bought the car, and now he's trying to set a high one when selling it. You need to do your homework in order to bring a more favourable anchor to the table.

The trick is to override his anchor using logical reasons for the figure (mileage, condition, CAP value) and then shut up. If there is a pregnant pause, savour the silence. On no account be the first to speak – even if it seems rude. There's an old negotiating phrase: "Whoever speaks first, comes second." It's now his job to attack your anchor. Do not accept the first counter offer but show your mettle by raising your offer by less than he dropped his, e.g. if he drops by £500, go up by £250. Ultimately, if he says no, walk away. There are other cars out there.

If you're in the market for a pretty decent second-hand car from a garage, the market is particularly healthy for buyers just after a new registration plate comes in. Lots of companies know the fleet cars their salesmen drive are key to creating the right impression for their customers. They might not know it's called the Devil Effect (see Section 56), but nevertheless, experience has taught them that driving an old car will undermine a salesman's standing and consequently his ability to persuade a customer. (In other words, customers will think that the salesman's abilities and his company's products are directly proportional to the standard of car he drives.) As companies want to maximise the time that their cars will give their salesmen the Halo Effect (the opposite of the Devil Effect), they look to buy them as soon as the number plates change. That, combined with individuals just waiting for the new plate before buying, means lots of vehicles are traded in at these times. That means showrooms have lots more second-hand cars to sell on. So, with the Law of Supply and Demand, the advantage shifts to the buyer, and your chances of getting a bargain at these times are noticeably increased.

The price of convertibles, especially from private sellers, drops considerably in the winter months. In the summer, you're buying the dream of whizzing down leafy country lanes with the wind in your hair, but, in the colder weather, you're buying a needs-to-be-garaged, inconvenient two-seater that no one's interested in (see *now-them, future-them,* Section 53).

Also, think about this. We all like that new car smell and those spotless carpets, but they are only short-lived benefits. Why would you pay £1000s for them? (See Distinction Bias, Section 50.)

And, finally, if you're selling your car privately, be aware that anchoring can work for you in areas not related to the price you're asking for the car. This short story will explain:

One of my friends went to buy a classic sports car from a private seller. As he arrived, the seller was highly apologetic. He explained that he had just noticed that one of the chrome wheel nuts had become tarnished. As the owner seemed to be nearly beside himself over a wheel nut which was only slightly less shiny than the others, my friend could hardly question the condition of the engine. Either knowingly or unknowingly, the owner had anchored my friend on the car's condition. As a result, the conversation then centred around how immaculate the car was as opposed to how many more miles it was going to manage before its pistons ripped through the bonnet. With the conversation kept in that zone, my friend's price-negotiating power had been, skilfully or otherwise, emasculated.

This is a technique you can use when selling a car. All you have to do is tell a quick story that speaks of your obsession with looking after the car. After that, the chances of you being confronted by a tyre-kicking, teeth-sucking chancer with a ridiculously low offer are far smaller. Simple but effective.

120 The power of nostalgia

The tendency to rate the past better than the present is known as Nostalgia Bias or Rosy Retrospection. It's common. We tend to remember mildly pleasant past events as better than they were. The indifferent holiday becomes one that is warmly remembered as the minor annoyances of that four-hour bus journey without air-conditioning and the spot of Dehli belly disappear from your recollection. This happens because emotional memories tend to be stored as a holistic feeling of an event, which is viewed as either a largely positive or negative feeling. If it is positive, then the minor bad feelings are forgotten and the whole memory becomes suffused with happy memories (and vice versa).

According to the journal *Scientific American*, feelings of nostalgia are actually good for you. They improve your mood and feelings of self-worth and well-being. Advertising companies know this, and, boy, do they make use of it. They recognise that these pleasant memories for things past can be used to influence the buying decisions of the present.

Musical tastes in most people tend to become fixed in their early 20s. At around this age, many of us stop listening to new types of music and remain wedded to whatever genres we grew up with.

Advertising companies have learned to target a specific age demographic by using the genre of the time that group was young. This appeal to our nostalgia sells us everything, including jeans, cars and airline tickets. Nostalgia also sells bread. The Hovis adverts are a superb example, with views of Yorkshire, an old mining town and classical music appealing to bygone simpler times. The idea that your past was somehow better is likely to be a fallacy. For example, the 1970s might be in your mind as a simpler, happier time if that's when you grew up, but, if you didn't and you read about that decade, it was one full of public unrest, rampant inflation and power cuts.

A number of companies (including Hovis) have taken the process a step further and include their old adverts in their new ones to make our nostalgic feelings towards old adverts part of the process. Coca-Cola are masters of this at Christmas, and they too have released an advert that celebrates all their previous Christmas adverts. They want you to watch the advert and remember where you were when you watched the previous versions. They want you to feel nostalgic for their old advert. From there, it's a very short mind leap to nostalgia for their product. It's genius. By linking the product to the past, you subconsciously want to buy the product to put you back in that feel-good place.

How can you use this information? Well, you might be in a position to use nostalgia in your adverts. If you are, that's fine. Do it. If, however, you're looking for a fix to ensure you're not influenced by advertising attacks on your nostalgia, then awareness is the key. Knowing that those jeans you are about to buy have been sold to you because of your memories of a great summer from your past will enable you to scrutinise that purchasing decision more rationally. However, my advice is don't look too hard to fix this part of your decision-making. Sometimes, just go with it. Feelings of nostalgia can be good for you.

(121) The science of selling sport

Sport shoes

As the developed nations get ever fatter, the marketeers are fighting a noble (but very profitable) battle to get us to exercise, and we spend hundreds of millions in gym memberships every year. A study by consumer magazine *Which?* showed that, in the UK, we waste about £37 million a year by not turning up to the gym – but that's another story (see now-you and future-you, Section 53). So, to help with our quest for the inner "Olympian", they are striving to sell us no end of stuff to get us to our fitness nirvana.

Let's take running shoes. Clearly, if you want to go running, you need shoes. The wellies you walk the dog in are not going to cut it. Luckily for us, shoe technology has advanced considerably over the last 30 years, and all the major shoe manufacturers have lines for every type of runner. The more specialised shoe shops will analyse your running style and recommend a shoe depending on how your foot and ankle move. We won't dwell on the technical names here – suffice to say the idea is that a "personalised" shoe will help you with your personal running quirks. Unsurprisingly, this all comes at a cost, and it's not difficult to spend well over £80 on a pair of specialised running shoes. It's a great idea for selling you an expensive pair of high-tech plimsolls, but are "personalised" supportive shoes really helping you?

The US Army (a large and technically adept organisation in the area of fitness, I would suggest) recently undertook a study to test whether they really do help you. They equipped one set of runners with supportive shoes tailored to their running styles and the other with neutral shoes which ignored their running styles. Over time, they analysed the number of injuries between the groups. They found no differences. Their study showed no discernible benefit from the supportive shoes. It's starting to look as if we've been wasting our money on those £80 marvels. There's now a growing suspicion that the manufacturers' foot wizards are no more than scientists with biases that made them uncover findings to support their marketeers' ideas. It seems they might have cherry-picked (see Section 97) their tests to ensure their statistics showed that tailored supportive shoes do help runners. The point here is that you need to look at the science behind expensive products with claimed benefits before handing over your cash.

There's also a new line of thought suggesting it's best to run barefoot (back to nature and all that), and a number of fitness companies now market shoes to help you run "barefoot" (i.e. as though you were running barefoot). At the moment, these shoes have even less scientific evidence to support their effectiveness, but let's not let that get in the way of profits. I've spent lots of money on sports shoes over the years and, if you have as well, it now appears that all our money could have been better spent. When it comes to purchasing decisions, we need to be less trusting of advertising and more rigorous in our research, otherwise we risk wasting money in the future too.

Sports drinks

Sports drinks and supplements are another area of growth. There are drinks to hydrate, drinks to improve performance, drinks to aid recovery, pills to improve muscle mass and pills to reduce injury. *The British Medical Journal* in 2012 found over 400 claims about sports drinks and supplements which it considered were "made with very weak evidence" or "not scientifically supportable". The journal stated the manufacturers had "a striking lack of evidence to back up their claims" about their drinks, protein shakes, etc.

Many of these claims feature an Appeal to an Unnamed Authority (see Section 71) or are backed by cherry-picked experiments (see Section 97) or obscure scientific papers. To add to this heady mix of "evidence" is our expectancy that the products will work for us. In essence, we expect these supplements to help us, so they do (see Section 113). A BBC *Panorama* programme which covered this same subject concluded with some pretty sound advice: Unless you like the taste of these products, just drink water when you're thirsty and eat a balanced diet, and you will achieve exactly the same effect. Isotonic salts replacement anyone?

(122) **People like to be told what to buy**

The recent rise in the number of book lists (e.g. "Richard and Judy's" and the "*Sunday Times* Bestsellers" and Oprah in the US) is quite noticeable. And, it's for a good reason. Book lists are an effective marketing method.

An experiment by Stanley Milgram (an American psychologist) in the 1960s showed people are more likely do something if told to do it by someone in authority. (See Appeal to Authority Fallacy, Section 71.) In Milgram's experiment, it was to test whether people would do something immoral when told, but subsequent experimenters have found that it also applies to more ordinary events, such as purchasing decisions. One study in the US found that individuals gave up decision-making if there was an "expert" on hand to tell them what to do. This is why book lists are so effective.

When you walk into a bookshop, you are overwhelmed with choices. Everywhere you turn, there are thousands of books, but which one to buy? We have already looked at how buyers like to make comparisons and how three is the optimal number of items (see Section 46 and Section 48). When there are hundreds of choices, decision-making becomes more of an effort. Well, as ever, help is at hand from those kind marketeers. They'll offer you a league table of about 20 titles, knowing you're likely to leave with one of the top five, safe in the knowledge that someone else has made your choice for you. Even less subtly, publishers can pay to have books at the front of the store as the "featured book". When this happens, there is not even the pretence of a critical review.

Book lists aren't the only way you can be told what to buy. These days, postings on social-media sites and peer-recommendation can also serve as that voice in your head. *Fifty Shades of Grey* is an excellent example of promotion of a book through social media. Before global connectivity, it would have been unlikely to have been such a runaway success because, given its subject (a relationship based on sadomasochistic sex), it wouldn't have sat comfortably on most traditional book lists. It did what's known in the film industry as a

Shawshank Redemption – it got out of the starting blocks through peer-recommendation. (The film *Shawshank Redemption* did quite poorly at the box office but became one of the most popular films of all time, according to a survey by film magazine *Empire*, due largely to personal recommendations.)

How can you use this information? Well, tell people that one of your products is your "best-selling item", and, if it isn't already, it probably soon will be. People will be more likely to buy it because other people (i.e. all the other buyers) are effectively telling them what to do.

"We recommend" is another line designed to tell you what to do, but unfortunately for the retailers, this comes with a "counter weight": there's an inherent mistrust associated with the seller, who's obviously out to make money. Therefore, "Our customers recommend" is likely to be more effective. It's why testimonials (see Section 56) are so useful. It's also the thinking behind Asda's "Chosen by You" range, which is really just "our best sellers" presented in a way that removes the inherent mistrust of the seller.

(123) Remember, it's not yours until it's yours

I remember my mother being close to tears when I was younger after a house sale fell through. When I asked my dad why she was so upset he said: *"Son, in her head, your mother had already put the curtains up and redecorated the lounge."* To my mother that house was already hers.

Car dealers know the power of this effect. That's why if they think you are a good prospect, they will often let you take a car home for a 24-hour trial. In the US, salesmen call this the "puppy dog close". They know that once you take that adorable "puppy" home, you will fall in love with it. And, they know you'll pay to ensure you're not parted from it.

As with that house my mum nearly owned, you don't even have to own the object temporarily to develop an attachment to it. You start developing a bond with it as soon as you imagine it as yours. That overvaluing of the things you own or the things you've imagined owning is known as the Endowment Effect (see Section 52). Of course, you can use the Endowment Effect to help you clinch a sale. But if you're not in the selling game, keep your guard up for those salesmen who try to make it yours before it's yours.

(124) A final word on shopping smarter

Think back to that "Now £2.99!" sign which actually represented a price rise. Think back to that bag of "budget" apples that was more expensive per apple than the individual ones. Think back to that £17 bottle of wine being indiscernible from the £7 bottle when your expectation is removed from the equation. Think back to that arbitrarily priced car at £14,579, and think back to all those unneeded items you put in your shopping basket when you were forced to walk the entire length of the supermarket just to buy some milk. These are just a few examples from the full range of attacks that bombard you every day.

Some of these attacks might seem like fair marketing ploys, but others are nothing short of exploitation that sail extremely close to the wind with regard to permissible trading standards. Retailers know you're too busy to defend yourself, and this allows them to get inside your head to ensure you keep emptying your pockets into their treasure chests. Remember, many of those brightly coloured bargain tags to which we all gravitate like moths to a candle are in fact baited hooks, and we're the fish.

Of course, you may like the fact that marketeers are more than willing to do your thinking for you and even advise you on what to buy, but, as a rule of thumb, it is worth remembering that, in the final analysis, convenience is always expensive.

When it comes to your daily shopping, you might be happy to endure the marketeers' influences and even to yield to them, but remember these influences will also be at play when you come to make your most important buying decisions. At that point at least, you must be in control and be able to counter all attempts to subvert you.

CONCLUSION

Well, that's it. We've reached the end. That means it's time for a quick wrap-up of everything we've covered in the book.

That's coming up next, but we're going to end with an idea that we didn't cover in the book. And it's the biggest idea of all. Before we get to that though, it is worth recapping some of the key ideas from each chapter.

In the first chapter, *Write to Get the Job Done*, we told you that no one cares what you've got to say unless it affects them or entertains them. We also warned you about the dangers of trying too hard to look "professional" with your writing, and we sought to discourage you from using too many Latinate words and unnatural sentence structures. The main message from that chapter was this: Put your key points at the top of your document (letter, email, whatever) and don't try to show off. Remember, if your writing reads like writing, then rewrite it. We were trying to encourage a bit more "starting" and a bit less "commencing", a bit more "preventing" and a bit less "militating", and a bit more "You have our promise" and a bit less "We can offer our clients a guaranteed assurance of the implementation of the aforementioned procedures".

There's also your credibility to think about, and the best way to protect that is to ensure your work is grammatically sound. Remember, if your readers think you're not on par with them intellectually, there's an increased risk they will not act on your requests. Now, you might think grammar is a bit tedious, and you might think that "as long as the message is understood, that's good enough", but they are not healthy thoughts. Just one incorrect "their" in an email to your boss can put you below a promotion rival, and just one misplaced apostrophe in a brochure can herd your customers towards your competitors. The key message regarding grammar was this: If it's important, get it proofread.

Oh, I nearly forgot. Parallel lists. Use parallel lists!

In the second chapter, *Guard against Your Biases and Exploit Theirs*, we covered the way your life experiences can influence how you make decisions and how they can leave "windows" unlocked in your brain that crafty folk can climb through to influence your behaviour. We suspect a fair proportion of the ideas presented in this chapter were known to you – even if you didn't know their names. However, instead of you perhaps half-knowing these ideas and dancing around the concepts to address them, we now hope you will be able to give them a title and pin them down neatly in your mind. Once you've done that, we hope you will use your improved understanding of these biases and cognitive effects to sharpen your thinking. This will empower you to argue more effectively, to form strategies to get your own way and to defend yourself against those trying to get one over on you.

The trick is to familiarise yourself with the key concepts covered in Chapter 2 and then scan all incoming messages (e.g. others' claims and assertions, adverts and factors for decision-making) for signs of these biases and effects. In essence, Chapter 2 was designed to install a virus checker in your brain to improve how you process and rationalise information. So, when somebody says something like "Well, scientists have proven that...", go straight on the offensive. "Whose scientists?"

In the third chapter, *Reading Body Language*, we touched upon how a person's body movements can sometimes contradict or confirm what he is saying. If you train yourself to notice how people hold themselves, shift their eyes, position their arms and legs as well as stroke or scratch themselves, it might be possible to turn how you deal with them to your advantage. The key term from that chapter was "in congruence". Remember, you are looking for a group of body tells that suggest the same emotion or trait. Far too many of us think that a person is lying if his eyes go top left before he talks. That is just one tell. That particular one usually just means he's trying to recall information. It could mean he's trying to recollect what happened or it could mean he's trying to remember the lie he's concocted. But, if it is accompanied by some neck stroking, a glancing down and fist clenching, you could be tracking a liar, and you might want to invest in asking some more pointed questions.

That said, identifying a liar through body language is hard. It's very hard. Unless you practise it for years, you probably won't improve your detection rate much more than if you were tossing a coin (heads he's a liar – tails he's not), but that shouldn't be what you're trying to get out of reading body language. In most cases when you observe someone, you're really just looking for indications of how confident or shy he is or whether he holds you in esteem or contempt. Having a good sense for how someone measures up on those kinds of traits will allow you to tune your actions towards him. For example, you might choose to praise a person early to boost his confidence or avoid giving a key task to someone whose body language, but not words, is showing signs of disdain towards you. That's the type of edge you should expect from reading body language. Just thinking about it will make you more observant and more aware of what is going on around you. Reading this chapter will not have turned you into a polygraph machine. And when you're making an effort to read someone's body language, be discreet. The Count Dracula stare is never conducive to you becoming more effective at anything… other than being the next nemesis for Peter Cushing.

The fourth chapter, *See Through Statistics*, was written to encourage you to be less trusting of the statistics presented in support of claims. The key point was that neither a professorship nor a doctorate means the person presenting the statistics is being honest. Those qualifications could just mean they're smart enough to twist the statistics to tell the story their paymasters want told. The other thing to keep an eye out for is comparators designed to influence you. If you notice a comparison that offers a seemingly random yardstick, be suspicious of why that yardstick was selected. For example, things that are described as "bigger than Wembley Arena" or "longer than the M2" are likely to be far smaller and shorter than most of us imagine as we picture the more familiar Wembley Stadium and the M1. And don't forget graphs. If someone truncates an axis of a graph, think about why he did it. Was the truncation required to fit it on the page or is he trying to make a canyon out of a pothole?

The key term from Chapter 4 was "confounding variables". Once you've decided what you think your data means, keep asking yourself "What else could have caused that effect?" And when you've finished asking yourself that question, go and find the office brainbox and ask him the same question before you present your findings.

In the fifth chapter, *Shop Smarter*, we covered how shops exploit your trust in them. When they print a "2 for £3" sticker, they know you'll make the assumption that the item was previously more than £1.50 and believe the offer represents a saving. Well, quite often (in fact, all too often), it doesn't. It's just an underhanded way of informing you that the item has gone up from, say, £1.30 to £1.60, but you can buy it at £1.50 if you buy two. So, not only do they get to knock their prices up, they get to sell you two at a higher price. In a fair world, the sticker would say "Was £1.30. Now £1.60, but we'll knock 10p off if you buy two". Just about every single square metre in a supermarket is set up to take a few extra pence off you. The trick is not to leave your brain in the car park. You have to take it shopping with you. You have to think of those yellow bargain tags as sirens beckoning you into pickpocket range. A suspicious eye in the supermarket can reduce your weekly shopping bill by 5%-10%. Honestly, it can. Try it.

The other big message in the fifth chapter was the idea that timing can be key to securing a bargain, especially with regard to buying cars, flights and holidays. The trick here is to have confidence that your timing is working in your favour. The seller will try to underplay the effect of the timing on him, but you must eat away at his feigned assuredness to strike the best deal for you. And that idea aligns quite nicely with our final, big idea, which is all about knowing where you're heading.

The chapters of this book were quite an eclectic mix of topics, and they were put together to help you sharpen the edges of the sword you'll use to cut through the chaos of modern life. That's all fine and dandy, but what does your actual sword look like? That's what we'll talk about in these last few paragraphs.

After he left the Royal Marines, a friend of ours became a bodyguard to the rich and famous for a few years. One of those rich and famous was the late Joseph Cyril Bamford, the founder of engineering giant JCB. One free evening, Mr Bamford and our friend were sitting on a balcony with a drink watching the Italian sun disappear over the Mediterranean. Mr Bamford quite unexpectedly broke the relaxed silence with a single piece of advice. He said: "Whatever you do in life, take a long time to make a decision, but once you've made it, stick with it." That is your sword right there.

At officer training school, this same advice is offered consistently. It is known as "selection and maintenance of the aim", and it is one of the principles of war. It works for everything – not just war. It is far too easy to spread yourself too thinly on multiple causes or to stumble without clear purpose towards unstated aims. The secret is give yourself a focused drive towards a well-understood end state, and if you do that, you are far more likely to leave others floundering in your wash.

A determined drive towards your goal will help you navigate past irrelevant hiccups, assist greatly in your decision-making and ensure that procrastination does not serve as an air brake to your progress. "Irrelevant hiccups" is an idea worth expanding on a little. As you move towards your end goal, you will undoubtedly encounter some disagreements and annoyances. The trick is to not let these consume you. If they're not blocking your path, don't hang around sparring with your protagonists.

> "If you're prepared to die in a ditch over an issue, you probably will."

That observation is offered to Commanding Officers in the British Army. In effect, it means choose your battles, because some things are not worth falling on your sword for.

With regard to procrastination, this Scottish proverb describes the condition well:

> "What may be done at any time will be done at no time."

Procrastination affects most of us, but those with a determined drive towards a clearly specified goal are far less affected by it. Jobs that "may be done at any time" just become easy jobs to tick off as done.

So, how determined do you have to be to succeed? Well, here's a short anecdote to give you a sense of the answer to that question.

In the early hours of a Sunday morning in deepest West Wales, a soldier we knew was taking a shortcut back to his accommodation after a long afternoon in town watching a couple of Five Nations (as it was then) rugby matches in the local pubs. He was armed with a wrapped kebab and chips. After such a long day, he'd forgotten about the four-foot drop onto a tarmacked car park, which he was nearing. The worst happened. He fell straight down it. He broke both collar bones, both arms and several fingers and smashed all but one of his front teeth out. When they found him hours later lying in the same spot, he was in a real mess, but, despite all his injuries, he had somehow managed to recover, unwrap and eat his kebab and chips. Now, that is selection and maintenance of the aim!

So, that's it. We've finally finished presenting our ideas, and we hope they were meaningful enough for you to enable you to apply them to your setting. It's a war out there, and we want you to win.

INDEX